Managing Web Projects

DEDICATION

To my wife Beverley,
a consultant and project manager for
web-space delivery

Managing Web Projects

The Management of Large Projects and Programmes for Web-Space Delivery

J. RODNEY TURNER

GOWER

Published by
Gower Publishing Limited
Gower House
Croft Road
Aldershot
Hants GU11 3HR
England

Gower Publishing Company
Suite 420
101 Cherry Street
Burlington, VT 05401-4405
USA

British Library Cataloguing in Publication Data

Turner, Rodney
Managing web projects: the management of large projects and programmes for web-space delivery
1. Web site development 2. Project management I. Title
658.4'04'0285

ISBN: 0 566 08567 4

Library of Congress Cataloging-in-Publication Data

Turner, J. Rodney (John Rodney), 1953-
Managing web projects: the management of large projects and programmes for Web-space delivery/J. Rodney Turner.
p.cm.
Includes bibliographical references and index.
ISBN 0-566-08567-4
1. Computer software--Development. 2. Web site development. I. Title.

QA76.76.D47T85 2004
005.2'76--dc22

2003057012

Typeset by Get Set Go, Epsom, Surrey and printed in Great Britain by MPG Books Ltd, Bodmin, Cornwall

Contents

List of Figures

Preface

I was excited when Gower asked me to write a book on the management of web projects. Project management has now come of age and there is a demand for books on more specific areas of project management. I hope this one may be the first in a series. (The next I am planning is a book on the management of projects in the health sector.) There is a body of opinion, with which I agree, that project management is a generic skill; that it can apply in all areas. But there are different types of project, and different types of project have different needs. I am involved in a project at the moment, sponsored by the North American Project Management Institute, to develop a classification system for projects. One reason for having a classification system is that you can choose appropriate methodologies for your projects. Projects of different types require different methodologies for their management. Project management may be generic, but it needs focusing in different ways for different types of project. Medicine is a generic profession, but there are different types of doctors; law is a generic profession but there are different types of lawyers; accounting is a generic profession, but there are different types of accountants; project management is a generic profession, but ... And so there is a need for books on the management of different types of project.

Before I started writing this book, I thought web project management was going to be a subset of information systems (IS) project management. Indeed, Chapter 2 is devoted to comparing web-delivery projects to mainstream IS project management. I thought I would need to research such areas as extreme project management, which have growing popularity in IS project management, and in fact I started to do so. But as I started interviewing managers involved in web-delivery projects, I was struck by the importance of the change management issues described in Chapter 3. Further, because the change management elements and the web technology elements need to be integrated in a project delivered over a relatively short timescale, web projects tend to be managed as an integrated whole, rather than salami sliced as suggested by extreme programming. Because HTML is by its nature fairly flexible, a large web space can be delivered as a programme, with the programme thick sliced into a number of smaller projects (see Chapter 16). You can start off with only a vague idea of what the final web space will look like, but deliver early projects with very specific objectives, as you refine your understanding of that final web space. The case study that runs throughout the book is the first step in the development of an integrated web presence for the company concerned. Thus my research led me to decide that techniques such as extreme programming were not relevant here, and so they are not covered.

This book is aimed at general managers, rather than information systems managers. One feature of web projects identified in Chapter 2 is that responsibility for their delivery tends to fall to general managers rather than IS people, operations managers, marketing managers or personnel managers. This was confirmed by the research I did into web project management. Therefore the book is aimed at them rather than at the IS professionals. I hope it may be of interest to IS project managers, but they may be interested in more technical project management, and techniques such as extreme programming.

This book is also about the management of web projects, not web-enabled project management. It is now common for people to maintain their project plans on a central server, but since the early days of project management in the 1950s, people have maintained central plans. The web is just changing the medium, not changing the idea. Planning on the central server is just an old idea in new bottles. Although, I guess, we expect people involved in web delivery to use the web for their project planning and control, I did not find that necessarily to be the case. Richard McBain, who was managing the electronic learning MBA (el-MBA) at Henley Management College was effectively using bits of paper.

Before I started writing the book, I researched web project management, and as a result the nature of the book changed. I found that web projects were not so much IS projects, but people, systems and organization (PSO) projects with a web component. That is they are projects where you need to change the people, systems and organization as much as you need to deliver the web component.

In recognizing that a different type of project requires a different type of methodology for its delivery, I have tried to use examples of web projects, IS projects or PSO projects thought to illustrate the principles. The case study that runs throughout is a web project, based on one from my own experience. It builds to show how the principles of each chapter apply to a real web delivery project. It is embellished, drawing on ideas from other web projects with which I have been associated. I have also tried to use other anecdotes and examples throughout to illustrate other points. I have gathered in new anecdotes – Ralf Müller contributed several. There are one or two places where I have used examples from other industries. For example in Chapter 13 I think the example of the Øresund crossing is such a good example of what can be achieved with risk management, I have used that, but I have also tried to relate it back to web projects.

Now there is the thorny issue of references. This is a book for practising managers, not an academic treatise. Therefore perhaps I should use no references at all. I certainly don't want the text to be littered with references to justify every opinion or comment I make by reference back to the literature. After all, this book is an expression of my opinions and I don't need to justify and reference every opinion I have. However, I found there was a need for references, for three purposes:

1 This book is not a comprehensive guide to the whole of the project management body of knowledge. For that you need to read the *Gower Handbook of Project Management* (Turner and Simister, 2000). So at points throughout the book, I say some topics are beyond the scope of this book, and refer you to the relevant chapter in the *Gower Handbook of Project Management* or one of the spin-off books, *People in Project Management* (Turner, 2003a), or *Contracting for Project Management* (Turner, 2003b).
2 This book is not an academic treatise; however, there are times when I feel as though I might sound as if I am making sweeping statements, and then I do want to justify what I say. For instance, in Chapter 13, in claiming the value of risk management, I didn't want it to sound like me on my hobby horse, when I know that research done by Terry Cooke-Davies (2002) has shown that effective risk management can improve project performance. Thus the reference to his work.
3 Finally, I must give due credit to my sources, as I don't want to be accused of stealing other people's ideas. I don't expect any of my target audience to go and read any of the three research dissertations I have quoted, but it is important to acknowledge the source of my own knowledge. When I am referring to another book, or professional standard, or even to a magazine article, I do think that some of my readers may be interested in following them up.

So I have tried to keep references to a minimum, eliminating references to any of my own research work. But I have included them where I hope they will be helpful, or it is important to acknowledge my sources.

I hope you find the book helpful, and would be grateful for any feedback. I am also happy to answer queries.

Rodney Turner
East Horsley
January 2004
rodneyturner@europrojex.co.uk
www.europrojex.co.uk

Acknowledgements

I am grateful to several people for the help and support I have received in editing this book.

I should give particular mention to Ralf Müller. He read every chapter of the draft at least twice, and made numerous helpful comments. Chapter 2 was substantially changed and the process flow diagram, Figure 2.6, was included at his suggestion. I have included two anecdotes he related while commenting on the text, and also included four topics he suggested – for example mention of super users in Chapter 15 was Ralf's idea. His contribution has been substantial.

Judy Morton proofread every chapter. As I say twice in the text, human beings find it very difficult to spot their own mistakes. I am no different. So it is useful to have the text read by an independent eye. Judy also highlighted several places where my style was somewhat unreadable. This was either because I was using project management jargon that may be a bit obscure to the lay reader, or because I just used turgid text. Either way it was useful to have the text read by a lay person to improve its readability. There were several places where the project management research community would have known what I was talking about, but they are not my audience.

In addition to Ralf I had a small committee of beta testers. Wim van der Voort (Anne Keegan's husband) made several useful comments, as did my wife Beverley. I am also grateful for the input from Martina Huemann and Xue Yan.

I undertook some research before beginning writing, talking to people involved in the management of web projects to discover what it meant for them. I mention in particular Matti Smith, Richard McBain, Richard Campin and Peter Race at Henley Management College. I also acknowledge the many other people I have talked to about the management of web projects over the past year.

Finally, several ideas in the text relating to the management of the project-based organization, but particularly the passage on innovation projects in Chapter 3, derive from research work I have done with Anne Keegan into the management of the project-based organization. I would not have been able to write those parts without that collaboration, and I wish to acknowledge that here.

Rodney Turner
East Horsley
January 2004

CHAPTER **1** *Introduction*

The Internet, intranets and extranets are now part of our lives. They are here to stay; and thus the management of the delivery of web projects has become an essential part of the project management armoury. Those doom merchants who said that the stock market shake-out of dot-com companies around the turn of the millennium spelt the end of the e-revolution are not students of history. It often happens with a new technology, from the South Sea Bubble of the eighteenth century, to the stock market shake-out of computer companies in the 1970s. It is a correction of early overenthusiasm, but a mere hiccough in the inexorable rise of the new technology.

Bill Gates in his book *Business @ the Speed of Thought: Using a Digital Nervous System* (2000) has a chart of the growth in utilization of new technologies, particularly the take-up in homes. From the telephone to the motor car to the home refrigerator, every new technology follows a classic S-curve building to around 95 per cent ownership. We are now about 40 per cent of the way through the growth in the ownership of personal computers (PCs) in the home and the use of the Internet. David Bicknell (2002) reports that in the UK 22 million people are online, with 15 million accessing the Internet via home computers. In the not too distant future 95 per cent of homes will have a PC and be using the Internet, just as 95 per cent of homes have electric lights, washing machines and colour televisions. It will happen, and people unable to manage web-delivery projects effectively will be left in the slow lane, joining some of history's other dinosaurs, such as the community laundry.

Most managers today, even those responsible for managing a function in the line organization, are often required to manage a unique, novel and transient endeavour to deliver novel business objectives or to bring about change in the organization. Normal management processes, which are designed to manage the status quo, are ineffective in such circumstances. We cannot expect processes designed to maintain the status quo and stability in the organization to also be effective at bringing about change. We need a different approach. That approach is project management. Project management is a process for managing change in organizations, for achieving novel business objectives. Most managers now have project management in their armoury of management skills.

But, as we shall see in Part 1 of this book, the management of web-delivery projects requires something additional to standard project management approaches. They have additional features, both in terms of the nature of the projects, and in terms of the scope of what they deliver, that requires an enhanced approach. This book describes the core skills of project management required in the management of web-delivery projects.

Before Part 1 I have provided an introduction to projects and their management and an overview of the book as a whole. I start by describing projects and their management, introducing the features of projects that require the adoption of project management processes. The book will draw on conventional project management, and so it is useful to give an initial overview. Web-delivery projects and their management have all of the features of conventional projects; they are a subset of projects and project management. (In Part 1, I also describe other elements of web-delivery projects that require additional features in their management.) In the second section of this chapter, I discuss some project typologies that influence some of the thinking in this book, before explaining the overall structure of this book in the last section.

PROJECTS AND THEIR MANAGEMENT

PROJECTS

I have previously attempted a precise definition of projects and their management, but I now prefer to think more in terms of the features of projects that require a different approach to their management than routine work. I find that some people take precise definitions of things and treat them as prescriptive (see Figure 1.1). That is facile. What we are trying to do is aid our understanding of the nature of the beast we have to manage, and choose appropriate management approaches. In this section I will consider the features of projects that require us to adopt project management processes for their management. Throughout this book I will draw on conventional project management thinking, and so it is worthwhile to start with a broad overview. This will form a precursor to Part 1 where I will describe the additional features of web-delivery projects that will require an enhanced approach to their management.

> When I was at Henley Management College, I had a student on the MBA programme who thought my definition of projects was wrong. The definition says they are unique, but he said he worked on maintenance projects in his job at British Telecom that were quite repetitive. He didn't have the humility to see that his use of the word 'project' might be wrong – but that wasn't the point. He found some value in viewing his work as projects, but didn't see that the point of a definition is to aid understanding, not to be precise and prescriptive.

Figure 1.1 *Being precise and prescriptive*

Having said that, I recently derived what appears to be a precise definition:

> A project is a temporary organization to which resources are assigned to undertake a unique, novel and transient endeavour managing the inherent uncertainty and need for integration in order to deliver beneficial change objectives.

However, this should be viewed as a list of features of a project. A project is an organization, not just a piece of work, created by a parent organization to bring about change. The change might be to exploit a new market, develop a new product or new technology, introduce a new computer system, change the organization in some way, or train managers. The project has a temporary existence, because it will no longer be needed once the change has been delivered. It is an agency to which the parent organization assigns resources (people, materials, money) to do the work required to achieve that change. The work required will be different than anything done before or in the future (though how different will be one of the typologies considered in the next section), and will therefore require novel processes for its delivery and be limited in time.

Being unique and novel, the work is risky, and so the project is an agency for managing that risk. Further, being novel, the resources of the project need to be integrated with each other, and the project and its outputs need to be integrated with the parent organization, so the project is an agency for that integration. (By this definition the maintenance 'projects' in Figure 1.1 are not projects. They are not temporary organizations created to bring about change; they are temporary tasks given to the routine organization, and fairly repetitive ones at that. I return to this in the definition of web projects in the next chapter.)

Organizations have two types of objectives:

- Routine objectives to do routine things to undertake the main line of business of the organization.
- Unique, novel, once-off objectives to bring about change.

In order to achieve the routine objectives, the organization needs to carry out routine activities. The emphasis of normal operations management is to keep things routine and maintain the status quo, because if they can repeat today what they did yesterday, there is a good chance they will achieve the same objectives. The emphasis of management in the second case is to upset the status quo – that is the whole point, to introduce change. Therefore a different approach to management is required. This is project management. In many organizations, the routine objectives are the responsibility of the front office, and the change objectives the responsibility of the back office, but in project-based organizations, the work of the front office will also be project work for external customers.

There are several functions that need to be managed on a project, including:

- scope of work
- organization of resources
- cost
- time
- quality and configuration
- risk.

Figure 1.2 lists some of the tools required to manage these functions and the chapters in which they are covered in Part 2 of this book.

Another concept we will meet repeatedly throughout the book is the difference between project objectives and business objectives. The project is a temporary organization, created to deliver a facility (project objectives). The facility may be:

- a new product or a new production process or factory
- a computer system
- trained managers or staff
- a new management process or change to the organization structure, and so on.

Function	*Tools*	*Chapter number*
Scope of work	Project definition	5
	Product breakdown	7
	Work breakdown	7
	Milestone planning	7
	Activity planning	7
Organization of resources	External organization	8
	Internal organization	8
	Organization breakdown	8
	Responsibility charts	8
	Stakeholder management	9
Quality and configuration	Quality control	10
	Quality assurance	10
	Configuration management	10
Cost	Cost breakdown	11
	Estimating	11
	Earned value analysis	11
Time	Estimating duration	12
	Bar charts	12
	Milestone tracker diagrams	12
	Networks	12
Risk	Identification	13
	Analysis	13
	Mitigation and control	13

Figure 1.2 *The functions of project management and the tools to deliver them*

Once the facility has been delivered and the work of the project completed, it is operated by the users to achieve the business objectives and provide benefit to repay the cost of the project. The business objectives are achieved over the medium to long term after the project is finished. They may be:

- to exploit a new market, or provide a new service to customers
- to increase efficiency or productivity
- to increase competitiveness.

This concept is expanded in Chapters 5 and 6.

PROJECT MANAGEMENT

Project management is the process by which a project is successfully delivered. What we mean by the word 'successfully' will be discussed in Chapter 6. There are many ways to describe the project management processes. The most common is through a project management life cycle. There are many views of the life cycle. Figure 1.3 contains what is now accepted as a standard format. Another sees the project as a problem to be solved: Figure 1.4 shows the resulting life

Stage	*Name*	*Process*	*Outputs*
Germination	Proposal and initiation	Develop proposals Gather information Conduct feasibility Estimate design	Functional design Commitment of resources to design Estimates ± 20%
Growth	Design and appraisal	Develop design Estimate costs and returns Assess viability Obtain funding	Systems design Money and resources for implementation Estimates ± 10%
Maturity	Execution and Control	Do a detailed design Baseline estimates Do the work Control progress	Effective completion Facility ready for commissioning Estimates ± 5%
Metamorphosis	Finalization and close-out	Finish work Commission facility Obtain benefit Disband team Review achievement	Facility delivering benefit Satisfied team Data for future projects

Figure 1.3 *The basic project management life cycle*

cycle. A third view adopts the ideas of Henri Fayol (1949), and says there are five basic processes of management:

- plan the work
- organize the resources
- implement by assigning work to resources
- control progress
- direct the work of the resources and provide leadership.

Step	*Management Process*
Perceive the problem	Identify an opportunity for providing benefit to the organization
Gather data	Collect information relating to the opportunity
Define the problem	Determine the value of the opportunity and its potential benefits
Generate solutions	Identify several ways of delivering the opportunity and associated benefits
Evaluate solutions	Identify the cost of each solution, the risk and the expected benefit
Select a solution	Choose the solution that gives best value for money
Communicate the solution	Tell all parties involved of the chosen solution
Plan implementation	Complete a detailed design of the solution and plan implementation
Implement the solution	Authorize work, assign tasks to people, undertake the work and control progress
Monitor performance	Monitor results to ensure the problem has been solved and the benefits obtained

Figure 1.4 *Management processes derived from a problem solving cycle*

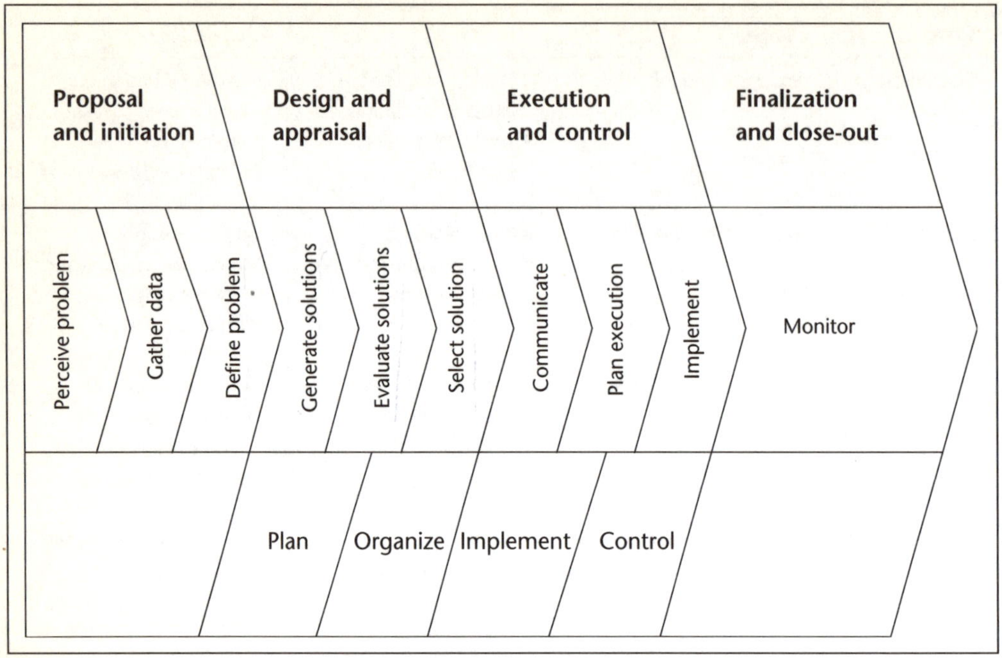

Figure 1.5 *Combining the three views of the life cycle*

These views are all similar, as shown in Figure 1.5. Figure 1.6 shows that project management is fractal management: each part of the project is almost a mini-project in its own right, and so is each element of that part. Thus the project management processes are applied on many levels.

Prince 2

Figure 1.7 illustrates Prince 2, the project process developed by the UK government for business development projects, including information systems (IS) (OGC, 2002). This has project start and project initiation followed by implementation. It also has two additional processes here, managing product delivery and managing stage transition. At the end of each implementation stage, the product the project will produce (the facility) must be checked against the business plan (the business objectives) as it is handed to the next stage. This produces a strong focus on the business case. Prince 2 also gives guidance as to the reports that should be produced at the start and finish of each stage.

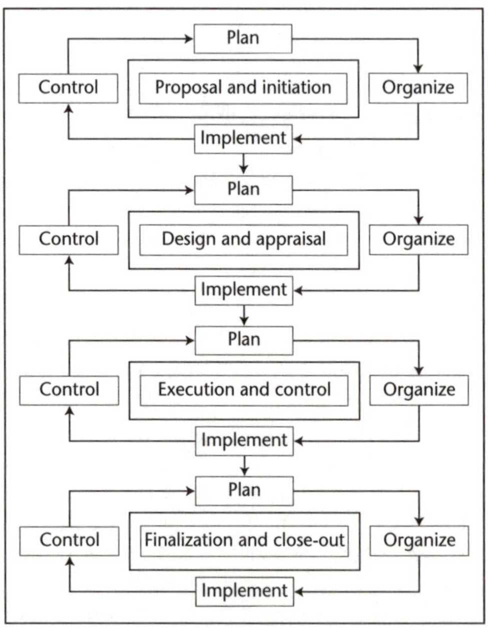

Figure 1.6 *Project management is fractal management*

Tailoring the processes

Prince 2 insists that the project management

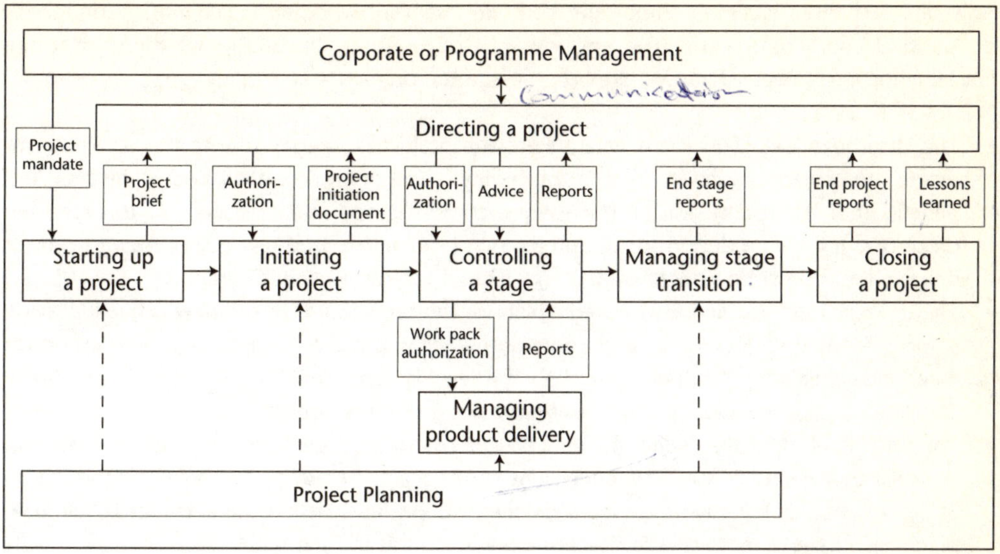

Figure 1.7 *The Prince 2 project process*

process should be tailored for each project. A company should have its standard process, but this needs to be reinterpreted project by project. Each project is unique, and so requires a unique process for its delivery. However, there is a problem. The more tailoring that is done, the more likely it is that a mistake will be made. Thus, a project-specific procedure needs to be produced for each project, but the closer a project's version is to the standard, the more likely it is to achieve a successful outcome.

PROJECT LEVELS

Finally in this section, we consider the levels over which the project is managed. We met the concept of a project being managed on different levels in Figure 1.6. Almost everything we do in life we manage over several levels, breaking it down to the next level as we understand the previous one. This helps define and control the scope. We do work because it will deliver an objective we want at the next level up, and we avoid doing work that does not deliver something we want.

I use the example of going on holiday to the south of France. I define my project by saying that I am going to go on holiday to St Tropez in the south of France, and I am going to travel overland by car. The project objective is to get to St Tropez; the business objective is to enjoy myself on holiday; the scope of work is to travel overland by car. At the next level of project definition, I define the towns I am going to travel through to get from where I live in the south of England (Guildford), to St Tropez. I will go from Guildford, to Dover, Calais, Paris, Beaune, Lyons, Aix-en-Provence, St Tropez. That defines the strategy for my project. At the next level I define the roads I will take between each town. To get from Guildford to Dover I will travel along the A246, M25, M26 and M20. From Dover to Calais I can take the ferry or train. I take roads that take me from one town to the next; I do not take roads that take me in a different direction or round in circles.

Projects should be no different. Unfortunately people seem to plan projects on just one level, usually a level of too much detail. They define work because it seems related to the project.

However, they often leave out important work, do irrelevant work, and even worse, sometimes do positively damaging work. The analogy with my journey illustrates that there are three fundamental levels over which we need to manage the project:

- *The integrative level:* This is the level where the project is integrated into the business. We define the project objectives, that is the facility it will deliver, and business objectives and benefits that the facility will produce when commissioned and operated. At this level we produce a functional design for the project, and define the business objectives and project deliverables. I describe how to do this for web-delivery projects in Chapter 5.
- *The strategic level:* We define a strategic plan for the project, a framework which will provide a focus for the project team and coordinate their inputs. In Chapter 7, I will introduce *milestone planning* as the tool to do this. This level is equivalent to the towns in the trip to St Tropez. At this level we produce a systems design for the project.
- *The detail level:* Here we define the work that needs to be done to deliver each milestone in the milestone plan. This level is equivalent to the roads between the towns on the trip to St Tropez. At this level we produce a detailed design, and define the activities required to reach each milestone. I will also describe how to do this in Chapter 7.

Each level should not be developed until the previous one has been properly defined. If you rush straight to the detailed level of planning, you will put a lot of time and effort into planning the project, only to find that it was never worthwhile. By planning down through the levels, you only commit resources to planning at a lower level after the project has been proven at a higher level. Because the lower levels give you greater accuracy, there may still be projects you reject at the lower levels, even though you accepted them at the higher levels. However, there will be many hopeless projects you reject at the integrative level, without devoting much time to their planning; there will be borderline ones you reject at the strategic level; and it will only be worthwhile projects that have been sanctioned that you will plan at the detail level. There are four breakdown structures for projects, three related to these levels.

- *Product breakdown structure (PBS):* This is the decomposition of the project's products through the levels above: business objectives; project outputs; milestones; and activity deliverables. It is equivalent to the Bill of Materials in a manufacturing context.
- *Organization breakdown structure (OBS):* This is the decomposition of the skill types to be used on the project: companies; functions; resource types; named individuals.
- *Work breakdown structure (WBS):* This is the work that will be done by the resources at a given level to deliver the products they are responsible for at that level.
- *Cost breakdown structure (CBS):* This is the definition of the cost types on a project, labour, materials, overheads etc. (described further in Chapter 11). This breakdown exists on one level only, and is not related to the levels above.

Figure 1.8 gives a wider view of the levels. This illustrates a cascade of objectives at different levels of management, from development objectives for the parent organization down to task objectives for individuals. At each level, the strategy for achieving the objectives at that level implies the objectives at the next level down. I quite like this model because it gets away from

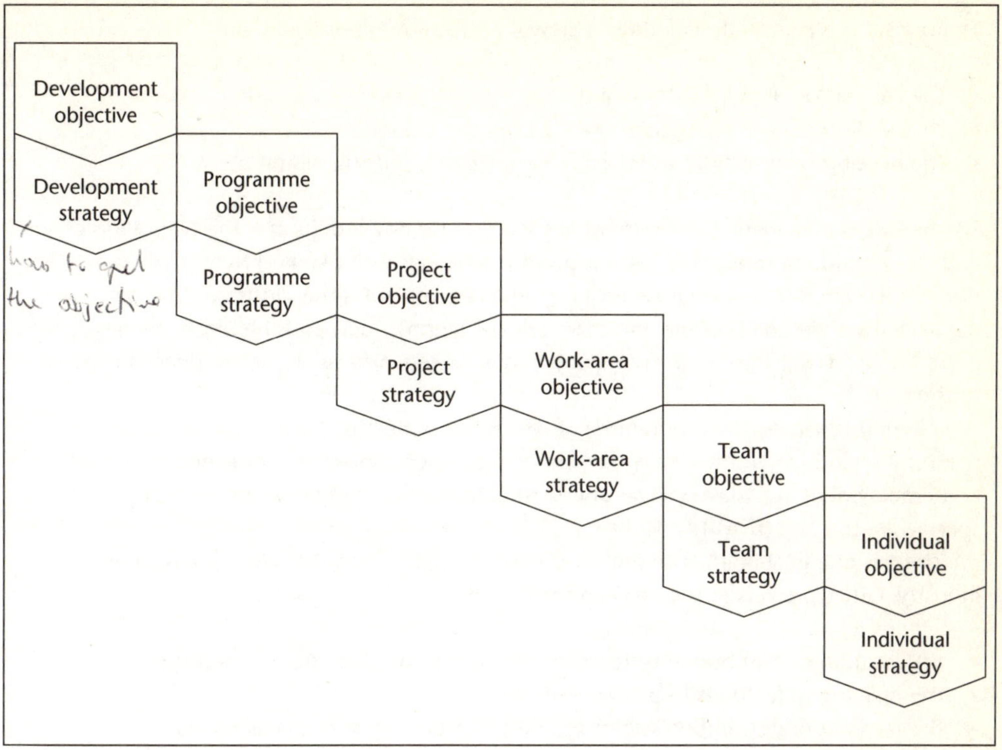

Figure 1.8 *Cascade of objectives*

hair-splitting arguments about visions, missions, aims, goals, and so on. We just have objectives at different levels of management. Figure 1.9 illustrates this cascade by reference to a project to develop a palm nut plantation in Malaysia. This example also illustrates another important point, that often our projects do not deliver their full potential until we have completed other projects in the programme of projects of which they are a part. Sometimes, as in the case of the palm nut plantation, we will get no benefit at all. Figure 1.10 shows the components in the PBS and the work elements in the WBS that result at different levels of this cascade. This also acts as something of a vocabulary for the use of these words in this book.

PROJECT TYPOLOGIES

I now wish to consider several project typologies which influence the thinking throughout this book.

CULTURAL VS TECHNICAL OBJECTIVES

Often, when undertaking projects, people focus only on the technical objectives:

- if installing new production machinery, it is all mechanical and electrical equipment;
- if implementing a new computer system, it is all hardware, software and peripherals.

The project is a palm nut plantation. The work areas are things like:

- the conversion of jungle to orchard;
- the development of an establishment to run the plantation;
- the development of systems for gathering, storing and shipping nuts.

The first work area involves milestones like the cutting down of jungle, the ploughing of soil and the planting of trees. One team is given the objective of planting trees, and on a given day, a member of that team is given a bag of trees to plant. (This illustrates that the lower the level the more the product and the work are synonymous, and the higher the level, the more the objectives have many ways of being achieved, and so are not so directly related to the work.)

Working upwards, the programme of which the project is a part is the development of a palm nut oil industry for Malaysia, and the development objectives are economic growth and employment in Malaysia. (This also illustrates that the higher up the hierarchy the less specific are the objectives.)

There is one final point. The project is part of a programme to develop a palm nut oil industry. Other projects in the programme include:

- the creation of distribution systems to take nuts from plantations to factories;
- the building of factories to process nuts into oil;
- the creation of distribution systems to take oil from factories to customers.

The palm nut plantation project will not deliver any benefit until these other projects are completed. If all we do is develop a palm nut plantation, we will end up with mountains of useless palm nuts. We can give those nuts a notional value, and work out the returns on the plantation, but we cannot realize those returns until we have completed all of the projects in the programme. Many of our projects are like this – we can only get the full benefit of our work when we have completed other projects in the programme.

Figure 1.9 *Cascade of objectives for a project to develop a palm nut plantation*

Level	*Product*	*Figure 1.9*	*Work*	*Duration*
	Vision	Good life		
Development	Mission	Economic growth		5 years
Programme	Aim or purpose	Palm nut oil industry		2 years
Project	Facility	Plantation	Project	9–18 months
Work area	Sub-facility	Cultivation	Work area	9–18 months
Team	Milestone	Orchards	Work pack	2 months
Individual	Deliverable	Planted trees	Activity	2 weeks
		Dig holes	Task	1 day

Figure 1.10 *Standard product and work breakdown structures (PBS and WBS)*

However, to make the new equipment work, it is also necessary to undertake what I call cultural activities (Andersen *et al.*, 1995). These are changes to:

- Management systems and procedures: describing how the new equipment will be used and operated (see Figure 1.11). New procedures need to be written.
- People, their number, skills and values: people need to be redeployed, trained and educated.
- The organization itself. You may need to create new functions or departments, change existing ones, or change management responsibility.

I was helping a company plan the implementation of their corporate intranet. They were going to transfer expense claims, reporting of sickness, holiday requests and other personnel issues to online reporting on the intranet. I asked whether they had written procedures for how online reporting would work. They said no, the systems would work the same as before. I pointed out that this was impossible, unless they were planning to print pieces of paper for the boss to sign, in which case it was pointless to put it online.

Figure 1.11 *New management procedures*

Projects with a mixture of technical and cultural objectives I call PSO projects; they create changes to people, systems and organization. These cultural changes need to be managed – they will not happen of their own accord. They need to be included in the project plan along with the technical activities. There has been a change in approach over the years:

- In the early 1980s, they were ignored. People expected the cultural activities to look after themselves.
- By the late 1980s, people were including them in the project plan, but almost as an afterthought. They were included as an appendage, not a core part of the project.
- By the early 1990s, people recognized that cultural changes need to be made an integral part of the plan. People changes are more difficult to achieve than the technical changes, and sometimes the technical work must be modified to suit what can be achieved on the cultural side. Cultural changes are a greater drag on the change than the technical activities. Technical activities are easy; cultural changes are difficult. The technology implemented has to reflect the cultural changes that can be achieved.

In Chapter 3, I will show that web-delivery projects include cultural activities in spades. They are cultural change projects, innovation projects, and business re-engineering projects. In Chapter 7, I show how to ensure that the plan gives due recognition to the cultural work and makes it an integral part of the plan. In Chapter 9, I show how to manage the stakeholders to try to make the cultural changes more acceptable to the people in the organization.

THE GOALS AND METHODS MATRIX

Projects can be judged by the uncertainty in the desired product or facility, and uncertainty in the method of delivering it (Figure 1.12). Some people say that you only have a project if the outputs are well defined (they only exist in the two left-hand quadrants). Further, many of the books on project management are written by engineers, who assume that both the methods and outputs are well defined, and so they are only writing about what I call Type 1 projects below. I think that you have a project once you have a reasonably well-defined business objective, but that there can be some uncertainty both about the facility that will deliver those business objectives and the method of delivering it. This is particularly true for web-delivery projects. This leads to the identification of four types of project:

Methods well defined		Goals well defined: Yes	Goals well defined: No
	No	**Type 2** Milestone planning Using known deliverables (Water)	**Type 4** Soft systems planning To define deliverables (Air)
	Yes	**Type 1** Activity-based Planning (Earth)	**Type 3** Milestone planning Using life-cycle stages (Fire)

Figure 1.12 *The goals and methods matrix*

- **Type 1:** *Projects with well-defined goals and well-defined methods of achieving the goals.* These are typified by engineering projects, which tend to be planned in terms of well-defined activities. The role of the project manager is that of a conductor, leading the team through a well-known score, just imposing his or her own interpretation and tempo.
- **Type 2:** *Projects with well-defined goals, but poorly-defined activities.* These are typified by product development projects. They tend to be planned in terms of the known deliverables, with the method of achieving them planned on a rolling wave basis (Chapter 7) as new information becomes available. The role of the project manager is that of a coach, training the team in standard plays, but leaving them to play the game as it evolves.
- **Type 3:** *Projects with poorly-defined goals, but well-defined methods.* These are typified by information systems projects, which are planned in terms of life cycle stages. The goals are defined in conceptual terms, but their specification is refined through the stages of the project. The role of the project manager is that of master craftsman, with a team knowledgeable in the techniques. But when they are painting their portion of the Sistine Chapel ceiling, they will have to paint around the unknown flaws they encounter.
- **Type 4:** *Projects with both poorly-defined objectives and work methods.* These are typified by research and organizational change projects and are planned in terms of gateways or hurdles. If a project is to be successful, it must pass through a gateway on a certain day. If it does not, the gateway closes forever. The role of project manager is that of an eagle. They must hover above the project, see it in the context of the parent organization, and then be able to dive down to deal with an issue, before rising up above the project again. These projects are more likely to be successful if the goals are defined first, and then the work methods.

We find web-delivery projects of all four types, but particularly of Type 4.

HOW UNIQUE IS THE PROJECT?

I said at the start of the previous section that projects are unique, but then implied that some are more unique than others. I also noted that organizations have two types of objectives, routine and novel, and that the work to deliver those will be repeat or unique respectively. In reality, it is not either–or; there is a spectrum from totally routine to totally novel, from totally repeat to totally unique. Projects lie toward the unique–novel end of the spectrum, but the last typology I describe here considers four types of projects on the spectrum:

1 **Runners:** These projects are very familiar for the people undertaking them; they are virtually repeats of earlier work. The only reason each project is different from the previous one is because it is done at a different time, so the weather is different. Very routine processes will be used to deliver them, and they will be very low risk. They almost don't count as projects, but as with the MBA student in Figure 1.1, there is some value as considering them as such. These tend to be Type 1 projects.
2 **Repeaters:** These projects are reasonably common for the organization, but not so familiar to the project team members. There will be knowledge within the organization about how this sort of project should be managed which the project team can draw on during the start-up process. However, there will be differences between this and the other projects which do need to be taken account of. These projects will be low risk, and indeed the greatest risk will be that differences from the other projects are not taken into account and mistakes made assuming they are totally identical. These tend to be Type 1 or simpler Type 2 or 3 projects.
3 **Strangers:** The organization has undertaken a very small number of similar projects before, but they are totally new to the project team members. There is some knowledge to draw on within the organization about how to manage this sort of project, but it still has to be planned and managed from first principles. In particular you should try to break the project down into familiar components, trying to identify as many parts as possible that can be made to repeat things done before by one or more team members. These types of project will be higher risk, and will tend to be Type 2, 3 or a simpler Type 4.
4 **Aliens:** These projects are totally new for the organization – there is no experience at all about their management. They are totally unique and novel, and so they will be very high risk. Again you should try as much as possible to find components that are familiar to project team members. If there are no familiar components you should seriously consider not doing the projects, but sometimes you have no choice. These projects tend to be Type 4.

HOW IMPORTANT IS THE PROJECT TO THE BUSINESS?

The final typology considers how important the project is to the business. One high street bank won't do any projects unless they can be assigned to one of these three categories:

1 **Stay-in-business projects:** These are to rescue the business, either because there has been an unforeseen crisis, or a change in government legislation. At the turn of the millennium, Y2K and Euro implementation projects were stay-in-business projects. Such projects ought to be strangers or aliens. If they are runners or repeaters there is something wrong with your business.
2 **Repositioning projects:** These are for the introduction of new products or new markets for your products. They tend to be repeaters, but may be strangers. For this type of project to be an alien, the new product or market being introduced will be very high risk. Don't go there. Many web-delivery projects are repositioning projects.
3 **Performance improvement projects:** These are to make changes to enable you to do your business better. They may be business process re-engineering projects, organizational change projects or training projects. They will tend to be repeaters or strangers, but may be aliens, in which case the performance improvement will be severe, and may be necessary to stay in business. But as we shall see in Chapter 3, some web-delivery projects introduce lateral changes to the business processes (business lateral engineering), and so will be aliens, though paradoxically not very high risk. Many web-delivery projects are for performance improvement.

THE STRUCTURE OF THIS BOOK

After this chapter of introduction, the book is divided into two parts.

PART 1: THE NATURE OF WEB PROJECTS

In the first part I describe the special features of web-delivery projects. As I said above they are a subset of projects, not a stand-alone entity. So everything that I have said above applies to web-delivery projects. But they have special features which make them an identifiable subset of projects.

In Chapter 1 I consider the differences between web-delivery projects and information systems (IS) projects. Web-delivery projects are a special type of IS project. However, they have many specific features, and these are discussed here in Chapter 2. I believe that many of these differences are due to the novelty of the technology and its speed of change. If someone had written a book like this about IS projects 30 years ago, they might have come up with a similar list for the differences between IS projects and engineering projects. However, some of these differences are inherent. I also describe life cycles suggested for web-delivery projects, and how some of the typologies apply to them.

But web-delivery projects are more than information systems projects. They are:

- organizational change projects
- innovation projects
- business process improvement (lateral engineering) projects
- creative projects
- publication projects
- marketing projects.

In Chapter 3, I describe the nature of these types of project, and what that means for web-delivery projects and their management.

PART 2: THE MANAGEMENT OF WEB PROJECTS

In Part 2 I step through the management of a web-delivery project. I use as my basis a project start-up workshop and work through one of these, describing the elements of a workshop, and the associated elements of project management. In Chapter 4 I look at the first step in the project life cycle, initiation, and in particular how to hold a project start-up or initiation workshop. Then the elements of the workshop and project management are dealt with in turn in separate chapters on:

- project definition
- project success and strategy
- managing scope
- organizing the project
- managing stakeholders
- managing quality and configuration
- managing cost
- managing time
- managing risk.

Figure 1.2 showed the chapters in which each of these is covered, except project success and strategy, which is covered in Chapter 6. You don't need to manage each of these on every web-delivery project. As I said above, you need to tailor the process to the project. But I cover all the topics and you can choose those that you need on your project. I believe you need project definition, success and strategy, a milestone plan and a responsibility chart for every project. The rest you choose as appropriate. Figure 1.2, and the agenda for the project start-up workshop, Figure 4.3, can act as templates to help choose the project management processes for your project. These are represented as a process flow diagram in Figure 2.4.

Following on from the topics listed above, the next two chapters in Part 2, Chapters 14 and 15, describe the two later stages of the life cycle, project control and project close-out. Finally in Chapter 16, I describe project portfolio and programme management. Many projects are implemented as part of a collection of projects. A project portfolio is a collection of projects managed together for administrative convenience, often to coordinate interfaces between them and share resources from a limited pool. A programme is a collection of projects with a higher order strategic objective. The projects contribute elements of the facility delivered by the programme. None of the projects can deliver the whole facility on their own, and the facility has little or no value until all the elements are delivered (for example the palm nut oil industry in Figure 1.9). In Chapter 16 I describe project portfolio management, and its two elements, coordination of interfaces and sharing of interfaces, and the management of a programme of projects of which a web-delivery project may be a part.

CASE STUDY: TriMagi

Throughout the book I use a case study to illustrate the concepts as they are introduced. As I work through Part 2, I will build up the project plan for the case study. I had intended to introduce the case study in Chapter 5 (Project definition) when I could introduce and describe it by defining it. However, I find I want to refer to it earlier, particularly in Chapters 3 and 4, so I give an initial introduction here. The case study is an intranet.

TriMagi provides financial services to the customers of the Highlands and Islands Bank (HIB). HIB has effectively outsourced the provision of a particular service to TriMagi. TriMagi plans to introduce an intranet. In the first instance this will cover three areas:

1 Processing of documents for personnel, including
   - expense claims
   - holiday requests
   - sickness reports.
2 Online availability of personnel information, such as
   - procedures to be followed to submit the above
   - information about the company car scheme
   - statement of the company's personnel policy and psychological contract with its employees.
3 Daily news reports on each person's desk top, including
   - news about the company
   - news from the financial services sector
   - briefings from the managing director.

The benefits are that the company wants to:

- communicate better with its employees, and hopefully improve the psychological contract
- speed up the processing of personnel documents, and reduce the administrative burden
- reduce administrative, printing and storage costs by making information available online rather than in paper form.

The project is to be implemented in four months.

PART 1 *The Nature of Web Projects*

CHAPTER

2 *Features of Web Projects*

What are web projects, and how do they differ from conventional IS (information systems) projects? In its issue of 23 November 2000 *Computer Weekly* said:

> As with any projects, from building a bridge to building a web site, the principles of sound project management apply. Just because e-business involves Internet technology, it does not alter the ground rules. But it does, nevertheless, throw up some new factors which the project management process needs to take into account.

In this chapter I consider what those factors might be. I give a definition of web-delivery projects, and describe ten features that differentiate them from conventional IS projects. I then suggest a model for managing web-delivery projects, including a life cycle and management process, derived to address those features, based on the concepts of the first chapter. As before, I don't want the definitions to be prescriptive, but to identify features which need to be taken account of in the management of web-delivery projects. Web-delivery projects are IS projects; they are just a subset with very special features that means their management requires a different focus from conventional IS projects.

In Chapter 3, I consider additional dimensions of web-delivery projects. As with all IS projects, web-delivery projects are not just about the information technology. They are PSO projects, they bring about change in the organization to improve performance, and to make them work it is necessary to re-engineer the business processes. They are also innovation projects often requiring considerable creativity. The impact of these dimensions is described in Chapter 3.

WHAT ARE WEB PROJECTS?

As with the definition of projects themselves, the literature throws up many definitions of e-projects, some of them quite prescriptive and limiting, and unnecessarily so. Peter Kulik and Robert Samuelsen (2001) give a very simple definition of web-delivery projects:

> An e-project is any project that involves creating or changing source code that is deployed on the Internet.

Anthony Onabanjo (2001) quotes IBM in defining web projects as:

> The transformation of key business processes through the use of Internet technologies.

This is narrower and more prescriptive than the first, but does focus on performance improvement through business process re-engineering as discussed in the next chapter. Peter Kulik and Robert Samuelsen go on to identify three types of e-project:

- *Construction projects:* This is the initial build of any web space. These are the closest to conventional projects with cost-benefit analysis, designs and approvals, and contracts important. They can take months to deliver – the authors liken them to the construction of a new house.
- *Remodelling projects:* These add new features to an existing space. Because of the dynamic modularity of HTML, new features can be added with little disruption, and be immediately available to users. Typically they take weeks to deliver and are like building an extension to a house.
- *Maintenance projects:* These correct bugs, or make minor changes to keep information current. They take days, or even as little as hours or minutes to do. They are like redecorating or repairing a house.

Using the definitions in Chapter 1, I would say maintenance and even smaller remodelling projects are not projects. They are not temporary organizations created to bring about change; they are temporary tasks given to the routine organization. Similarly, some very small construction activities, such as the creation of a home web page are not projects; they too are temporary tasks undertaken by a routine organization. I will therefore be focusing in this book on larger construction and remodelling projects, ones which last months, where a temporary organization is created to bring about a change to a parent organization, to transform business processes, as suggested by IBM.

Peter Kulik and Robert Samuelsen's definition just mentions deploying code on the Internet. There are three major media, the Internet, intranet and extranet, with 'the Internet' sometimes used as a generic word for all three. Tim Rahschulte (2001) describes the opportunities offered by all three media:

1. *The Internet:* This is the worldwide web that started it all. Information held on a server, either within the organization, or at a remote service provider, is made available to the outside world 24 hours a day, 365 days a year. It enables an organization to establish a global presence, makes its product catalogues available for inspection and its products available for purchase to people globally, around the clock. Time-sensitive data can be updated in real time. It enables an organization to open its markets globally.
2. *The intranet:* This is information only made available to internal staff. It enables management to communicate with staff on a real time basis, publishing for instance a daily newsletter. Members of the organization can share data and collaborate with each other and internal business processes can be expedited. Tasks such as the reporting of sick leave or annual holidays, making expense claims, or completing time sheets can be automated. Information such as terms and conditions of employment, or information about company car schemes or health insurance can be made permanently available and always current. The management literature talks about a psychological contract between the employer and employee; an intranet can help maintain the psychological contract.
3. *The extranet:* This is information that is made available to specific customers or suppliers with password protection. It enables customer or supplier contact information to be tailored to a specific firm. It enables organizations to integrate the supply chain, linking first, second and third tier suppliers, and make links to first, second and third tier customers. Motor car companies, for instance, can create an integrated supply chain from third tier suppliers, through the forecourt to consumers.

A fourth and growing use of the Internet is *application service provision*. Rather than buying their own software licenses, users access applications over the Internet, effectively from the extranet of their application service provider (ASP). However, I think this is sufficiently different from the uses of the extranet implied above to stand as a fourth use. The advantage to users is that they can gain access to real time updates to their applications, and they can access integrated applications that more specifically meet their needs.

At the end of the last chapter, I introduced a case study which I will use to illustrate the application of the project management techniques described in Part 2. It is the development of an intranet at TriMagi Financial Services.

Kulik and Samuelsen say web construction projects need to be subjected to all the disciplines of conventional projects, particularly cost-benefit analysis. On the other hand, Bill Gates in *Business @ the Speed of Thought: Using a Digital Nervous System* (2000) quotes Andrew Grove, chairman of Intel, as saying: 'What is my return on investment on e-commerce? Are you crazy? This is Columbus in the New World. What was his ROI?'

Mehari Akalu (2003) showed that conventional investment appraisal techniques such as net present value (NPV) and internal rate of return (IRR) (Turner 1995; Lock, 2000b) are not valid in the case of IS and innovation projects, and since web-delivery projects are both, they need to be appraised in other ways. A more recent example than Columbus of a national level innovation project that satisfied no investment criteria was the construction of the interstate highways in the US in the 1950s. It was something President Eisenhower just thought had to be done, and it repaid itself many times over. However, excessive optimism leads to the South Sea Bubble. Web-delivery projects must still deliver value. A balance is needed between stifling innovation through rigid control, and allowing anarchy to reign. I discuss this when dealing with innovation projects in the next chapter.

KEY FEATURES OF WEB PROJECTS

Anthony Onabanjo (2001) identified ten differences between web-delivery projects and conventional IS projects. Web-delivery projects have ten features that make them a special case of IS projects. All of these features can be viewed as a continuum, and some IS projects may even share them. Some of the dimensions in the next chapter apply equally to IS projects, particularly that they are change projects, and the need to re-engineer the business processes. Innovation and creativity are not so significant on most IS projects. Some of the differences Anthony Onbanjo identified are inherent to web-delivery projects, and others will disappear with time. When he was presenting his results at the IPMA World Congress in Berlin in June 2002, members of the audience said some of the 'differences' would have applied to IS projects 30 years ago. It was because the technology of IS projects was now more familiar that the 'difference' now exists, and it would disappear as the technology of the web became more familiar. I have recast and reformulated the features and split them into inherent features and temporal differences that may disappear with time. The features are listed in Figure 2.1.

INHERENT FEATURES

Shorter timescales

Web-delivery projects usually have shorter timescales than conventional IS projects. Durations are measured in weeks or months, rather than quarters or years. Peter Kulik and Robert Samuelsen say the duration of web construction projects is months, remodelling activities weeks and

Difference?	*Web projects*	*IS projects*
Inherent	Short time horizons, months	Longer time horizons, quarters
	Global reach with diverse user requirements	More localized with narrower user requirements
	Managed from outside the IS Department	Managed from within the IS Department
	Multidisciplinary teams with high focus on creativity and usability	Less creative features and visual design less important
	Wide range of user requirements	Narrower range of user requirements
Temporal	Diverse technologies, less proven applications, rapidly evolving	Integrated technologies, proven and stable designs
	Immature industry with skill shortages	Developed industry with skills more widely available
	Undefined methodologies integrating all elements of web projects	Well-defined methodologies such as SSADM, Rapid applications development (RAD), Prince 2, etc
	Fast changes in the industry	Fewer changes due to 'legacy' systems
	Perceived greater risk	Perceived stability of conventional business model

Figure 2.1 *Ten key differences between web-delivery and IS projects*

maintenance tasks days. Larger IS projects will last 9 to 18 months, and very large IS programmes may last for years. (There is a growing view in the project management community, which I share, that most projects cannot have a duration of more than 18 months. If they become longer, the end deliverable is not that clear, and they become a programme and not a project: see Chapter 16.) Linked to the short project durations is reduced release frequency. Mean time between releases is directly proportional to mean time to market: new construction will have a release frequency of months, remodelling a release frequency of weeks, and maintenance a release frequency of days or even hours with rolling updates.

The reason e-projects have short duration is that time to market is regarded as crucial. Personally, I think the reason is slightly perverse, and organizations have created a rod to beat their own backs with. With web technology it is possible to meet short timescales, and so customers expect it will happen. Organizations get caught on a treadmill. They are able to deliver rapid releases, they do so, and so customers expect they will continue to do so against ever shorter timescales. Reuters told me in the mid-1990s that they aimed to release their updated products once every two years. Some enhancements were ready to add almost as the latest version was released. But if updates were drip fed onto the market, customers expected to get them for free. Reuters would save all the updates for two years and release them together, charging a premium for the update package. Symantec now do release updates for the Norton suite of products about once every two or three weeks. Virus definitions are updated weekly, or even daily if some significant new virus is found. This would not be possible without the Internet. Norton Anti-Virus 2003, which I have just installed at the time of writing, now automatically updates virus definitions while I am online downloading my e-mail. (I am sure McAfee does the same.) The technology has created the possibility of frequent releases, and customers expect it. The way Symantec overcome the problem perceived by Reuters of not being able to charge for the releases is to build the price for the first year's updates into the price of the product, and then charge a subscription for future years – a simple solution. Henley Management College, when launching their el-MBA, made the first release in six months, and the first remodel four months later. The course starts once every four months, and so between cohorts they set the target of making the first release for the cohort after next. They were able to achieve about 70 per cent of the desired functionality for the first release, and built the remainder into the first update. The technology makes that feasible.

A consequence of the perceived pressure for short project delivery and rapid releases is that quality suffers. Project managers bypass proper control processes. It is essential to maintain quality and functionality. Simple techniques for managing quality and configuration will be presented in Chapter 10.

Wide-ranging and even global reach with many stakeholders

One of the objectives of many e-projects, particularly the Internet and extranet, is to achieve global reach, to access customers or suppliers in much broader, more diverse market segments. An intranet may have narrower focus, but is often still aiming to a chieve a wider audience than conventional communication systems within an organization. My wife was responsible for implementing a standard, corporate intranet within BOC, who are a multinational company, so even an intranet can have global reach. This means the users of the systems will hold a much broader range of cultures, beliefs and values, which also means that they will have a more diverse set of requirements for what they want from the system. Also the designers of the system must be much more cautious of not causing offence to a wider range of potential customers. This is leading to the new role of usability engineers who can design the system for this broader range of needs and tastes. It is not my intention to give a detailed description of managing cultural differences in this book. I will briefly touch on it when describing the management of stakeholders in Chapter 9. For a more detailed description see David Rees's chapter in the *Gower Handbook of Project Management* (2003).

You might say that information systems are also becoming global in their reach, and therefore this feature is temporal. However, it is the Internet that is enabling the global sharing of information. Thus, I suggest this as an inherent feature of web-delivery projects. Perhaps that just illustrates that in the end all of these features will become temporal, as the boundary between web-delivery projects and all other IS projects disappears. I described above how many users are now accessing their software applications over the web from ASPs. Ralf Müller (2002) has suggested that one result is that the number of users for these applications is growing from thousands, as it has been in the past, to millions in the Internet era. IS systems can no longer be perceived as technical solutions of business or entertainment. They are becoming social systems that pervade the everyday life of people in many societies. Thus managing web-based software development can mean migrating a system from a purely technical system with limited user base, to a widely used system with social impact.

Managed from outside the IS department

In the past, IS projects tended to be led by the IS department. They worked on their own to establish the user requirements and deliver the system. We could discuss how appropriate this was. I believe the users should be kept informed throughout the project, through configuration reviews (Chapter 10). Indeed, this is now changing, with upwards of 50 per cent of IS projects now managed outside the IS department. For instance, it may be the Marketing department that is driving the creation of an Internet presence, the Personnel department that is interested in the intranet or the Operations department that is leading the creation of an extranet.

Multidisciplinary teams

E-projects require a wide range of skills whereas conventional IS projects tended to be led by the IS department which worked on its own to deliver the system. The range of skills required for the delivery of web space includes user experience, technical knowledge, content delivery and other skills. Those people that may need to be included on the project team are listed in Figure 2.2. Figure 4.6 shows team members for the intranet at TriMagi. The situation is further complicated by the fact that many of the team members are located in different sites and even different countries, increasing the coordination and control requirements. Paul van Fenema (2002) has shown that globally distributed IS projects require more formal coordination and control mechanisms than more localized projects. Globally distributed projects need to be treated like high reliability organizations, but:

- People find it difficult to conceive the information needs of project team members on another site.
- People tend to use less informal communication when working across remote sites, whereas it ought to be increased to give the team a feeling of belonging.
- People can be unaware of task dependency, leading to inappropriate control mechanisms.

User experience	*Technical knowledge*	*Content specialists*	*Others*
Creative director	Programmer or web developer	Copywriter	Management consultant
Art director	Technical architect	Editor	Brand consultant
Designer	Security expert	Content manager	Quality assurance expert
Animation	Audio or video engineer		Business representative
Usability expert	Network analyst		Customer representative
	Tester		

Figure 2.2 *People who may be included in the project team*

In Chapter 7, I show how to use the milestone plan to delegate work to different units, making the dependency of work clear at that level, and enabling the adoption of simple, robust coordination mechanisms. The issue of a feeling of belonging to the project team is important. It can be increased by bringing the team members together for the start-up workshop, as discussed in Chapter 4. You might think it is a waste of money flying people around the world for a three day workshop, but doing it once at the start can be invaluable. After that, you can use the web space to post a team newsletter, and develop a team identity. A team logo and identity can be important, with a virtual noticeboard for team news (Reid, 2003). Posting photographs can also sustain the sense of belonging beyond the start-up meeting.

A wide range of user requirements

Web projects have global reach with many stakeholders. All of the project team members listed in Figure 2.2 are stakeholders of the project. There may also be a large number of additional stakeholders, including sponsors, employees, suppliers and customers in the integrated supply chain, partners and other collaborating organizations, shareholders, government, etc. All of these people have a view about the requirements of the system, the design of the web space and the nature of the changes and new business processes that will be introduced. These diverse requirements need to be taken account of. However, you must not overcomplicate the system. I saw a Dilbert cartoon recently where Dilbert was telling the user that with 400 requirements the system would be too complicated, and the user said, 'Oh! There was an additional requirement, the system should be simple'. Using the project definition processes in Chapter 5, you must carefully define the requirements of the system. But you must keep them simple, use the stakeholder management processes in Chapter 9 to communicate the chosen requirements to the extended team, and persuade them to accept the system as delivered. Do be sensitive to the needs of the users, but also keep the web space simple and useable.

The non-standardization of technology and jumble of legacy systems discussed below puts additional pressure on the user requirements. The systems need to be able to deal with a range of different technologies, including different browsers (Internet Explorer, Netscape Navigator), versions of the browsers, hardware technology (IBM compatible, Macintosh), operating systems (OS Windows, OS X and Linux), and modem speeds (from the slowest to broadband). Often it is necessary to limit the requirements for initial implementation.

Another problem with user requirements occurs when an old system is being migrated to a new (web-based) system. Sometimes, a customer may have important databases using legacy source code, perhaps decades old such as COBOL. It is old-fashioned but it still works. Or they may have just invested in a very expensive system and don't want to lose their investment. The web applications must then use the legacy systems to retrieve, process and change the database content. A risk averse customer may want the new system to replicate the old, preserving current processes, and delivering exactly the same output. Only once the old system has been replicated is the customer willing to accept new functionality, business processes and outputs. Inevitably, the new system is almost never able to deliver exactly the same output. It either delivers better (more accurate) results or is not capable of displaying or printing output in the same way as the old one. Given this phased approach of replicating the old system before adding new functionality, the buyer is usually disappointed after the first phase and sometimes cancels the project simply because it cannot mirror old technology. Similarly, the vendor can spend huge amounts of money to mirror old technology, just to throw it away when the new version works. I talk in the next chapter about the need to define the new business processes, and in Chapter 9 about the need to manage the stakeholders. They must accept that the web is a new departure, resulting in lateral changes to the business processes, and accept the changes from the start.

TEMPORAL DIFFERENCES

Technological challenges

As a result of the newness of the technology, there are many uncertainties. The technical architecture has to deliver performance requirements to handle loads associated with high and unpredictable volumes. Typically the hardware and software architecture is multi-tiered having to integrate many disparate legacy systems, and encapsulate existing business logic. The technical architecture should be able to meet the following requirements, to fit the following set of FRAMES:

Flexibility: it needs to handle the wide range of user requirements

Reliability: it needs to be able to cope with unexpected surges in demand

Availability: it may need to be available 24 hours a day, 365 days per year

Maintainability: it needs to be easily adaptable to deal with new technical or business requirements

Elasticity: it needs to be well integrated with other technical components

Security: it needs to be resistant to unauthorized access to data, and to viruses.

The rapidly changing nature of the technology means that technical integration is a concern. Legacy systems often cannot be mapped forward in their entirety, leading to hours of rekeying data, which can be prone to error. The speed with which systems become obsolete is another technical risk. Frequent updates can be necessary, but the benefit of updates needs to be balanced against time and cost. E-commerce would benefit from much greater standardization of systems, and as that happens web projects will become closer to conventional IS projects.

Skill shortages

One consequence of the newness of the industry is that there is a short supply of skills. Whereas in conventional information systems and technologies there is a ready supply of skilled resources, this is not the case in the new Internet technologies. Anthony Onabanjo reports that skill shortages can result in projects being delayed for months – which is significant when you consider that the duration of projects is measured in months. The result is that investors become more cautious with their e-commerce budget, and may delay investment decisions if they think that the results cannot be delivered in time.

Lack of methodologies to integrate all components

Conventional methodologies associated with IS projects, such as SSADM (structured systems analysis and design methodology) and the waterfall model (Turner, 1999) are not effective at integrating all the elements of a web-delivery project described in the next chapter. Rapid applications development (RAD) can been used to develop the software elements of web projects, but it ignores the business processes and change requirements, the people, systems and organization (PSO) elements. The result is the software develops out of phase with enabling business processes. To me this is scary, because the business process improvements are an essential part of IS projects, and it is frightening to think that IS systems design and project management methodologies that don't support the PSO elements have been developed. However, the problem is magnified on web-delivery projects because the business process changes are total, lateral re-engineering. We are not talking about modifying the business processes; we are talking about doing things completely differently through the web. Thus the PSO elements of an e-project are an essential part of it, and need to be addressed by the design and project management methodology. The Prince 2 methodology (Figure 1.7) which adopts a business focus, would be appropriate for web delivery.

Fast changes in the industry

The e-business environment is changing rapidly, with changing technologies and evolving business models. This can lead to changes during the course of project delivery, further impacting on quality and requiring careful change control and configuration management (Chapter 10). There is evidence that this difference with IS projects is already beginning to disappear.

Risk factors on IS projects	*Associated features of web projects*
1 Technological acquisition	Diverse technologies Immature industry Fast changes in the industry
2 Size of project team (and number of stakeholders)	Global reach Multidisciplinary teams
3 Team expertise	Managed from outside the IS department Multidisciplinary teams Immature industry Fast changes in the industry
4 User support	Global reach Wide range of user requirements
5 Role definition	Global reach Multidisciplinary teams
6 Lack of user experience on systems development	Managed from outside the IS department Lack of methodologies

Figure 2.3 *Risk factors on IS projects*

Perceived greater risk

Put all of this together, and web-delivery projects appear to have much greater risks. Each one of these differences from IS projects is a potential risk. James Jiang, Gary Klein and Selwyn Ellis (2002) have shown that there are six significant risk elements on software projects (Figure 2.3). You can see from the above discussion that each one of these is a problem on web-delivery projects. Some of them are technical risks, but many are people risks. It would be easy if it weren't for the people. I describe risk management in Chapter 13.

A MODEL FOR MANAGING WEB PROJECTS

In this section I propose a model for managing web projects which forms the basis of this book. The model draws on the principles of project management as described in the previous chapter to address the nature of web projects as identified in the last section. It also takes account of the nature of web projects as PSO, change projects as identified in the next chapter. I start by describing life cycles for web projects as commonly proposed. I then suggest a process for managing web projects which is the process followed in this book. I end with ten commandments for web projects.

A LIFE CYCLE FOR WEB-DELIVERY PROJECTS

In Chapter 1, I gave several versions of a project life cycle. Specific versions of the project life cycle have been also developed for web-delivery projects. Peter Kulik and Robert Samuelsen (2001) suggest a four step process, which they call their 4Ds to E-projects:

1 *Discover:* business analysis
2 *Design:* requirements documents, technical specification and acceptance criteria
3 *Develop:* programming, graphic design, technical implementation and quality assurance
4 *Deploy:* marketing and benefits realization.

As presented the middle two steps focus only on the software elements. However they are easily recast to encompass the PSO elements. Tim Rahschulte gives almost the same life cycle, except he calls it: decide, design, develop, execute. He focuses much more on the PSO elements, and thinks that an holistic approach is required which generates value through innovation in the following:

- human resources
- finance
- business development
- business process re-engineering
- marketing
- operations
- distribution
- business portfolio, including markets, products and services.

Henley Management College have used a similar cycle in the development of their web presence. They call it ADDIE:

- Analyse
- Design
- Develop
- Implement
- Evaluate.

This is the same as the previous two except with the addition of the last stage, evaluate. The post completion review has real meaning on a web-delivery project, since improvements in the system can be made in real time. Henley Management College also emphasize that each stage of the life cycle should end with a review, a stage gate before proceeding to the next step. The system and its components need to be constantly tested as they are delivered. Figure 2.4 suggests a stage gate model for web-delivery projects based on the above life cycles. This is essential in innovation projects (see Chapter 3). Figure 2.5 shows the key issues that form the basis of decision criteria at each stage gate in Figure 2.4. At each stage gate there are three possible decisions:

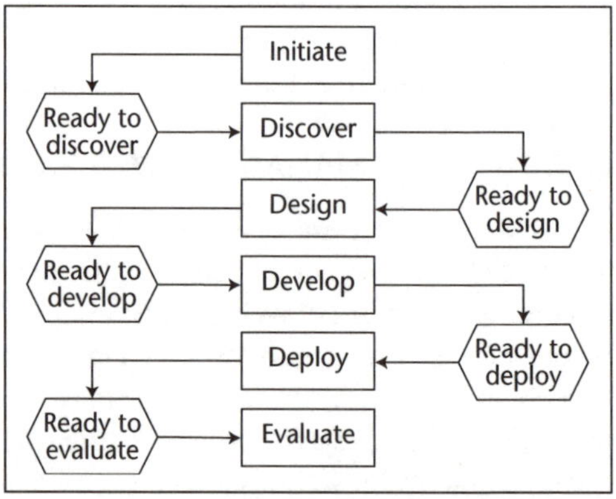

Figure 2.4 *Stage gate model for web-delivery projects*

- proceed
- repeat
- cancel.

Stage gate	*End of stage*	*Key issues and decision criteria*
Ready to discover	Start	Background, context, problem High level options Project deliverables Order of magnitude cost User consultation Appoint project champion
Ready to design	Feasibility – Discover – Analyse	Purpose, scope, outputs Feasibility, options assessed Milestone plan ± 30% estimate Review user requirements Appoint project manager
Ready to develop	Design	Business plan Design complete Activity plans ± 10% estimate Finalize user requirements Appoint team members
Ready to deploy	Construction – Develop	Work complete Acceptance tests User training Documentation complete Operation and maintenance procedures in place As-built design recorded
Ready to evaluate	Closure – Deploy – Implement Evaluation	Assess benefits realization Assess achievement of user requirements Record out-turn time and cost

Figure 2.5 *Stage gates for web-delivery projects*

When undertaking a project, you may plan one stage at a time, with each stage of the project treated as a sub-project in its own right, Figure 1.6, or your plan may cover the project from discovery to final evaluation. One approach that is quite common is for feasibility (discovery or analysis) to be planned and managed by the project champion. Subsequent stages cannot be planned until that stage is complete. When it is complete, the project manager is appointed, and the project planned through to the end. What you do will depend on the size of the project and its uncertainty:

- a large project will be planned one stage at a time; on a smaller project, the plan may cover several stages
- Type 1 projects (Figure 1.12) may be planned from start to finish, on others you may need to complete one stage before being able to define the next.

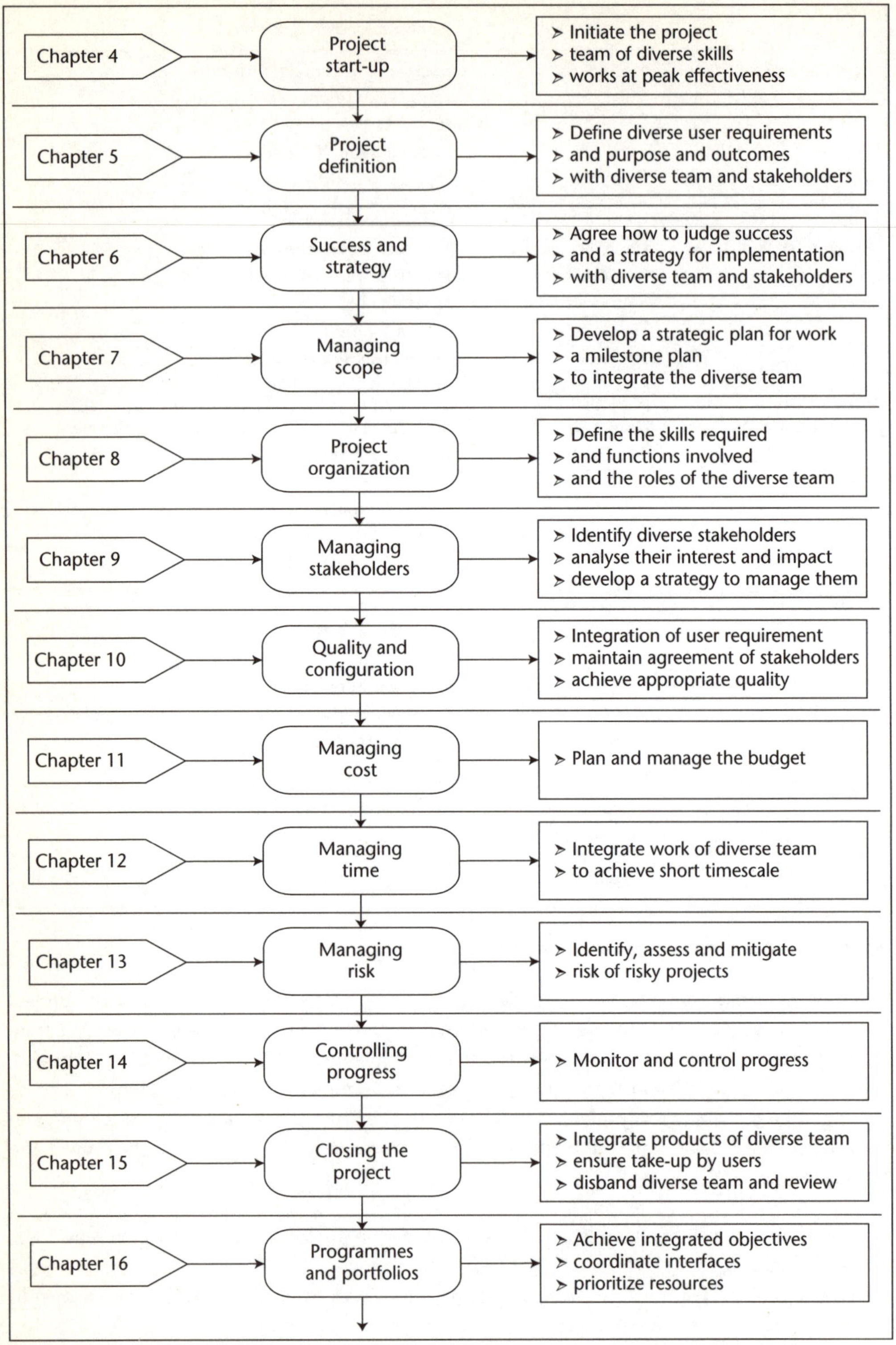

Figure 2.6 *A process for web-delivery projects and the structure of this book*

A PROCESS FOR WEB-DELIVERY PROJECTS

There are no widely accepted methodologies for the design and management of web-delivery projects. I propose a process for managing web-delivery projects (Figure 2.6), which builds on the generic project process shown in Figure 1.2, and the agenda for a start workshop shown in Chapter 4, Figure 4.3. As I have just said, you may apply the process one stage of the life cycle at a time. Or you may follow the whole project through from start to finish, depending on the size and uncertainty of the project. During this process I recognize the need to link to system design and development processes, but this is a book about web project management, not web design. However, Figure 2.7 illustrates that a significant overlap occurs between web design and web project management through the use of a life cycle and the application of configuration management. The suggested steps for undertaking a web delivery project are:

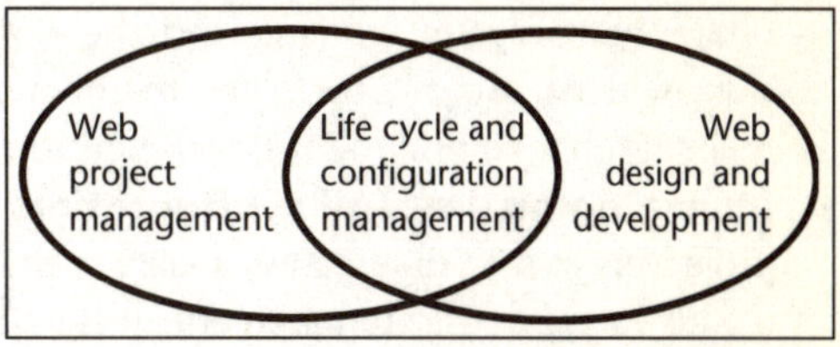

Figure 2.7 *Linking project management with web design and development*

- **Project start:** It is essential the project should achieve a proper start. With short time horizons, you cannot afford to have the team working at less than peak efficiency for any length of time. Time needs to be set aside for the project start process: this can range from one to five days. You may say that with short time horizons you cannot afford the time, but with three months to undertake a project, it is better to spend a week planning and initiating the project, and then have a team of eight people work at 100 per cent efficiency for twelve weeks, than work at 50 per cent efficiency for thirteen weeks. The project start process can also be used to build team identity and psychological attachment between team members.
- **Project definition:** With a wide range of potential stakeholders and a team with a wide range of skills drawn from several departments, it is essential that everyone clearly understands what the project is about. Everybody needs to understand the reason for the project, the problem to be solved, and the strategy for undertaking it, so they can clearly plan their role in the project and align their effort with the project goals. If the project is managed from outside the IS department, it is important to gain the commitment of the team and other stakeholders to the project definition. Project definition is the first step of the project start process.
- **Success and strategy:** A necessary condition for project success is for all the stakeholders to have the same visions of project success, what the purpose of the project is and how that will be achieved, and how the project will be judged successful when that purpose is achieved. There must also be a clear understanding of what user requirements will be delivered from the wide range proposed. After defining the project, you need to ensure the wide range of stakeholders have the same vision for the project and the strategy for achieving it.
- **Managing scope and milestone planning:** The work of the project needs to be planned. Because of the uncertainty of end-deliverable of web projects (they are type 2, 3 or 4 projects), I suggest you follow the principles of goal directed project management, developing a strategic plan in terms of milestones, and then defining the lower level plan on a rolling wave basis. By clearly assigning milestones to different project teams or team members (using the responsibility chart), you can coordinate the inputs of different people, especially where they are working remotely from each other.

- **Organizing the project and responsibility charts:** You need to define the wide range of skills needed for the delivery of the web project and source those skills from inside or outside the parent organization. Having built the project team, you need to gain the commitment of team members to their role. I suggest the responsibility chart as a tool to gain and maintain that commitment.
- **Managing stakeholders:** Web-delivery projects have wide, potentially global, reach, and so have many stakeholders. As we will see in the next chapter, they may also threaten established ways of working and therefore meet resistance. It is essential to identify the stakeholders, to gain their commitment to the project's goals and success criteria, and maintain that commitment throughout the project.
- **Managing quality and configuration:** With tight timescales, the quality of web-delivery projects is at risk, so effective quality management processes must be applied. Further, with a wide range of user requirements it is important to know how those user requirements will be delivered, and to manage the construction of the web space to deliver them. Configuration management processes help achieve that. As illustrated in Figure 2.5, configuration management is a key link to the design and development of the system. The configuration management processes also help us to respond to changes in the industry and diverse and evolving technologies. We can deliver a product that meets the user requirements while meeting the need of FRAMES.
- **Managing cost:** As with many projects, web-delivery projects will have a limited budget. We therefore need to manage the project cost. Because of their inherent risk, there may be some uncertainty in the project's cost and the cost management processes suggested address that.
- **Managing time:** Web-delivery projects have short time horizons, making the need for managing the timescale critical. The team need to work at peak efficiency throughout the project, and that requires each team member to know what they have to do week by week, but also where they are reliant on other team members and where other team members are reliant on them. Clear dates against the milestone plan help achieve that.
- **Managing risk:** Web-delivery projects are risky (Figure 2.3). That risk needs to be managed. There are simple tools for identifying, assessing and mitigating risk, which are easily applied to improve the chances of success.
- **Controlling the project:** Not only must all of these things be defined in the project start processes but they must be managed throughout the project.
- **Closing the project:** With a wide range of skills on the project team, their work needs to be pulled together at the project completion. There is a last step of project integration, where you need to ensure that all the different resources finish their work at the same time, and their different outputs are tied together. With a wide range of stakeholders and users, you also need to ensure that they all come online together to achieve maximum benefit from the project and the web space delivered. It won't happen of its own accord. You also need to say your thank yous to the project team members for their contributions, and review how you did. Like all projects, the project review process can generate learning to improve performance on future projects. But with web projects it is also possible to make quick and immediate corrections through a remodelling or maintenance project.
- **Programme and portfolio management:** Like many small to medium-sized projects, web-delivery projects may take part as a group of projects which need to be managed in a coordinated way. Sometimes, and especially with construction projects, the web-delivery project will be one of several projects bringing about an integrated change in the organization. To

achieve the desired change, not only will there be the web-delivery project itself, but other PSO projects introducing other changes in the organization. The programme of projects needs to be managed together to ensure the higher order strategic objective is achieved. At other times, there will be no connection between the projects apart from the fact that they use common resources. This will especially be the case with remodelling and maintenance projects. Then it can be useful to manage the projects as a portfolio. There are several advantages; in particular it is easier to give priority for resources to the whole portfolio than the projects individually, and by managing the projects together they can be completed efficiently and effectively.

Figure 2.6 shows how this process is followed through the book.

TEN COMMANDMENTS FOR WEB-DELIVERY PROJECTS

In an article in *Director* magazine, David Bicknel (2002) gives ten commandments for web-delivery projects, the first two of which reinforce the first three steps of this process, and the last two of which reinforce the need for effective close-out. The other five relate to systems design and development, but I thought it would be useful to relate all ten commandments.

1 *Ensure your objectives are clear:* You cannot judge the success of your site unless you know the criteria against which it will be judged. Know what you want from your Internet presence and how it fits with your overall business plan.
2 *Write a clear brief:* We saw above the need for clear user requirements. Write a clear statement of requirements including project objectives, target audience, timescale and budget.
3 *Ensure the site is thoroughly planned:* Define the design, technical and functional requirements needed to meet your objectives.
4 *Use relevant and engaging content:* Ensure your web presence matches your company culture and philosophy. Capture user interest and encourage two way communication.
5 *Improve navigation:* Ensure the site matches the user's expectations and is attractive, informative and easy to navigate. Plan the navigation so users find what they want before abandoning the site.
6 *Include a search option:* A content-rich web site will usually include a search engine to help the user navigate.
7 *Make the most of graphics and images:* A picture is worth a thousand words. They improve the visitor's experience. Make sure they fit your message, and the image you are trying to convey.
8 *Optimize your search engine listing:* To maximize the number of visitors to your site, you must appear high in the rankings of the search engines. This can be improved by including links to other sites and have them link to you.
9 *Test your site:* As part of the evaluation step, test your site. This is good project management. Test usability and functionality before final commissioning. Don't wait until you are online before finding faults.
10 *Constantly monitor your web site:* Monitor the number of hits. This information provides information on attracting new visitors.

This chapter has focused on web-delivery projects as a special case of IS projects, describing the features that set web-delivery projects apart from conventional IS projects. In the next chapter, I describe additional dimensions of web-delivery projects that make them PSO projects, implementing changes to the people, systems and organization of the parent firm.

CHAPTER 3 *Web Projects Are …*

When I told some people I was writing a book on managing web-delivery projects, they said that the problem with such a book was that the technology is moving so fast it will be out of date before it is published. This is a very blinkered view that sees web-delivery projects as just IS/IT projects, using a novel and rapidly changing technology. In the previous chapter I considered some of the consequences of that aspect of web-delivery projects, but concluded that in spite of that, project management principles can be applied to their management, and their application is not dependent on the current configuration of the technology. However, web-delivery projects are more than just IS/IT projects. That is their main feature, but as with most IS projects, web-delivery projects are not only about the information technology, they are:

- change projects
- innovation projects
- business process re-engineering projects
- publishing projects
- marketing projects.

IBM's definition of web projects given at the start of the last chapter mentioned the first and third of these. Overall they are PSO projects (Chapter 1) bringing about changes to the people, systems and organization of the parent firm. In order to make the new web space work:

- the people of the organization require new skills and values, requiring education and training
- they need new management systems and procedures to operate the new technology
- the firm may need changes to the organization structure, new management roles or even new departments to look after them.

Remember, these changes have to be managed as part of the project. They will not occur of their own accord; they need to be built into the project plan and managed. But worse, these changes will be more difficult than the technological changes and may require more time. Yes, the main element of web-delivery projects is the IS/IT work, but that is the easy bit. Changing the people is the difficult bit. In this chapter, I consider these additional dimensions of web-delivery projects.

CHANGE PROJECTS

Above all, web-delivery projects are change projects; the web-delivery project manager is a change agent within the organization. He or she therefore needs to be aware that:

- change is inevitable in organizations, and necessary to bring about performance improvement
- they need to implement the right change and not unnecessary change

- change will meet with resistance, requiring the stakeholders to be managed
- the life of a change agent is dangerous.

I have a series of quotations which I think illustrate the issues faced by the web project manager as change agent.

CHANGE IS NECESSARY TO BRING ABOUT PERFORMANCE IMPROVEMENT

Change is inevitable

First, change is inevitable and necessary within organizations:

> There is nothing permanent except change.
> *HERACLITUS (540BC–480BC)*

This is something of a modern cliché that you hear quoted all the time in the management press, but its source is surprisingly old. It seems to be an inevitable part of the human condition that change will occur. It has been that way for 2500 years, it will go on being that way for the next 2500 years. As managers we need to recognize change and embrace it. The introduction of web technology and the changes it brings about are part of the inevitable march of technology.

Performance improvement

> If you are second best in the world, you don't become best by gradual improvement.
> *JOHANSSON ET AL. (1994)*

Change is undertaken because it enables organizations to be better at what they do. What Johansson *et al.* are saying is that it is not enough to make gradual improvements, what in the 1980s in the Total Quality Management era was called *habitual incremental improvement*; slowly and gradually inching forward. If you do that you will remain a laggard. No! You need to make large step-wise improvements to overcome your competitors and win. Some years ago, a firm of consultants called Andersen Consulting (now Accenture) had an advertisement on British television showing a snail morphing into a frog, again emphasizing the need for performance improvement to be leaps forward, not inching forward.

Changes in organizations can be in several areas (Figure 3.1). What this figure tries to illustrate is that the bigger changes, taking longer to implement, lead to bigger improvements in performance. Web-delivery projects can lead to changes in all of these areas:

- *Operational efficiency:* Many web-delivery projects lead to improvements in operational efficiency. When Henley Management College introduced their el-MBA, they made improvements to operational efficiency which enabled them to switch resources from administration to teaching, increasing the value for the student. With the case study, the intranet at TriMagi, personnel procedures will be processed more efficiently. Other web developments, such as Amazon, benefit the customer; it is easier to buy a book online than go to a bookshop. All these cases are about trying to reduce the transaction costs, either reduce the cost of the vendor providing the product or service, or the customer of obtaining it. But you need to beware that you don't decrease the cost to one, but make a bigger increase to the other. When Henley first introduced e-learning, it led to internal efficiency

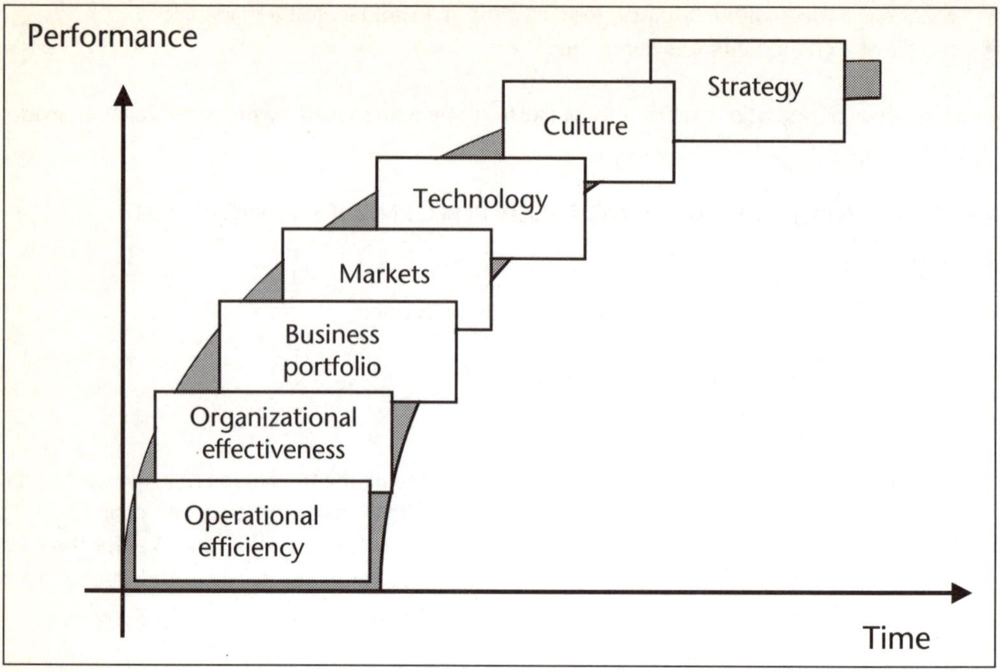

Figure 3.1 *Business performance improvement*

improvements, but their students suffered huge telephone bills. Broadband has overcome that problem for the students, so they have the efficiency improvements, and students have better access to tutors, without suffering huge telephone bills.

- *Organizational effectiveness:* This is the ability of the organization to deliver products or services to the customer which add value. The el-MBA at Henley enabled the students to get better access to tutors and improvements in operational efficiency were used to pay for improved organizational effectiveness. But the tutors can also be more readily accessible. As a tutor I log in two or three times a week to give feedback to students on their work. And I can log in anywhere in the world (as long as I can plug my modem into the telephone system, or gain access to the web). TriMagi will use the intranet to give employees better access to personnel records, and to give management improved communication with employees through daily newsletters and briefings.
- *Business portfolio:* The greatest performance improvements come from changing the business portfolio and the elements it is composed of. The business portfolio is the products or services the business supplies, the markets it supplies them to, and the technology it uses in their production and distribution. Clearly, web-delivery projects are making radical changes to the technology, but they can also change the

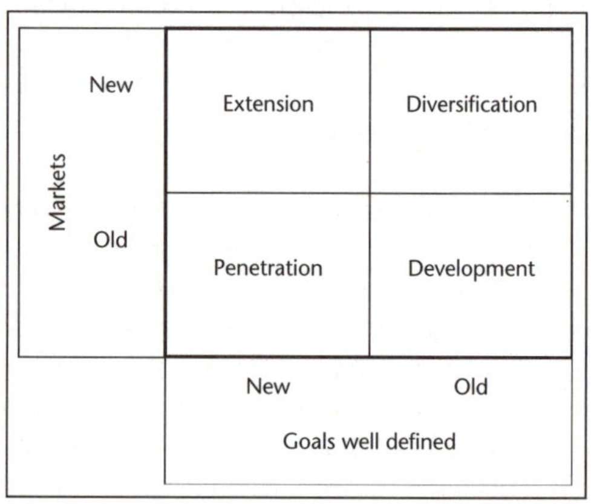

Figure 3.2 *Ansoff's matrix*

products or services and the markets they are supplied to. Figure 3.2 illustrates Ansoff's matrix (see Turner, 1995, 1999) which suggests that in introducing new products or services or in exploiting new markets, an organization has four strategies:

1 *Penetration:* selling more of the same products to the same markets. A web presence may enable a company to reach more of its existing customers, by making it easier or cheaper for them to buy, or by making the product add more value. This was the case with the el-MBA at Henley. Amazon was originally a new concept, but now that it is established it may try to increase market share by improving its portal.
2 *Extension:* selling more of the existing products to new markets. A web presence may enable an organization to reach new markets, to break out of its existing geographical region or even to make contact with a different group of people in the same region. Henley already had a distance learning MBA (dl-MBA) being sold around the world, but the el-MBA may widen its appeal. Amazon has opened outlets in new countries.
3 *Development:* selling new products to existing markets. Having established a web presence, it may provide an opportunity to sell new types of products. Henley have not yet tried that with their MBA programme. However, an American training organization called the International Institute for Learning (IIL) runs so called webinars, online seminars. These are a substantially new product, but sold to the existing customer base. Amazon widened its product line from books to include music and films, and so on.
4 *Diversification:* selling new products to new markets. This is high risk. You are dealing with products you don't understand and markets you don't understand. Unfortunately many companies got carried away with enthusiasm in the early days of the web, blinded by the infinite possibilities, leading to the implosion of household names such as Marconi and Cable and Wireless. This is dangerous. Obviously many new-start companies, such as Amazon and Lastminute.com when they were both first established, are selling what for them are new products to new markets. But that is to be expected, and there were many failures. For more traditional companies, the web offers opportunities for penetration, extension and development, but you should be wary of diversification.

- *Culture:* The web can also enable an organization to change its culture. People talk of bricks and mortar companies entering the electronic super highway. That is fine. As Ansoff's matrix illustrates, a web presence can offer organizations many new opportunities. This can include changing the basic culture of the organization, and it may be necessary, especially if selling to new markets. But I would urge caution. The fourth commandment at the end of Chapter 2 suggested your web profile should match your company culture and philosophy. If you are trying to extend the market or develop new products, you can set up a separate business unit to take responsibility. That is what many banks did when they introduced Internet banking. Using new technology or selling to new markets may demand a new culture; but if you change the culture of the whole organization, it is very difficult to retrench if the new venture fails. Better to prototype the new way of working and then retrofit it to the rest of the organization once it has been proven. (This can also be a way of overcoming the resistance to change. If people say 'It won't work,' but it has been shown to work on a prototype, that argument disappears.)
- *Strategy:* The adoption of a web presence should be something that is done as part of a coherent strategy. I don't have space here to deal with all the tools for developing a company strategy. David Partington (2000) and Ruth Murray-Webster and Michel Thiry (2000) give an overview of the link between corporate strategy and projects. Most large web projects should

be undertaken because it can be clearly shown that they are expected to lead to performance improvement, not because the technology is there. By all means experiment and prototype, but that is research not development. If the research demonstrates that the new technology has potential value, be ready and willing to change your corporate strategy (Figure 3.3).

> The man who invented the graphical user interface worked for a well-known IT vendor. The company said that they did not think there would be great user demand for such a thing: it was not part of their current business plan and he should stop work on it. So he left and joined Apple Computers inc. – the rest, as they say, is history.
>
> On the other hand, there was a man working for 3M who invented the glue that wouldn't stick. 3M are praised for allowing people in their research department 15 per cent of their time to work on their own projects. The company lives by its ability to innovate, and they take the view that allowing their best brains this time leads to some of their best innovations. The man who invented the glue that wouldn't stick did so in this project time. The company initially said they could see no great need for such a thing: very interesting, but he would be better advised to devote his energies to other things. However, he sang in the choir at his local church, and wanted a way of marking hymns at the start of the service so such that he could flick between them without the risk of the bits of paper falling out. But he needed to be able to remove the markers at the end of the service. So he pasted his glue on to bits of paper, and marked his place with them. He went back to his company and said he had found a use. Not many people sing in choirs, was the response. So he started pasting his glue onto pads of yellow paper and giving them to the secretaries in 3M. Bits of yellow paper started appearing everywhere, 3M changed its strategy, and again the rest is history. In this case perseverance, and the demonstration of the value of the new technology, saw it adopted.

Figure 3.3 *Changing corporate strategy*

Doing the right change and the change right

Having identified the need for change, you need to ensure that you do the right project. For web projects, that means not just designing the web space properly, but also designing appropriate changes to people, systems and organization. The process of project definition described in Chapter 5 will help to ensure the right project is done. However, it is essential that the project definition should be linked to a clear organizational strategy as just described. The first, second and third commandments at the end of Chapter 2 were all about defining business strategy and the project requirements properly.

However, beware! We are dealing with a technology where mass psychosis is evident. People have become so persuaded by the apparent promise of the web that they rush headlong into adopting the technology because it is there. The dot-com bubble in 2001, and the implosion of Marconi and Cable & Wireless are cases in point. Think through what you want to achieve, clearly linking it to your organization's strategy, and beware siren voices trying to lull you onto the rocks. Figure 3.4 is one of Aesop's fables which is as valid today as it was 2500 years ago. Once the project starts, you will be inundated with suggestions about what should be done, what wonderful benefits the web can deliver, and how you should adopt them all. For your web projects:

> The miller and his son were taking their donkey to town to sell it. They were walking alongside their donkey, when they passed a group of people who started laughing. 'Look at them walking alongside their donkey when they could be riding it.'
>
> The father said to his son, 'You get up on the donkey and I will continue walking alongside.'
>
> Soon they passed a second group of people who began to scorn the son. 'What is the youth of today coming to? Why are you riding, you lazy bones, while your father walks?'
>
> The father and son swapped places. Shortly they came to a third group of people who scorned the father. 'Look at the man riding, while his son, a mere child, walks.'
>
> The son's legs were getting weary, so the father suggested the son join him on the donkey. Shortly they came to a fourth group of people who asked the miller and his son where they were riding the donkey to. 'We are taking it to market to sell it.'
>
> 'Well, you'd better not ride it or you will tire it out and nobody will want to buy it. In fact, you had better carry it the rest of the way.'
>
> The miller and his son got off and started carrying the donkey. As they crossed the bridge coming into town, the town's people started laughing at the sight of the man and his son carrying their donkey. They laughed so loud, the donkey began to wriggle, so that they dropped it over the edge of the bridge. The donkey was drowned. The miller and his son went home.
>
> The miller said, 'I wish I had never left home this morning. Then I had a donkey. I tried to please all those people and now I have nothing.'

Figure 3.4 *The miller, his son and their donkey*

1. Be sure the change is necessary: link it clearly to your corporate strategy and the identified need for the web and the performance improvement it is expected to deliver. But do change corporate strategy if necessary (Figure 3.3).
2. Do the right change: carefully follow the project definition process as described in Chapter 5 to undertake the right project to achieve the outcomes you want.
3. Do the change right: apply appropriate project management processes from Chapters 5 to 16 to achieve a successful result. Particularly manage the expectations of the stakeholders (Chapter 9) to avoid siren voices, but also so that by the end of the project they are expecting what they get.

As a footnote, I want to say that I don't want to imply that Marconi and Cable and Wireless did not have a clear strategy. In business you don't make profits if you don't take risks and occasionally you back the wrong horse. You just need to back the right one more often than the wrong one.

RESISTANCE TO CHANGE

Changes in an organization can meet with resistance, and this is especially true of web projects, which can be a radical departure from established ways of doing things.

> If you put a frog in cold water and slowly raise the temperature, it will eventually allow itself to be boiled to death.
>
> *HANDY (1995)*

Apparently this really is the case. Frogs cannot tell absolute temperature, they can only tell temperature difference. If you try to put a frog in hot water, it will jump out. But if you put it in cold water and gently raise the temperature, it will sit there quite happily. Handy uses this as a metaphor for people in organizations. They sit cosseted by their organization, and can't see that the world around them is beginning to boil. 'This way of working was effective five years ago, it should be effective now.' Unfortunately it may not be, because the world has changed. But people can't see the world changing from within their organizations. They are like the frog surrounded by warm, cosy water. When I was a consultant with Coopers and Lybrand, I would often go into a company and instantly see their problems and know what the solution was. But saying that to the directors makes them feel stupid. They are intelligent people; it is only because they are too close to the problem, the environment having changed imperceptibly, and the consultant was at another company last week with the same problem that the consultant could see and the directors couldn't. You need to help people find the solution, not make them feel stupid. That is part of the art of stakeholder management (Chapter 9). The skill as a consultant or change agent lies in helping people find the solution and think it is their idea, but recognize that you were instrumental and essential in catalysing their thinking.

All new ideas go through three stages:

- first people think it is stupid
- then they think it is dangerous
- then they think it was their idea all along.

I am not sure of the source of this quotation, but it is core to my thinking on stakeholder management. There is a science programme on British television called *Horizon*. Often, as they discuss a new concept, you see their experts go through this process. First they scoff at the idea, then they find it threatening to their established positions, and then when the evidence becomes overwhelming they say, 'Well, it was obvious all along.' When you introduce a new way of working in an organization, you will meet this reaction. You need to manage the stakeholders through the three steps. Usually, they won't go of their own accord, or at least not quickly enough. You need to build an education process into the project plan to manage people through the three steps to the point where they have internalized the new process as the way they now want to work. Further, if you do it well, you can keep the second stage to mild concern rather than outright fear. Figure 3.5 suggests the process that people need to be taken through when implementing change in organizations. There are two major stages: first where people hear

Stage	*Step*	*Reactions*
Winning approval	Brief	I've heard something
	Inform	I know what it is about
	Understand	I see what it means
	Positive perceptions	I think it's good
Trying and liking it	Start-up	Let's give it a go
	Implementation	Let's see how it works
	Common understanding	This is the way we do it
	Internalization	We like doing it this way

Figure 3.5 *Reactions to normal change*

Stage	*Response*
Stability	Management communicate their vision, the need for change and the consequences.
Immobilization	People are taken by surprise. Their reaction is anxiety and confusion.
Denial	People defend themselves against the threat to their life or livelihood: • 'They can't mean me!!!' • 'Is that what we get for years of loyalty!!!' • 'Management is overreacting; it can't be that bad!!!'
Anger	Openly displayed anger towards management emerges. People try to take control, through their power base in the organization, trade unions, and so on. Alliances are formed; efforts to divide management are made; all means are tried to reverse the situation. Management must persistently argue the case, and not indulge in warfare.
Bargaining	People begin to try for a modified solution. All kinds of remedies will be proposed in order to try to reduce the impact of the change: • 'If we take a cut in salary?' • 'If we increase our productivity?'
Depression	Frustration, and a feeling of having lost, spreads. People find it difficult to work, and organizational paralysis sets in. Management must help. They must have plans containing supporting packages, and must actively assist individuals in taking responsibility for themselves in the new situation.
Testing	The individual and the organization start working with alternative exit strategies to try to facilitate the individual's transition: • 'Did you say I could have six months pay while looking for a new job?' • 'Being paid through a year's MBA programme would help the transition.' Management helps to find realistic alternatives.
Acceptance	Individuals and the organization deal realistically with the situation. They may not like it but they accept it. Management gives recognition and support towards future plans. New stability is achieved.

Figure 3.6 *Reactions to extreme change*

about the change and build up positive perceptions; and second where they are helped to internalize it.

Sometimes, a change can have extreme consequences. People lose their jobs and livelihoods. You will not get the reaction in Figure 3.5; they can never have positive perceptions of the change, and never internalize it. But they can have positive perceptions of the new opportunities in their lives outside the current organization. Web projects may bring about such changes in an organization. If the organization is diversifying, then there may be no room for the forces of conservatism. Or if a new business unit has been established to implement the web presence, and it doesn't work, people may need to be made redundant. Figure 3.6 shows reactions to extreme change, and the process people go through. This cycle was first observed with people told that they have fatal illness. But the same can happen with people facing extreme change, especially if it is threatening to their livelihoods. There is an episode of *The Simpsons* where Homer has eaten some sushi, and thinks he has eaten the poisonous part of a blowfish. He goes to the hospital and the doctor takes him through this cycle. If you are introducing extreme change, you need to build this cycle into your project plan and help people through it. They need to be allowed time for each step, though for immobilization, denial, anger and bargaining, one day each may be enough. You need to give people time to grieve. But during this stage you need to be fairly hard-hearted, 'You have to be cruel to be kind.' Giving people false expectations is more cruel in the long run. Hopefully if the cycle is well managed, depression will be short and shallow, and people can build hope for the future. Often organizations making people redundant will give them career counselling.

> Human nature is like a stick of Brighton Rock; bite all the way down it still says Brighton Rock.
> *Grahame Greene in* Brighton Rock *(1938)*

Change may be part of the human condition, but individuals usually prefer a certain amount of predictability and stability in their lives, especially as they get older. However, they don't resist all change. Indeed, if Heraclitus is right, then a certain amount of change will always be occurring within organizations. It is only as the level of change rises above this normal background level that you may begin to get resistance. It is said that people resist change, but my view is that what they resist is having it imposed on them. If you engage people in the change, inform them early on, and make them feel they are contributing to it and have some influence on the outcomes, then they will be much more responsive and accepting of it. That is the thinking behind Figure 3.5. In Chapter 9, I describe the management of stakeholders, giving a stakeholder management process. I also discuss how to inform people about the change process and avoid the conflict that it can engender. However, that is not to say that there won't be sticks of Brighton Rock in the organization, usually older people who want to hold on to the old technology and old ways of working (see Figure 3.7). These people will be more difficult to persuade, but they need persuading all the same.

> In 1989 and 1990, I worked with a team in British Telecom, implementing an early call centre. Everybody under 40 thought the project was wonderful, introducing new technology that would change their working lives, making their jobs more interesting and richer, and make the organization more efficient and more successful, offering them careers into the future. Everybody over 50 thought the project was awful, introducing new technology at a time of their careers when they would like to stick with the familiar, and threatening their jobs as the organization made itself more efficient and more successful, at a time of their lives when they would find it difficult to get another job. About the only person between 40 and 50 was the project manager, whose game plan was to gain experience implementing this new technology (call centres), and then have himself made redundant so he could work as a highly paid consultant.
>
> At the time I was under 40, but I have just passed 50. Have I turned into a stick of Brighton Rock, or is that not a fate that waits people of my generation?

Figure 3.7 *Encountering resistance to change*

THE PROJECT MANAGER AS CHANGE AGENT

> The reasonable man adapts himself to the world; the unreasonable one persists in trying to adapt the world to himself. Therefore all progress depends on the unreasonable man.
> *George Bernard Shaw in* Man and Superman *(1903)*

It is the role of the project manager to implement the change. He or she will meet resistance, as we have just seen. Thus the project manager can often appear unreasonable in pushing through the change. In a recent course I was challenged about this quotation. A student said it is the sticks of Brighton Rock resisting the change who are unreasonable – the project manager is the agent of the management who want the change. There is also truth in this. I was also once challenged that I do not describe how to manage irrational people. I don't think anyone is irrational, not even the sticks of Brighton Rock. Everybody behaves rationally within their world view; they work to optimize their economic position as they see it. Not everybody shares your world view, not everybody's economic position is optimized in the same way as yours. The stakeholder management process of Chapter 9 will help you identify other people's world view, identify what will optimize their economic position, and how to influence them and their involvement in the project to achieve the outcome you want.

> There is nothing more difficult to arrange, nor doubtful of success, nor more dangerous to carry through, than initiating change ...
> *Machiavelli in* The Prince *(1513)*

Being a project manager and change agent is a dangerous role. Some years ago I did a series of courses with the IS/IT project managers from a well-known bank in the UK. They said that being a project manager was a thankless task. If the project went well, they got none of the praise. The project had been so well specified by the users and designed by the IS/IT engineers that any one could implement it properly. If the project went badly, it had been well specified and well designed, so it must be entirely the project manager's fault. Praise for the uninvolved and blame for the innocent.

INNOVATION PROJECTS

As we have just seen, web projects lead to innovations in an organization's markets, its products and services, and the technology by which it makes and distributes them. Innovations in technology occur almost by definition. To facilitate these innovations, the organization needs to create an environment to support innovation, and ensure that it adopts an appropriate management process to deliver it. In this section I discuss how to create an appropriate environment and whether you should adopt a rigid, linear-rational, or a flexible, organic approach for implementing innovation projects.

CREATING AN ENVIRONMENT SUPPORTIVE OF INNOVATION

There are many things you can do to create an environment supportive of innovation, including:

- making appropriate information available
- creating channels for formal and informal communication
- blurring organizational boundaries

- integrating boundary spanners
- creating flexible roles and multidisciplinary teams
- decentralizing authority
- allowing some stress and ambiguity
- facilitating projects rather than rigidly controlling them
- encouraging effectiveness rather than efficiency.

I will discuss some of these and then consider whether project management encourages them.

Information and communication

Communication is essential to innovation, to ensure the right people have the right information. But you need both formal and informal channels. When establishing the project you need to ensure that everybody who may have knowledge or information or opinions about the design and specification of the web space is properly consulted, and those people who need to know are informed of the solutions. But just as importantly, you do not want to be flooded with too many conflicting opinions from people who have no real input to make. Further, if you inform everybody on the project about every decision, those people who need to know may ignore the bit of information targeted at them. The responsibility chart introduced in Chapter 8 helps define the channels of communication on the project.

Informal channels of communication are also important for innovation. New things happen and new ideas are generated because people who do not normally talk to each other make new contacts, and through those contacts generate new ideas. I discuss how to encourage new contacts between people later in the section on organic approaches to innovation. Having people work in cross-discipline teams is also essential to that. Web-delivery projects are more than IS/IT projects, they need to involve people from across the organization. We meet this again in the next chapter, where Figure 4.6 shows the people required to work on the intranet at TriMagi.

I often say that management is a series of dilemmas, and information and communication on innovation projects can be no different:

- Communication can be too formal, stifling cross-functional working, innovation and people's ability to perform (Figure 3.8).
- Or it can be too informal, with too many conflicting opinions, too many siren voices, too much hype about the possibilities of the web (Figure 3.4).
- You can talk to too many people, again with too many conflicting opinions, informing so many people about your progress that nobody bothers to listen to you.
- Or you can talk to too few, behaving in a cloak and dagger fashion, so that nobody knows what you are doing and nobody cares.

You need to manage your information and communication on web projects carefully to achieve the innovations you want. This can be somewhat ironic on a web project, which is all about informal communication and making information available to the maximum number of people. But even on a web project you need an appropriate balance between formal and informal communication.

Boundary spanners

Projects require cross-functional working. They are temporary organizations used to create change, and change, by definition, involves people working together in novel ways. We have just seen that

I wrote a case study on an IS/IT project in the Civilian Aviation Authority and one of the people I interviewed had just joined from the private sector. He said he was working on a project involving people from other departments, but found it impossible to make progress. If he needed to write a memo to somebody in another department to make a decision, he had to write a draft of the memo to give to his boss to critique. He would then revise the memo, and it would go to his boss's boss to critique, and so on until it got to the lowest common boss when it would be sent to the relevant person. The reply would come back the same way, and the whole process would take weeks. He said you cannot work on a cross-functional project in this way.

You can understand why people are doing this. If a plane crashes, the media will be on a witch-hunt, and managers want their stamp on decisions for which they will be held accountable. But in the temporary organization that is a project you do need to empower people to make progress.

The next person I spoke to was a Royal Air Force Officer on secondment. I asked him if it was true. He said he was afraid it was. What he did was to send the first draft of the memo to the person he was trying to communicate with and they got on with it. You can see the military is used to empowering people. In the heat of battle you cannot refer decisions up the line; there isn't time. Projects are like the heat of battle; you need to empower people (within firm guidelines).

Figure 3.8 *Excessively formal communication*

people working across functions can lead to new ideas through new contacts. But it also needs people to be empowered to make progress together; the project must be a rugby scrum, not a relay race. The communication methods described in Figure 3.8 can result in projects being artificially extended, as they go from one department to another. People must work in flexible, cross-discipline teams, with decentralized authority. This is especially true of web projects, as we saw in Chapter 2. They are more than IS/IT projects, being as much about marketing or production as they are about IS/IT. The implementation team must include people from all departments. The team implementing the el-MBA at Henley Management College included faculty, administration, marketing and course design as well as the IS/IT people. In the case study, the team implementing the intranet at TriMagi includes personnel and marketing (see Figure 4.6). People can be given roles to act as boundary spanners – those whose role it is to bridge the gaps between people, and get them working together in a team. Figure 3.9 (adapted from Fong, 2003) illustrates the need, bridging boundaries between disciplines, hierarchies and areas of expertise to achieve new thinking and innovation in the organization.

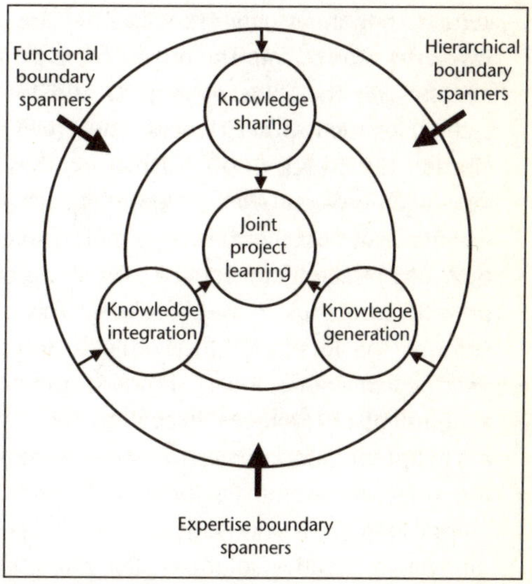

Figure 3.9 *Boundary spanners*

Stress and ambiguity

Surprisingly, or perhaps not, some stress and ambiguity can lead to better innovation.

Necessity is the mother of invention, and necessity, which creates stress and ambiguity, helps innovation. It is well known that people work better under reasonable levels of stress than they do under no stress at all. But this is another dilemma. Too much stress can be harmful. Likewise ambiguity can encourage innovative solutions. It is recognized by psychologists that it is not risk that people fear; but ambiguity and the chance of loss. People will respond to risk if they see it as a chance of gain. Further, if it is unclear whether the risk will result in loss or gain, they fear that as well. Thus where ambiguity exists, people will try to eliminate it, leading to innovative solutions to their problems. You should encourage reasonable levels of stress and ambiguity on your web projects to find the most innovative solutions.

Facilitation vs. control

Projects involve stress and ambiguity, they involve cross-discipline teams with boundary spanners, and they involve communication between team members. They should therefore encourage innovation, right? No! Wrong! The project environment often kills innovation through too rigid control. I will talk below about the need to achieve a balance between the rigid linear-rational approach usually adopted on projects, and the organic approach sometimes adopted. But as an introduction let us consider some of the problems of too rigid control.

- *Competency traps:* Projects are more exposed to competency traps than routine operations. This is where you have an established way of working that you know works, though it may not be optimal. But you fear trying an alternative for the risk of failure. In a routine environment it is easier to try out something new. If it doesn't work at the first attempt, you can always try to improve next time, and if it doesn't work at all, you can go back to the old ways of working. It is much easier to experiment in a routine environment. On a project you only do it once. If it doesn't work first time it doesn't work at all. There may be a way of doing your project that is twice as good as your preferred way, but with say a 20 per cent chance of failure. So if you were going to do it several times, on average you would be 60 per cent better off doing it the better way. In a routine environment, you can give it a go, find out where the flaws are and get it right second time around. But on a project, you only do it once, so people prefer the certain, though less efficient way. They are trapped in the inferior way of working.
- *Rigid evaluation criteria:* The project management industry has developed rigid evaluation criteria for assessing the value of projects and their contribution to corporate wealth. In particular techniques such as net present value (NPV), and internal rate of return (IRR), are suggested (Turner, 1995; Lock, 2000b). However, these do not properly evaluate both IS/IT projects and innovation projects (Akalu, 2003). For such projects a technique known as option pricing gives a better view, but unfortunately is much more difficult to apply. Mehari Akalu (2003) showed that most organizations are reduced to applying qualitative assessment criteria to IS/IT and innovation projects, and thus to web projects. This can create problems in organizations wanting to compare the IRR of all of their projects, and applying strict hurdle rates.
- *Rigid resource utilization:* Standard project management techniques also suggest tight assignment of resources, allocating the precise number required to do the job. This is not really appropriate for most projects, except possibly type 1 projects in Figure 1.12. Projects are risky, and some flexibility is required to deal with uncertainty. But it is especially inappropriate for innovation projects. People with time to think develop much more innovative, creative solutions. For many organizations, web-delivery projects can be quite new at first implementation, what in Chapter 1 I called strangers or aliens. So substantial

creativity is required, coupled with high uncertainty. That is stress enough, without adding additional stress by making the project team work to tight resource limits.

- *Rigid control:* Traditional project management approaches also suggest tight control. Again, this may only really be appropriate for type 1 projects. On innovation projects it may be appropriate at the development stage, but not at the research stage. Innovation projects should still be managed, but at the research stage more organic approaches are appropriate, emphasizing facilitation and coordination of the people working on the project. At the development stage there can be more rigid deadlines, the new product needs to be delivered to market by a certain date, the web space needs to be online by a certain date. Thus the appropriate form of control, organic or linear rational, depends very much on the type of project and the stage it has reached.

LINEAR-RATIONAL VERSUS ORGANIC CONTROL

There are two opposing approaches to managing innovation projects:

- The linear-rational approach which emphasizes rigid evaluation criteria, rigid resource utilization, rigid control and the following of a strict process
- The organic approach which emphasizes more fluid and flexible approaches.

The linear-rational approach is about keeping to the straight and narrow, moving as briskly as possible to your final objectives, whereas the organic approach is more pagan, following the seasons through cycles of development to your end objectives. Which is appropriate for your innovation project depends on the nature of the project, and the stage of development the product has reached. If your project is a type 4 project, a stranger or alien, at the research phase, organic approaches may be more appropriate. If it is a type 1 project, a repeater or runner, at the final product delivery stage, more rigid control may be appropriate.

The linear-rational approach

The linear-rational approach to innovation is usually based on some version of the life cycle, based on toll gates or stage gates. Innovation projects must move through a series of go/no-go decisions, being evaluated against strict criteria at each stage-gate before being allowed to proceed. The Prince 2 process, Figure 1.7 is in essence a stage gate model, though the number of stage gates can be varied to meet the needs of the project. At the completion of each stage, the project is evaluated against business and project control criteria. Figure 3.10 illustrates Ericsson's PROPS process. At each stage gate, the product is evaluated against business, project and operational criteria. Stage-gate 3 is the most significant, where the main business case is made. Figure 3.11 is the stage-gate model used by a financial services supplier to assess the data products they supply over their own network, and over the web. They suggest that at each stage gate, half the surviving projects fall. Thus 64 product proposals need to start for one to be released to market. Even at the last stage gate, one out of two products falls; two

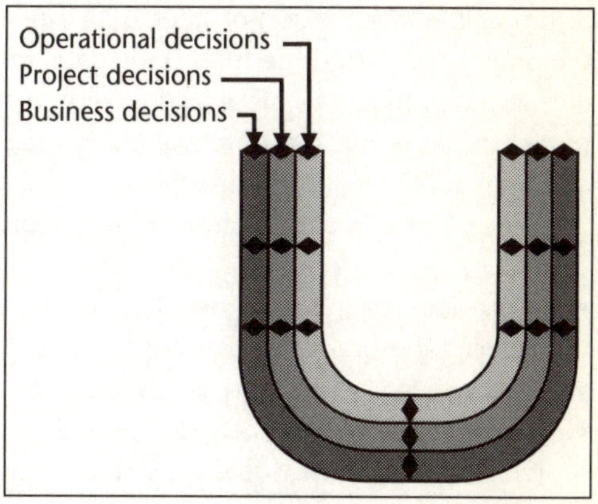

Figure 3.10 *Ericsson's PROPS process*

Stage	*Time*	*Action*
Identify market opportunity	One week	Sales prepare a brief description of the customer's requirement
Initial product description	One month	Marketing appoint a product manager who develops a product description and initial project plan
Project portfolio committee	Three months	As the resource requirements are quantified, the product portfolio committee prioritizes products for development based on resource availability
Requirements definition		Functional and system requirements are defined
Assess risks, and reconcile project success criteria		The project planned in detail, a formal risk analysis is conducted, and success criteria and factors evaluated
Approve release		The product is ready for release to market. Likely maintenance costs and profitability assessed

Figure 3.11 *The stage-gate model for a financial services supplier*

have made it all the way through the product development process, and only one is released to market. I attended an innovation conference in Ireland a few years ago, and a speaker from Ericsson described the 63 that don't make it as 'failures'. They are not failures. To be an innovative organization, it is necessary to try out many things in order to have the one successful one. The mistake is not shutting the projects down quickly enough. Figure 3.11 illustrates that seven-eighths of the projects should be shut down within three months. The same speaker said that out of every four products that Ericsson releases, two make a loss, and only one makes a profit. The financial services agency tried to stop that with their last stage gate, so every product released at least breaks even.

In Chapter 2, I suggested standard life cycles for web-delivery projects. They are not incompatible with the sort of stage gate models I have just described. They would be used once the project has passed the third stage gate, for managing the development and implementation of the web product. An organization with many potential web products may apply a stage gate model to prune out the potential contenders and choose those products for implementation, and then apply the life cycle suggested in Chapter 2 for implementation of those selected.

The advantages of the linear-rational approach are that:

- it provides clear no-go decisions encouraging the development of a business plan, and allowing the project to be matched to company strategy
- it allows ideas to be tried and tested; closure is not seen as a failure
- it provides clear, strict control, through the stage gates and through milestone planning
- it helps manage risk; ideas are tested before progressing, and the stage gates are clear review points.

The disadvantages of the linear-rational approach are that it:

- favours efficiency and control over creativity
- can artificially extend projects if you insist that one stage gate is passed before work on the next begins.

The organic approach

The organic approach overcomes these weaknesses, but at the expense of efficiency and control. It is still possible to provide vision and direction for the project, and coordinate the input of resources. But the organic approaches favour more flexible management. The organic approach involves innovation through:

- deliberate redundancy
- sampling
- chance encounters
- creative communications
- creative tensions.

Deliberate redundancy: Advertising agencies, when starting work on a new account, often create three or four teams to work independently to develop ideas. They then sample those ideas to come up with an overall proposal for the client. Also, many high-tech companies often have two people do a job where strictly one will do. The advantage of this is that two people working together can come up with more creative solutions to the client's need, and when the job is over, two people have the new skill, improving learning in the organization. I call this the creation of Nellies. In traditional companies, the new recruit learns the work of the company by serving an apprenticeship, sitting next to an experienced person, sitting next to Nellie. There are no Nellies in high-tech companies because the technology is changing so fast, so firms create Nellies in the way described. Some people ask how you can afford this inefficiency. But if you obtain more creative solutions, with better learning for the organization, then the cost is repaid. Unisys, Intel and Hewlett Packard have all told me they adopt this approach. So for your web projects, consider having several people or teams work independently to design the web space, and then choose the best solution. And have people work together to deliver more creative solutions and communicate those solutions to the rest of the organization.

Sampling: Having generated several different solutions to the problem, you need to choose the best solution. That is what advertising agencies do. The best solution may not be one of the proposals, but a mixture of them all. So the sampling needs to be more a blending process, where the best solution emerges as a mixture of the proposals. In the financial services company mentioned above, the one product that emerged at the end was not one of the 64 that started, but a mixture of them. This led to a tension between the product development personnel and senior management. Senior management wanted to shut half the projects down at each stage gate, but the product development personnel wanted to keep them alive, as they couldn't know which ones would contribute to the final product. Somebody described it as being like blending whisky. Sampling from the different casks, you couldn't know you had the right blend, and what it would comprise, until you had it.

Chance encounters: I said above that innovation comes through people making contacts that have not existed previously. New ideas come from old ideas reforming in new ways. An Irish advertising agency decided to try to reduce office rent and commuting costs for their employees by having them work from home. All their creative people were given laptops and an ISDN link at home. Creativity plummeted! Sir Alexander Fleming, who discovered penicillin, deliberately left petri dishes lying around to see if something unexpected happened, and it did. I spoke above about the need for cross-discipline teams and boundary spanners. On your web projects, don't let the IS/IT people work in isolation.

Creative communications: Chance encounters lead to creative communications and vice versa. The Danish hearing aid company, Oticon, encourages people to chat at the water fountain. At Henley Management College, morning and afternoon tea are something of a ritual, but creative communication occurs at these sessions.

Creative tensions: Differences between people, rather than being avoided, should be encouraged, as they too can lead to new ideas by reforming old ones in new ways. In advertising agencies, the tension between the suits and non-suits (business people and creative people) is encouraged. On your web project, rather than avoiding differences between IS/IT people and marketing people, you should encourage it to find the best solution.

The linear-rational and organic approaches are quite different, but not entirely incompatible. Clearly, deliberate redundancy is incompatible with efficiency, but not with effectiveness. Further, you can have deliberate redundancy and creative communications for the work for the first and second stage gate, sample at the second stage gate, and then apply more strict project management processes from that point on.

BUSINESS LATERAL ENGINEERING PROJECTS

I started this chapter by saying that almost all web-delivery projects are PSO projects; that is, they change the processes of the business. In the early 1990s, people talked about business process re-engineering, defining the business processes and improving on them. The quotation by Johansson *et al.* (1994) above comes from their book about process re-engineering. But even though they are suggesting that to become best in the world you need to make stepwise performance improvement through changes to your business processes, there is still an implication that this is achieved by reconfiguring your existing processes. Web projects are often more than business process re-engineering; they are business process lateral engineering, finding wholly new ways of doing things. For the creative organization they offer the opportunity of truly breaking the china and starting again. However, that can be risky, which is why I suggested above that you should prototype the new ways of working in a temporary organization, and retrofit them to the routine organization once they have been shown to work. If the new ways don't work, you need to be able to recover the old ways while they are made to work. Overlaying radically new ways of doing things on to an existing business could lead to a competency trap, as people try to limit the extent of the changes out of fear that they won't work. Prototyping and then retrofitting them overcomes that fear.

In Chapter 1, I described the history PSO projects, from when the cultural changes were ignored, to recognizing they need to be planned as an integral part of the project. The new business processes won't design themselves, and you shouldn't think that they will be implied through the design of the web space. The web space should be designed to deliver the new business processes. Thus you need to design the business processes as an early step in the project. While running a start-up workshop at TriMagi, I asked how they were going to process expense and holiday claims and sickness reports using the new system: they responded that they thought it would work like the old system (Figure 1.11). But that is impossible. In particular it is necessary to define principles of security and access for approving things such as expense claims, and how they will be passed to accounts for payment.

Euro Projex

Procedure

Department:	Personnel
Procedure:	Online expense claim
Owner:	Frances Seeker

1 Claimant logs in via password access

2 Claimant completes relevant screen
- Name
- Department
- Date of trip
- Date of claim
- Expense type
- Amount, split gross, net, VAT
- Total of claim

3 Claimant nominates authorizing manager

4 Claimant submits

5 Authorizing manager informed by automatic e-mail of claim awaiting authorization

6 Authorizing manager logs in by secure access

7 Authorizing manager checks and authorizes claim

8 Claim enters accounting system for payment

Author:	JRT	**Date:**	21 Jan 2003	**Issue:**	A

Figure 3.12 *Process for online filing of expense claims at TriMagi*

Various techniques exist for defining the business processes. They can be a simple list of tasks. The drawing menu of the Microsoft Office suite contains symbols for drawing more formal flow charts under <Autoshapes>. Or you can use the milestone plan (Chapter 7) or responsibility chart (Chapter 8). The IDEF0 technique (Turner, 1999) developed by the US Airforce is particularly suitable for more complex business processes. Figure 3.12 is a process for online filing of expense claims at TriMagi.

OTHER PROJECTS

In the sections above I have discussed the implications of web-delivery projects as change projects, innovation projects, business lateral engineering projects and creative projects. I have also implied that you should encourage cross-functional working on your web-delivery projects. Also, features of web projects we encountered in Chapter 2 were that they may be led from another department and involve multidiscipliniary teams. The corollary is that the project may take on the features of a project from another discipline. Rather than being primarily an IS project, it may have the features of:

- a publishing project (extranet)
- a marketing project (Internet)
- a personnel project (intranet)

Many of the content specialists I suggested in Chapter 2 that should comprise your multidiscipinary team were publishing experts (copywriter, editor, content manager), and some of the user specialists I recommended were artistic production personnel (creative director, art director, designer, animator).

Different types of project need to be managed in different ways. I am not going to say any more here than that you need to be sensitive to the management needs of the project, managing it according to the needs of the appropriate discipline, not just addressing its features as a web-delivery project.

PART 2 *The Management of Web Projects*

CHAPTER

4 *Project Start*

In this chapter I consider project start. The process in Figure 2.6 showed that on web projects project start processes are important to get the team working at peak efficiency from the outset, and not at 50 per cent efficiency for the four months of the project. They are also important for building psychological attachment of the team members, making them feel part of the team, and committed to the task. Figure 1.7 shows project start-up and project initiation as the first two stages of the project, ending in the *Project brief* and *Project initiation document*, as described in the next chapter. The emphasis of this chapter will be more on project start, getting the definition and delivery of the project underway. Project start is not strictly a stage of the project. It is something that may be repeated at the start of every stage, or it may not be done at all. It may be done every time there is a significant change in the members of the project team, whose commitment to the project objectives and to the way to proceed needs to be won. Morten Fangel (1987, 1991) drew the distinction between project start and project start-up by likening it to the difference between flicking the ignition of a car, and an extended process to start up the steam engine of a ship. The former is a single action, the latter a process requiring concerted action (a little like the difference between the French *soir* and *soirée*). This chapter focuses on the project start-up processes, but mainly as applied during discovery and design. I consider the objectives and methods of project start and then describe how to conduct a project start workshop and how start-up differs for each of the four types of project shown in Figure 1.12.

OBJECTIVES OF PROJECT START

In Chapter 5 and 9, I will show that the most significant determinant of project success is to gain the agreement of all the stakeholders to the success criteria and key success factors. Project start is a way of ensuring this, particularly to gain the commitment of the immediate project team to the project's objectives (Chapter 5), success criteria (Chapter 6), and method of delivery (Chapters 7 to 14). Many stakeholders are in a strong position to make failure a self-fulfilling prophecy if they do not agree with the approach being taken. Figure 4.1 illustrates the process of team formation and maintenance, with four stages commonly described as: forming, storming, norming and performing.

1 *Forming:* The team comes together, with a mediocre level of performance. They have disagreements about the project's purpose, the nature of the outputs and how they should be delivered. They fumble around in the dark. Second worse case scenario is that they stay forever at this mediocre level.
2 *Storming:* The disagreements come out into the open. The team argue and their performance falls. Worse case scenario is that they never recover.

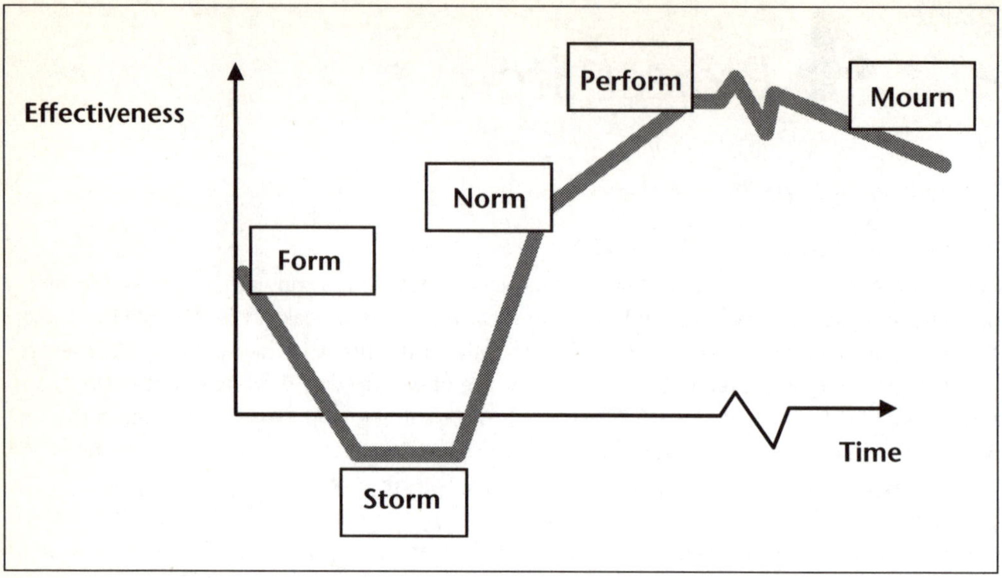

Figure 4.1 *A process of team formation and maintenance*

3 *Norming:* The team agrees on the project's purpose, its outputs and methods of delivery. They also gel as a team, and form patterns of behaviour (norms) for how they are going to work together.
4 *Performing:* They are firing on all cylinders as they deliver the new web space in record time.

When some teams form they stay forever in the forming stage as they try to avoid disagreement and conflict in the team; others spend too long in the storming stage. The purpose of project start is to take the team into the storming stage, to get the disagreements out into the open, and then to take them as quickly as possible into norming and performing stages to get peak performance. When you have four months to deliver a web construction project, you cannot afford to spend the first month in the forming, storming and norming stages. You need to take them through that in the first week. With remodelling and maintenance projects, the delivery time of which is measured in days, you need to take them through in the first day.

The objectives of project start-up are therefore:

1 To agree the business objectives and deliverables of the project (Chapter 5):
   - the background and problem faced by the organization
   - the strategic need of the parent organization, the purpose of the project and expected benefit
   - the nature of the web space to be delivered at the end of the project to achieve that purpose.
2 To agree the success criteria of the project and the strategy for its implementation (Chapter 6):
   - the success criteria and key performance indicators
   - the key performance indicators
   - strategy for implantation.
3 To develop and agree the plans for implementation of the current and future stages, and agree people's roles:
   - milestone plan and responsibility chart (Chapters 7 and 8)
   - agree these with the stakeholders (Chapter 9)

- quality and configuration plans (Chapter 10)
- associated time and cost schedules (Chapters 11 and 12)
- define risks and how they will be managed (Chapter 13).

4 To agree the project management method and control process (Chapter 14)
- when and how will progress review meetings be held, and who will attend.

5 To get the project team functioning (Chapter 7)
- how will early milestones be delivered?
- what will be done tomorrow?
- get the team marching in the same direction to the same tune, and in step.

6 To brief new team members
- at any significant change in the project team
- or at the start of a new stage or a significant milestone.

There is a shift in emphasis as you move down this list from problem identification and problem solving, to negotiating agreement in the middle, to briefing new members on existing agreements at the end. This represents a shift in emphasis as you move through the project. Figure 4.2 shows how the objectives of a project start-up, definition or launch workshop change as you work through a project.

Stage	*Name of workshop*	*Objectives*
Initiation	Initiation	1, 2, 3
Discovery	Definition	2, 3, 4
Design	Launch	3, 4, 5
Delivery	Launch	4, 5, 6
Major work package	Briefing	5, 6
Deployment	Task force	3, 5 – mop up what is left

Figure 4.2 *Start-up through the life cycle*

METHODS OF START-UP

There are three recognized methods of project start-up:

1 Workshops
- definition
- launch.

2 Reports
- project definition report
- project manual.

3 Ad hoc assistance
- experts in that type of work
- experts in team dynamics.

WORKSHOPS

Workshops can be of help throughout the project, to launch a stage, to brief the team, to gain their commitment, or to plan the coming stage of the project. The emphasis of the workshop and its objectives change throughout the project as illustrated in Figure 4.2. An example agenda for a start-up workshop is given in Figure 4.3.

A frequently asked question is how can the team afford to spend the time in a workshop when they have a project to be getting on with. A related question is how long the workshop should last. The response to the first question is to ask what is better:

Agenda item	*Duration (hours)*	*Timetable 1 day:time*	*Timetable 2 day:time*	*Chapter number*
Definition				
– purpose				
– scope				
– objectives	1.5	1:1600	1:1000	5
Success criteria	1.5	1:1730	1:1130	6
Milestone plan	3.0	2:0900	1:1400	7
Responsibility chart	2.0	2:1300	2:0900	8
Analyse stakeholders	1.0	2:1500	2:1100	9
Quality plan	1.0	2:1600	2:1200	10
Calculate durations	0.5	2:1700	2:1400	11
Schedule milestones	0.5	2:1730	2:1430	12
Risk analysis	2.0	3:0900	2:1500	13
Activity plans for early milestones	1.0	3:1100	3:0900	7
Control plan	1.0	3:1200	3:1000	14

Figure 4.3 *Agenda for a project start-up workshop*

- Is it better to have a team of six people fumble around in the dark for the first months of a four month web construction project, and achieve nothing?
- Or is better to take two or three days out, and then spend four months minus three days performing at peak effectiveness?

No contest, in my view. I once worked with a team developing an internal network in British Telecom who had just seven weeks to complete a critical project. They devoted the first week of the project to doing nothing but planning the project, including three days with me in a project start-up workshop, and then went on to complete it with days to spare. In response to the second question, research done by Roland Gareis and Martina Huemann (1998) showed that you should spend between half a day and two days (at least) on the workshop, depending on the size and complexity of the project or package of work being planned. I typically spend two and a half days with teams, as shown in Figure 4.3.

Item	*Description*
Management summary	**One page summary for senior management**
Background	Strategic need for the project
Definition	Purpose, scope and objectives
Work scope	Milestone plan, work areas, work package scope statements
Organization	Roles and responsibility chart including the schedule
Stakeholder register	Stakeholders, their objectives, impact on the project and influence plan
Cost plan	Resource and costs estimates
Schedule	Network and bar charts
Quality plan	Quality of key deliverables
Risk register	Identified risks and mitigation strategies
Appraisal	Rough cost and benefit analysis (to commit resources to design)

Figure 4.4 *Possible contents of a project definition report*

REPORTS

Reports produced in one stage of the project can be used to help launch the next stage. Two specific reports are:

1 *The project definition report:* This is a report of the results of the project initiation. It will cover the issues outlined in the next chapter. The suggested contents are shown in Figure 4.4. Figure 4.5 is a possible contents page for a report. The Appendix contains a pro forma for the entire report. In Figure 1.7, this is called the project brief.

Euro Projex

Project Definition Report

Project: **Project Champion:** **Project Manager:**	

CONTENTS

1	Project context	Background
2	Project mandate	Purpose/scope/objectives Work areas
3	Project strategy	Key performance indicators Mission statement
4	Work definition	Milestone plan Work package definition Work package scope statements
5	Organization	Departments involved Project roles Responsibility chart Stakeholder register
6	Project plans	Activity plans Network and bar chart Quality plan Risk register
7	Project control	Planning and control system
8	Project appraisal	Cost estimate Revenue estimate Project appraisal

Author:	JRT	**Date:**	21 Jul 2003	**Issue:**	A

Figure 4.5 *Contents page for a project definition report*

2 *The project manual:* This will be a complete description of how the project is to be implemented. It will contain the complete design of the web space, new processes and procedures to support it, and a project plan for its delivery. It will have similar contents to Figure 4.4, but in greater detail. In Figure 1.7 this is called the project initiation document.

AD HOC ASSISTANCE

Finally, you may use the assistance of experts to aid the definition of the current project. These experts may be of one of two types:

1 *Experts in the web technology and web space design and delivery:* These will be people who have done similar projects in the past, who can advise the current project team on issues such as
   - mistakes made previously
   - successes
   - web technology, and ideas for design and construction which did or did not work
   - project strategies which did or did not work.

2 *Experts in team dynamics:* These will be people who are skilled in managing the working of the team. They will look for disagreements to get the storming going, and agreements to get the norming and performing going. They will aid the problem-solving, ideas generation and analysis of results. Because they get the storming going, they are not always the most popular people with the project team members at the end of the project. What works well is to have the facilitator start the storming, and the project manager to appear to start the norming and performing. The project manager is then left at the end of the workshop having the full backing of the project team as it is he or she who has seemed to lead the obtaining of consensus.

HOLDING A PROJECT START-UP WORKSHOP

Figure 4.3 gives a possible agenda for a Project start-up workshop, with timings. This is a long two days or a comfortable three days. I often start at 4.00 pm on the first day, and finish with dinner on the third, or start at 10.00 a.m. on the first day and finish with lunch on the third. It never works quite as smoothly as the timings given, and you will see there is contingency built in, but hopefully you get the idea. I usually insist on holding the workshop off-site, away from the distractions of the office. Back in the 1980s that meant we were completely isolated, and people could focus on the task at hand. Now I have to insist that they also leave their mobile phones in their bedrooms, or at least switch them off, and only switch them on during the tea breaks. Holding the workshop off-site in a hotel also helps team building. The team can relax together in the evening and get to know each other. I held several workshops with a company where the project champion was a keen snooker player, and we played snooker into the small hours most nights. On another the champion was a keen cribbage player.

The people who may be invited to the workshop are:

- *The sponsor or owner:* the person paying for the project, and who will receive the business benefit to pay for the investment.
- *The champion:* the senior user responsible for ensuring the project's outputs are properly implemented, and the business benefit delivered.
- *The project manager:* the person responsible for delivering the outputs, on time, on cost, to quality.

- *The project support office manager:* who will help with project planning, prioritizing resources with other projects, and coordinating interfaces.
- *Key line managers:* managers of key stakeholders whose support is required, such as Marketing (Internet), Personnel (intranet) or Operations (extranet).
- *Resource providers:* people who will provide the resources required to implement the project, as listed in Figure 2.2.
- *Designer managers:* people responsible for the design and delivery of the web space.
- *Users:* people responsible for operating the key project deliverables, such as the web space and its design, or the processes and procedures required to support the operation of the new web space, or changes to the organization brought about by its operation. On larger construction projects they will tend to be represented by their line managers. On smaller construction projects, remodelling and maintenance projects, they will attend the meeting.
- *Marketing:* who may have identified the business opportunity.
- *Key external consultants or contractors:* people providing resources from outside the organization.

The process works best with between six and twelve people, with eight or nine the optimum. Figure 4.6 shows who might fulfil the above roles for the intranet at TriMagi, and who would be invited to attend the project start-up workshop (PSW).

Project role	*Person with role*	*Attend start workshop?*
Sponsor	Managing Director	Part-time
Champion	Personnel Manager	Yes
Project manager	IS Assistant Manager	Yes
Key line managers	Operations Manager	Yes
	Finance Manager	Yes
Resource providers		
Design managers	IS Department	Yes
Users	Departments	Yes
Marketing	Not involved	
External consultant	Rodney Turner	Yes

Figure 4.6 *People fulfilling project roles on the intranet at TriMagi, and those attending the start-up workshop*

PROJECT START-UP FOR DIFFERENT TYPES OF PROJECT

The approach to project start-up will depend critically on the type of project, particularly how well-defined the goals and methods of delivering them are understood (Figure 1.12). Figure 4.7 illustrates different approaches.

- **Type 1:** The goals and methods are well understood, particularly if this project is very similar to ones done in the past. The emphasis will be on adapting well-understood processes to this project, using specialist implementers. The facilitator will therefore probably be an expert in this type of project. The project manager's role will be that of a conductor, leading the team through a well-defined score, and imposing his or her interpretation. As this is likely to be a maintenance or remodelling project, the meeting may only last half a day, focusing on key points.

Methods well defined	Goals well defined: Yes	Goals well defined: No
No	**Type 2** Brainstorm techniques ***Invite many disciplines*** *Experts in work* COACH	**Type 4** Problem solving and strategy ***Invite many disciplines*** *Experts in teams* EAGLE
Yes	**Type 1** Tailor known techniques ***Invite specialists*** *Experts in work* CONDUCTOR	**Type 3** Agree end stage milestones ***Invite specialists*** *Experts in teams* MASTER MASON

Key: **Project Type**
Emphasis of the workshop
Type of people to invite to the workshop
Type of facilitators to invite to the workshop
ROLE OF THE PROJECT MANAGER

Figure 4.7 *Start-up and the goals and methods matrix*

- **Type 2:** The goals are well understood, but they are novel, so it is not yet known how best to achieve them. The emphasis will be on brainstorming the techniques, using multidisciplinary teams comprising people who may be able to contribute to the process. The facilitator may again be an expert in this type of work, somebody who may be able to advise how similar things have been done in the past. The project manager will be a coach. The objective is to get the ball into the goal at the end of the field as many times as possible in the next 90 minutes (very clear). How is completely unknown. The coach instructs the team in standard plays, but then can only shout instructions from the sideline as the game unfolds.
- **Type 3:** The exact specification of the goals is now unclear, but a well defined life cycle will be followed in defining them. The emphasis will be on agreeing the milestone and stage review points at which progress towards the definition of the goals will be reviewed, and agreed. Specialist teams who have done similar things in the past will be invited since they will have experience in the standard life cycles to be followed, but the facilitator will be someone who can guide the team in their problem solving. The project manager will be a master mason. Exactly what the cathedral will look like or how it will stand up is not known as the team starts. But they will follow very well-defined stone-crafting techniques, under the guidance of the master mason, in order to put it up.
- **Type 4:** Neither the goals nor the methods are known. What is known is the business problem to be solved, and so the emphasis is on solving that problem, identifying the deliverable that will solve the strategic problem, and then treating the project as type 2, once the deliverables are defined. Multidisciplinary teams will be invited again to give a broad range of views about possible solutions to the problem, but the facilitator will be somebody who can guide the team in their problem solving. The project manager must be an eagle, able to hover above the project and see it in the context of the business, but then be able to spot small details and go down to deal with them, before returning to hover above the project again.

Note that the team invited depends on whether the goals are well defined or not, but the facilitator invited depends on whether the methods are well defined or not.

The size and duration of the start-up meeting also depends on the type of project, but more on whether it is a construction, remodelling or maintenance project. As we saw in Chapter 2 the last two will tend to be fairly small and repetitive. If a project start meeting is held at all, it will be very short, typically half a day, to clearly define what needs to be done. On web construction projects, the project start meeting may last one to two days (even three depending on the impact on the organization). It will need to go through most of the suggested steps.

FOLLOWING THE START-UP PROCESS

Most of the remainder of this part of the book follows the project start-up workshop, explaining what needs to be done at each step, as shown in Figure 4.3. Tools are introduced to manage each project step, and it is suggested how they can be completed in the start-up workshop. One thing I should say is, don't feel compelled to use each tool. Use those you need to use for your project.

CHAPTER

5 *Project Definition*

In Chapter 3, we saw the need to link the definition of the project to corporate strategy, to ensure that the project delivers an outcome that will deliver benefit to the business. That was supported by the first two of the ten commandments listed at the end of Chapter 2, which suggested that you should ensure your project objectives are clear, that they are clearly linked to corporate objectives, and that you should write a clear brief for the project. That is the first step in the development of the project model, and the topic of this chapter. Here we define:

- The background to the perceived need for the web page, the context within which it will be developed, and the pressures for change which make it necessary;
- The business objectives that it is intended to deliver;
- The project objectives, the definition of the project outcomes, the nature and contents of the web space that will enable you to achieve the required business objectives; and
- A basic understanding of how they will be delivered and what needs to be done to achieve those ends.

Thus we start by defining the project at the top, or integrative level. We start by integrating the project into the business. This should be done on almost all projects. By and large, projects should only be undertaken if they will deliver some essential business objective to the organization. But remember the cautionary tales in Figure 3.3; sometimes consider changing the business when a really good idea comes along. In this chapter I describe project definition – how to define the project starting with the background, and then the purpose, scope and outputs, and areas of work. I will begin by reinforcing the need to integrate the project into the business.

INTEGRATING THE PROJECT INTO THE BUSINESS

Figure 5.1 illustrates the top level of breakdown, what I called the integrative level in Chapter 1, the level where the project is integrated into the business. It corresponds to the top three levels in Figure 1.8. It shows that there are three sub-levels, which are, starting from the bottom:

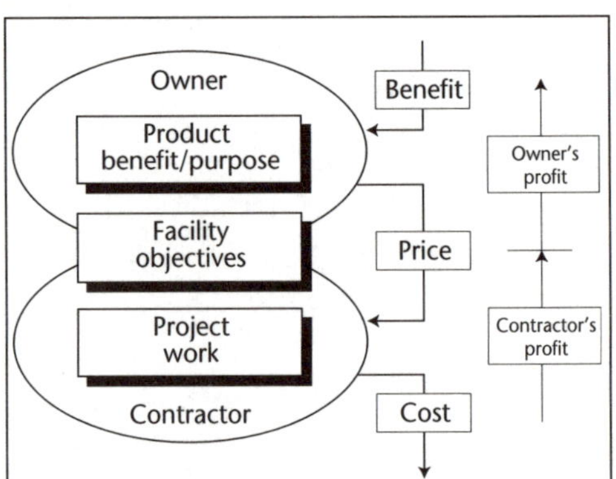

Figure 5.1 *The owner–contractor model*

1 The project is an endeavour, or temporary organization, created to deliver the web space (the project's outputs). However, because both the web space and business objectives are not achieved until some time in the future (the web space is

delivered at the end of the project, the business objectives some time later), people undertaking the project tend to focus on the work to be done, not the objectives. The project takes on a life of its own, independent of its objectives. Work is done, web components developed, because it seems like a good idea at the time, not necessarily because it will deliver some useful result.

2 Thus the team should not lose sight of the fact that they are doing the work to deliver the desired web space (and supporting PSO changes). All the work should be oriented to producing essential components of those outcomes, and configuring them into the whole. Anything else is of no value and should be avoided. But the web space is not being built for its own sake either.

3 Once commissioned, it will be operated by users. They will operate it on behalf of the owner, to achieve the business objectives and deliver business benefit. This benefit will repay the cost of the project. It is to achieve this business benefit that the project is undertaken, that is its purpose, the reason for its existence, its *raison d'être*. Everything done on the project should be oriented towards this end. Thus the definition of the project should start with the business benefit. From that we should determine the project's output, and the method of delivering it.

Figure 5.1 also shows two groups of people associated with the project: the owner and the contractor. The owner buys the web space (for a price), and operates it to receive the benefit, and thereby pay for their investment. The contractor undertakes the work to deliver the web space. They receive the price from the owner, and spend money (the cost) to do the work. The owner's profit is the difference between the price and the benefit; the contractor's is the difference between the cost and the price. If the owner can get the price down, they increase their profit. If the contractor can get the price up, they increase theirs. So we have a basic tension between the two main parties involved, with seemingly conflicting objectives. The best results are obtained if they can align their objectives, so they increase the benefit at a given cost (increase value), and thereby set a price which allows them both to make a reasonable profit. This, in the famous cliché, is the win-win solution. Thus two parties to the project can have opposing objectives. When the contractor is an external supplier or consultant, we accept that, it is part of the contract. When it is the back office supplying the front office, we assume they are all part of the same organization, and should have the same objective. They don't. But it is complicated even further on web projects. We saw in Chapter 2 that on traditional IS projects the contractor (or back office) was the IS department, supplying the Operations department (the front office). But for web delivery, the project can be led by the Marketing or Personnel department, on behalf of the Operations department, with a wide variety of resources, including the IS department, in support. This increases the need of ensuring that the project and its components are clearly defined, to stop people slipping their own personal wish lists into the project definition, and to achieve a balance of the desired outcomes of the project to satisfy everyone's needs. I talk further about balancing the basket of success criteria in the next chapter, and about managing the various stakeholders in Chapter 9. It also increases the role of the project champion, also discussed in Chapter 9.

THE PROJECT BACKGROUND

The first step in project definition is to write a statement of the project's background. This will be prepared before the project start-up meeting and circulated to the people attending. The background:

TriMagi
Project Definition Report

Project:	Intranet Phase 1
Project Champion:	Martin Pacific
Project Manager:	Frances Seeker

Background

TriMagi is investigating the way it can use web-enabled technology to improve its operations and its contact with its customers and its employees. It is expected that in the medium term it will develop:

- a home page to market its products and services to potential customers
- an extranet, to provide Internet and home banking services to customers
- an intranet.

The intranet will be the first step in the process. Reasons for this are:

- TriMagi can gain experiences with web-enabling technologies testing them out on employees, before customers, so that the company has gained experience by the time it goes live externally
- all employees will automatically be logged on to the TriMagi home page at the start of every day, so as services for customers are introduced, employees will be familiar with the system, and automatically be online to support the new services.

The system will also automate several personnel processes, and enable information about the company benefits programme to be readily available online. The system will support:

1 Processing of documents for personnel, including
   - expense claims
   - holiday requests
   - sickness reports.

2 Online availability of personnel information, such as
   - procedures to be followed to submit the above
   - information about the company car scheme
   - statement of the company's personnel policy and psychological contract with its employees.

3 Daily news reports on each person's desktop, including
   - news about the company
   - news from the financial services sector
   - briefings from the managing director.

The benefits are that the company wants to

- communicate better with its employees, and hopefully improve the psychological contract
- speed up the processing of personnel documents, and reduce the administrative burden
- reduce administrative, printing and storage costs by making information available online rather than in paper form.

Author:	JRT	**Date:**	21 July 2003	**Issue:**	A

Figure 5.2 *Statement of background for the intranet at TriMagi*

- describes the context of the new web space, and the reasoning behind it
- begins to give an understanding of the problem to be solved or opportunity to be exploited, describing symptoms of the problem or opportunity, how it manifests itself
- suggests the possible benefit of exploiting that opportunity or solving that problem.

Figure 5.2 is the statement of background for the intranet at TriMagi, using the pro forma in the Appendix.

PURPOSE, SCOPE AND OUTPUTS

The first thing considered at the project start-up workshop is the project mandate, the purpose, scope and project outputs. This defines the three levels in Figure 5.1. You should start with the purpose, the reason for doing the project, the business objectives. Whether you next consider the scope and then the project outputs, or vice versa, depends a little on the project and what stage you have reached. Sometimes you need to go through the basic problem-solving first, to think about how to achieve the project's purpose, and then derive the project's outputs. At other times you will have a reasonably clear idea of the nature of the web space the project will deliver and will need to think about how to do that. It tends to be the case that at early stages of the project (at the start of discovery), you need to do the problem-solving first, working out how to do the project, and then trying to define the outputs. At later stages (at the start of systems design) you know what you are planning to deliver, and the emphasis of the scope is on ring-fencing the project, deciding what is part of the project, and what is not.

PURPOSE (WHY?)

The purpose is the reason for doing the project. This should follow fairly obviously from the statement of background. It is some problem to be solved, or opportunity to be exploited. There may be some inefficiency that is costing money and can be eliminated. Or there might be some market niche that can be exploited. It might be some legislative change that needs to be accommodated or the company will be forced out of business. Most projects should be one of the three types in the third typology in Chapter 1, a staying in business project, a repositioning project or a performance improvement project.

The statement of purpose will define the benefit derived from the new web space, the savings from the improvement in efficiency, or the income from exploiting the market niche. (There is no benefit from responding to the legislative change, other than staying in business. There is no income, so the emphasis is on minimizing cost.) At this very early stage, the benefit will be only very coarsely defined, to an order of magnitude, say ± 50 per cent. Remember that at the discovery stage we are only trying to demonstrate viability sufficiently to assign resources to systems design, not full implementation.

Figure 5.3 gives the purpose for the intranet at TriMagi using the pro forma from the Appendix.

OUTPUTS (WHAT?)

Then you can define the project's outputs, the components of the web space and associated PSO changes to achieve that purpose. This defines the end points of the project, what the project team hands over to the operations team. The operations team will then take this away, and use it to achieve the benefits defined above. The definitions of the project's outputs should be measurable, so the users can accept them, say 'the project is over', and assume responsibility for the operating web space.

TriMagi
Project Definition Report

Project: **Project Champion:** **Project Manager:**	Intranet Phase 1 Martin Pacific Frances Seeker

Purpose: **Why?**	The purpose of Phase 1 of the intranet will be to: • communicate better with employees to improve psychological contract • speed processing of personnel documents and reduce administration • reduce personnel administration costs There is also the additional purpose of gaining experience of web-based technology for further development of the intranet and for introduction of the Internet home page and extranet.
Outputs: **What?**	The project will deliver an intranet comprising: • internal home page to automatically appear on employees' screens when they log on at the start of the day, containing news for employees, and linking to other pages containing further current information • document processing pages for essential personnel information such as holiday requests, expense claims, sickness reports, and others as agreed; these pages will include information on when to complete these forms and how to complete and process them • personnel information pages containing essential information relating to terms and conditions of employment, and information about company personnel schemes, such as the company car scheme The project will also a deliver a report describing experience for Phase 1 to be used in the implementation of Phase 2 and the implementation of the Internet home page and the extranet. The project will be complete when the system has gone live, and the report on experience for Phase 1 has been accepted by the managing director as a basis for proceeding to Phase 2.

Scope: **How?**	**Discovery:**	The overall content of the system will be planned and new procedures written. An audit will be conducted to produce an inventory of current hardware.
	Design:	The site will be designed and developed and the new procedures piloted. New hardware requirements will be identified and orders placed.
	Delivery:	The new procedures will optimized, and the site assembled and approved.
	Deployment:	The new hardware will be installed and the data entered or migrated. The system will go live.
	Exclusions:	Phase 1 will not include the management information and production pages.

Areas of work:	There will be four areas of work: M: Management approval D: Design and development P: Procedures and systems H: Hardware and data

Author:	JRT	**Date:**	21 July 2003	**Issue:**	A

Figure 5.3 *Project mandate for the intranet at TriMagi*

I think that at the very end of the project, the system should have been put on load – not necessarily to full load, but sufficiently to test it is working. You should define the target level of load as part of the project definition. Then at the end of the project you can test whether or not it has been achieved. If it has the users can take responsibility for the system, and the project team can have a party and disband. If not, then you need to decide whether it is because the project team have made a mistake, or the users aren't using the system properly. If the former, the project team need to put it right; if the latter, the system should still be handed over to the users so they can learn to use it properly.

Remember also that the project outputs will not just include the definition of the technical elements of the web space, they should also include the cultural elements, the changes to the people, systems and organization. They should include a statement of new management processes required, training of the people in the use of the new system, an education programme to encourage them to accept it (Chapter 9), and any organizational changes required to support the new system. It is here that you recognize that these PSO changes are required. In Chapter 7, I will show you how to use the milestone plan to ensure they are given due emphasis in the plan.

Figure 5.3 gives the outputs for the intranet at TriMagi using the pro forma from the Appendix.

SCOPE (HOW?)

The definition of the scope fulfils a number of needs:

Exactly how the purpose will be achieved, and the problems solved, may not be clear initially. So it may be necessary to perform basic problem solving, following the cycle in Figure 1.4, to determine the best way of achieving the solution. This will create several options for achieving the project's objectives. You need to determine the advantages and disadvantages of each. Each option will deliver some or all of the expected benefit and cost varying amounts of money. You should choose the highest value option, that is the option that gives the optimum ratio between benefit and cost, not the cheapest option (that is doing nothing), nor necessarily the option that gives the most benefit (if that is excessively expensive) but the one that gives the best value. (However, Figure 5.4 is a cautionary tale about what you need to include in the assessment of the value of an option.) The statement of scope may set out the various options considered and explain why you chose the one you did.

> In the 1990s I worked with a company supplying electronic financial data products over its own networks. They told me that in designing their new products the cost–benefit ratio conformed to a Pareto principle or learning curve. For a certain cost they could achieve about 80 per cent of the full functionality: full functionality would cost them five times as much. They would design for the 80 per cent point, as that gave best value for money, four times the value of the point giving full functionality, 0.8/1 as opposed to 1/5.
>
> The problem was that in the early 1990s they had a worldwide monopoly, but another company began to provide products to fill the 20 per cent gap. Having gained market share this company began to supply products to compete with the 80 per cent and the first company soon lost its monopoly. (The founder of the second company is currently mayor of New York.)
>
> The first company should have priced the threat to its monopoly into its value equation.

Figure 5.4 *Choosing the best value option*

Having chosen the option to carry forward, you now need to ring-fence the project. You need to decide what work has to be done to implement the chosen solution, and what will be excluded from the project. You need to decide what is in the project and what is out.

- **In:** At this stage this is a fairly high-level description of what has to be done, specifying work areas. The definition of the work will be expanded over the coming steps.
- **Out:** There are at least three reasons why work may need to be excluded:

1 *Nice-to-haves:* As the project begins, some of the stakeholders will try to include their pet topics in the web design. Many of these will add cost for little benefit, and thereby reduce the value of the project. In the worst case some will even stop the web space working.
2 *Sharing work:* Often, several projects taking place at the same time share a component. Rather than all projects developing that component, it is clearly more efficient for just one to do it. It may not matter which one does it, but it is critical to decide which, and make that clearly understood.
3 *Delegating work:* Another approach is to set up a separate project to look after that component. This is quite common, for instance, where several related projects need to redeploy and train people. Again, it usually doesn't matter what decision is made, it just needs to be clear.

Figure 5.3 gives the statement of scope for the intranet at TriMagi using the pro forma from the Appendix.

AREAS OF WORK

At the end of the initial project definition process, we can now more formally state the areas of work of the project. This merely restates what was contained under 'In' from the scope statement, but in a more specific manner. There should be one area of work delivering each project outcome as stated under the outputs, defining all the technical and cultural elements of the work to be done.

Figure 5.3 gives the areas of work for the intranet at TriMagi using the pro forma from the Appendix.

CHAPTER

6 *Project Success and Strategy*

The first of the ten commandments at the end of Chapter 2 not only dealt with defining the project objectives, but also with ensuring that you know the criteria against which you will be judged. It is essential before you start a project to agree the success criteria for the project with all the stakeholders. We also saw in Chapter 2 that web-delivery projects can have a large number of potential stakeholders, with many of them involved in the project's delivery. John Wateridge (1995) showed that it is a necessary condition for project success to agree the success criteria with all the stakeholders before you start. Unfortunately it is a necessary condition but not a sufficient condition; other things can still cause the project to go wrong. (In Chapter 9, I will say that it is essential to go on agreeing the success criteria at review points throughout the project to ensure success.) In his book, *Alice in Wonderland*, Lewis Carroll relates a conversation between Alice and the Cheshire Cat. Alice asks the Cat, 'Which road should I take from here,' to which the Cat replies, 'That all depends where you want to get to.' Alice, who is lost in the forest, says, 'I don't much care where,' to which the Cat replies, 'Then it doesn't matter which road you take.' If you don't know where you are going, any road will take you there. And if the project team members don't know where they are going, then they may all be travelling along different roads. So before the project starts its is important to agree:

- what the project will deliver and when (the project deliverables or outcomes)
- how achievement of those deliverables will be judged to be successful (success criteria)
- what measures of the success criteria we can track throughout the project to ensure we are on course for a successful outcome – key performance indicators (KPIs)
- what project delivery techniques increase the chances of successfully delivering those project outcomes (success factors)
- that you have the support of all the project stakeholders to these decisions (which implies that you know who the stakeholders are).

So this is the next step in the project start-up workshop, agreeing the success criteria and identifying the potential stakeholders. In this chapter, we consider these questions. I start by suggesting three questions that can be used in the project start-up workshop to tease out how the project will be judged successful, and who the stakeholders are who will have a view on this. I then consider what potential success criteria might be and introduce key performance indicators, measures of the success criteria you can track throughout the project. I then describe potential success factors, things you can influence to increase the chance of a successful outcome.

THREE QUESTIONS FOR PROJECT SUCCESS

Francis Hartman (2001) proposed three questions you can use in the project start-up workshop to help identify the project success criteria and the stakeholders. First the team should agree the end date of the project. Then they should be asked the following three questions. You should ask

Francis Hartman describes running start-up workshops with two companies, where the project teams gave contrary answers to his three questions.

The first project was the development of a large system for a company in Alberta, Canada. There were two project managers, one for the design stage of the project and the other for development. In response to question 1, one said the project was over when the system had been tested and was ready for commissioning, and the other when the system had been evaluated and shown to be working as intended. These two dates are at least a month apart, and yet both gave the same completion date.

The other team were implementing replacement accounting software for their organization. About 30 people attended the workshop, and responses to the first question ranged from:

- beta test successfully completed
- the system has run for twelve months without fault (roughly 15 months later)
- 30 people have been made redundant.

The first two of these are at least 15 months apart. The third was unfortunate because some of the people in the room were those to be made redundant and this was the first they had heard of it.

If the teams had continued with this level of misunderstanding, they probably would have blamed failure of their projects on circumstances beyond their control, saying 'We were unlucky.'

Figure 6.1 *Failure to agree completion criteria*

the team members (or attendees at the start-up workshop) to complete these questions separately, and then it can help identify differences of opinion within the team. The three questions are:

Q1: On the last day of the project, what will the project team hand over to operations?

Q2: How will success of the project be judged?

Q3: Who has an opinion on questions 1 and 2?

Question 1 defines the web space to be delivered, and its components. The answer is the same as for the project outputs in the project definition, as described in the last chapter. But the question can be very useful not only for identifying the technical deliverables, but also the PSO elements. It can also be very useful for helping to identify precisely the stage of development of the deliverables when handed over to the operations team. It is amazing how different team members can have quite wildly different understanding of what the configuration of the deliverables will be when handed over to the users, and even though they are working to the same end date the different configurations may be months apart (Figure 6.1). If that is allowed to continue into the project itself, the project team members will not only be trudging along different roads, but at different speeds. At the end of the project some will then think the project a success and some will think it a failure. So unless you can get the team members to agree the

TriMagi
Project Success

Project: **Project Champion:** **Project Manager:**	Intranet Phase 1 Martin Pacific Frances Seeker

Deliverables	*What will the project team deliver to operations on the last day of the project?* The project will deliver an intranet comprising: • internal home page to automatically appear on employees screens when they log on at the start of the day, containing news for employees, and linking to other pages containing further current information • document processing pages for essential personnel information such as holiday requests, expense claims, sickness reports, and others as agreed; these pages will include information on when to complete these forms and how to complete and process them • personnel information pages containing essential information relating to terms and conditions of employment, and information about company personnel schemes, such as the company car scheme. The project will also a deliver a report describing experience for Phase 1 to be used in the implementation of Phase 2 and the implementation of the Internet home page and the extranet. The project will be complete when the system has gone live, and the report on experience for Phase 1 has been accepted by the managing director as a basis for proceeding to Phase 2.
Success criteria	*How will the project be judged to be successful?* The project will be a success if: • it delivers a web design that matches the corporate image and is generally acceptable, but particularly to the board and marketing • the new method of processing personnel documents is acceptable to the users • the online availability of personnel information is well received • agreement is obtained to proceed to Phase 2 on the basis of experience from Phase 1 • the project is completed within an acceptable timescale and budget.
Stakeholders	*Who has an opinion on the above?* The managing director and other members of the board The general managers from personnel, marketing, IS and production Staff generally
Key performance indicators	*Qualitative:* User acceptance, corporate image, ease of implementation *Quantitative:* The project is completed at a time and cost that makes progressing to Phase 2 worthwhile

Author:	JRT	**Date:**	21 July 2003	**Issue:**	A

Figure 6.2 *Answers to the three questions for the intranet at TriMagi*

success criteria before you start, not everyone will agree on whether or not it has been a success at the end.

Question 2 identifies the success criteria and question 3 the stakeholders. In the next section I consider what potential success criteria might be. In Chapter 9 I describe how to manage the stakeholders. Figure 6.2 gives possible answers to the three questions for the intranet at TriMagi.

I would just like to reinforce a point made in Chapter 4. Usually you need to do the project definition before considering the project success criteria. You cannot think about the success criteria until you know what the project is about. The answer to Francis Hartman's first question is something that was considered under project definition, and is the link from definition to success. It is worth considering it again to ensure the team have the same view about the configuration of the web space as it is handed over to the users. However, sometimes you already have an idea of what the space will look like, the feasibility study has been completed and you are about to start design and delivery. Then you do success before definition. The emphasis of definition will be on the purpose and ring-fencing the project under the scope, deciding what the project will and will not include.

JUDGING SUCCESS

So what are the criteria by which a project is judged to be a success? The conventional view, now widely discredited, is that the project is a success if it is delivered

- within budget
- on time
- to the defined level of quality or functionality.

This perspective is from the point of view of the project team, and on the last day of the project. It is now accepted that there is a basket of success criteria, reflecting different people's interests and judged over different timescales (Figure 6.3). Some success criteria are judged on the last day, some months later, some years later. Furthermore these criteria may not be compatible. They are usually not mutually exclusive, but some effort is required to align them. It is part of the

Success criteria	*Interested stakeholders*	*Timescale*
Increases shareholder value	Shareholders, sponsor	End + years
Makes a profit for the owner	Owner	End + years
Satisfies owner and sponsor	Sponsor, owner	End + years
Satisfies consumers	Consumers	End + years
Satisfies users and champion	Users, champion	End + years
Achieves purpose	Users, champion, owner	End + months
Meets specification – Functionality – Flexibility, reliability, availability, maintainability, elasticity, security	Users, champion, team	End + weeks
Time, cost, quality	Project team, users	End
Satisfies project team	Project team	End
Makes a profit for the contractor	Project team	End

Figure 6.3 *Success criteria for projects*

development of the project organization to ensure that the various stakeholders' objectives are aligned (see Chapter 9).

John Wateridge (1995) asked participants on information systems projects to think of previous projects they had worked on, to consider whether they were a success or failure, and against what criteria they were making that judgement. He also asked them their role: sponsor, user, designer, or project manager. On successful projects, all four groups were looking for the project to provide value for the sponsor. On unsuccessful projects:

- the sponsors were looking for value
- the users were looking for good functionality
- the designers wanted to produce the best design
- the project managers wanted to finish on cost and time.

What is sad is that what the various parties were focusing on in unsuccessful projects was important. To be successful and produce value for the sponsor, the project must deliver good functionality, through a good design, completed at or near cost and time. However, it is possible for the parties to focus on what is important to them to the exclusion of everyone else, which results in the team being torn apart. Or there is a way in which the team members focus on what is important to them, but oriented to the common good. This may require them to suboptimize what is important to them, to achieve the overall global optimum.

This is a feature of projects very different from routine operations. In operations, the parts of the system are disconnected, so the overall optimum is obtained by optimizing the parts separately. In a project, the parts are integrated, one part affects the other, so the system must be optimized as a whole, and that may not optimize the parts separately. The project team must determine in advance what the overall optimum is, what the success criteria for the project are, and what that means for their individual parts of it. The manager must agree the success criteria with all the stakeholders before the project starts. It is impossible to pull the project into the optimum at the end if it has not been the target from the start. It would seem the overriding aim should be to produce value for the sponsor, to achieve the project's purpose. All the other team members' goals should be aligned with that overall aim. As I said above, achieving goal alignment should be the main aim of project organization.

Figure 6.3 shows a basket of success criteria, the stakeholders concerned with each criterion, and the timescale over which the assessment is made. Note that the criteria that are of importance to the project team (time, cost and quality), are perceived at the end of the project. Good functionality, which is of importance to the users, is perceived over the coming months. Whether or not the project achieved its purpose, and the owner made a profit, is perceived over a period of years. This leads to an initial focus on time, cost and quality, the conventional, but discredited, criteria. Research done in Australia showed that projects finishing on cost and time were less likely to be perceived as a success over the long term than those delivering good functionality. Research done in the US in the late 1980s showed that on product development projects, achieving good functionality was the most important outcome. Finishing on time was reasonably important, but money could be thrown at the project to achieve the other two (Turner, 1999).

KEY PERFORMANCE INDICATORS AND PROJECT CONTROL

Key performance indicators (KPIs), are quantitative measures of the success criteria that can be judged throughout the project, to ensure it is progressing towards the successful achievement of the success criteria. It is no good waiting to the end of the project, saying 'How did we do?' and finding the project has failed. The project team need to track progress throughout the project against measures of the success criteria, and take action early on to counter any shortfall.

Now we come to another mistake frequently made by project managers. The success criteria as defined are good functionality, good quality, within budget, or makes a profit for the owner, but the project progress reports track time only, because that is all their project management software tracks. The project team must choose their control methods (methodology) and their key performance indicators to reflect the success criteria. That is if the key success criteria is to:

- *Make a profit for the owner:* the team need to track the expected benefit (first year's revenue) of the new web space and compare to the predicted costs as below
- *Make a profit for the contractor; or finish on cost:* they need to track the forecast cost at completion (Chapter 11)
- *Deliver appropriate functionality:* configuration management is used (Chapter 10)
- *Deliver the new web space within the defined timescale:* then the schedule needs to be tracked using bar charts or milestone tracker charts (Chapter 12).

The project team may need to track a basket of these KPIs, but they must agree in advance their relative importance, so when faced with a critical decision during the project they know whether to give priority to first year's revenue, functionality, cost or time (see Figure 6.4). To maximize first year's revenue, functionality should almost always take precedence. The relative importance of time and cost depend on the circumstance. However, there are some projects where if they are not done by a certain date they have no value; the Olympic Games for instance.

> Ralf Müller tells me that when he worked for NCR, he would ask his clients at the start of a project to prioritize time, cost and functionality. At the start, they would almost invariably say that timescale was the most important in order to deliver the project by the deadline. But at the end of the project the clients would now be saying functionality was important; without appropriate functionality, the users would not accept the system. He says he would be working on two projects with one client, one at the start and one at the end; on the project starting the client would be saying time is important, and on the project finishing the same client would be saying that functionality was important. Organizations did not seem to learn from one project to the next what was truly important on their projects.

Figure 6.4 *Agreeing the priority of success factors and KPIs*

Somebody was telling me recently that they were involved on a project in the National Health Service which had 125 key performance indicators. If you have 125 performance indicators, at least 119 are not 'key'. Around six is the maximum number of key performance indicators you should have for your project. Typically you might have:

- schedule
- cost
- predicted first year's revenue
- stakeholder satisfaction.

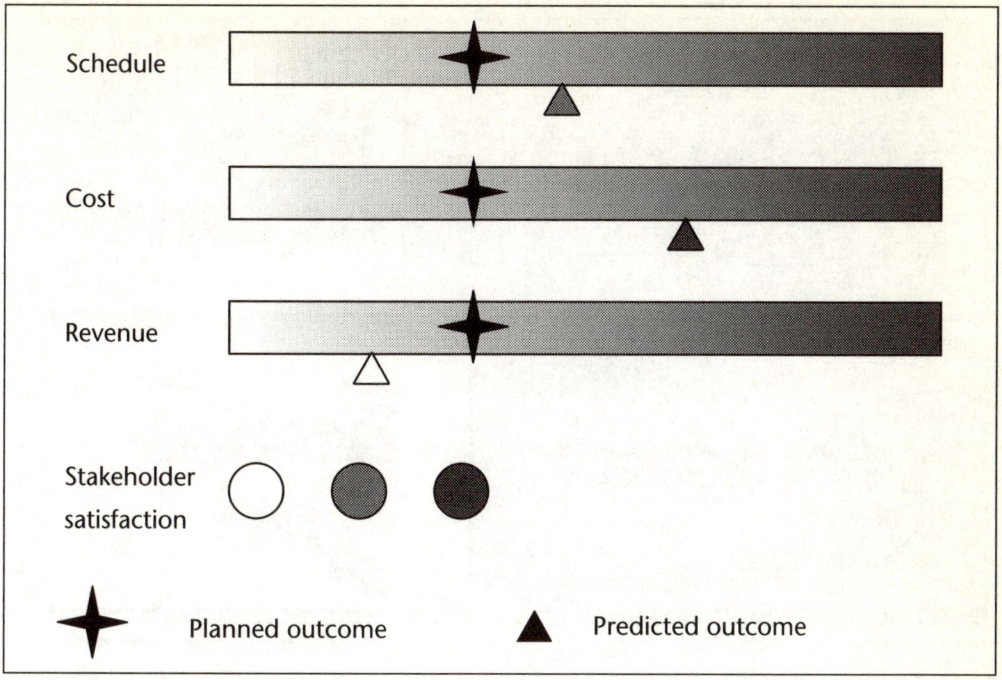

Figure 6.5 *Project dashboard*

You will also monitor configuration (Chapter 10) at the project reviews, but that is not a quantitative measure. Predicted first year's revenue is the quantitative measure of configuration.

KPIs can be turned into highly visual project control tools. I chaired a conference recently where a speaker suggested a project dashboard (Figure 6.5). For the first three measures above, there is a dial showing the target and the current prediction. In Figure 6.5, the target is shown as a cross, and the current prediction is shown as a triangle under the dial. The dial can go from green to red, success to danger. (This unfortunately cannot be shown in a black and white version here.) Stakeholder satisfaction is a qualitative measure, and is shown as a red, amber or green traffic light. Another visual representation of the KPIs is shown in Figure 6.6. This monitors:

- milestones (Chapter 7)
- time (Chapter 12)
- cost (Chapter 11)
- risk (Chapter 13).

The content of the boxes will be explained in the coming chapters as indicated.

SUCCESS FACTORS

So what can you do to increase the chance that your project will be a success? Well, for a starter, agree the success criteria with the stakeholders before you start, and go on agreeing at the project review points throughout the project. What else have people identified? The first work was done in Norway by Kristoffer Grude while working as managing director of an information systems supplier (Andersen *et al.*, 1995). He looked at pitfalls, things that cause projects to go

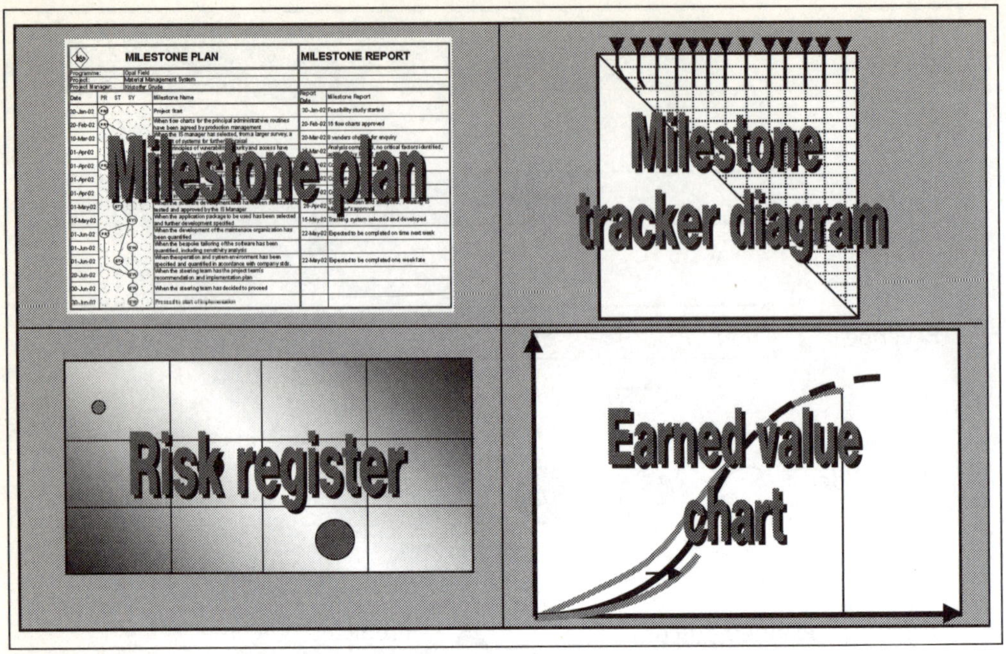

Figure 6.6 *Project performance tracking sheet*

wrong. I recast these as success factors in Figure 6.7. The definitive study was done by Jeffrey Pinto and Dennis Slevin (1988). They identified ten critical success factors from a survey of 400 projects (Figure 6.8). Applying these success factors, people found that success of projects rose, but from 30 per cent to 60 per cent. More recently, Terry Cooke-Davies (2002) has analysed project success factors, and found the most significant contributor is to manage risk (Chapter 13). The major risks likely to be encountered on web-delivery projects were listed in Figure 2.3. Putting Figures 6.7, 6.8 and 2.3 together, we can develop a seven point strategy for the successful delivery of new web space:

1 *Project vision and mission:* make sure purpose of the web space is clearly defined and agreed, agree the expected business benefit and success criteria with the stakeholders before you start
2 *Top management support:* don't proceed without political support
3 *Schedule/plans:* have good clear plans
4 *Client consultation:* agree the specification, the plans and the success criteria with the client before you start. The client is a multi-headed beast, consisting of the sponsor, the users and the consumers
5 *Project team:* gather a competent, motivated team to undertake the project
6 *Technology:* ensure the technology used is flexible, reliable, available, maintainable, elastic and secure
7 *Risk analysis and management:* develop a clear risk management plan, identify and prioritize risks, and monitor and control risk as the project progresses.

These points are eerily reminiscent of the ten commandments at the end of Chapter 2, especially the first three. We see again the need to define the goals and agree the success criteria as described in this chapter and the last. It is very important to be clear about the project's objectives, the design of the web space to be delivered and the business objectives it is expected to achieve. The features of web projects will make them difficult to manage and give them a high risk of failure.

Project stage	*Success factors*
Foundation	Align the project with the business Gain commitment of involved managers Create a shared vision
Planning	Use multiple levels Use simple friendly tools Encourage creativity Estimate realistically
Implementation	Negotiate resource availability Agree cooperation Define management responsibility Gain commitment of resource providers Define channels of communication Project manager as manager not chief technologist
Control	Integrate plans and progress reports Formalize the review process – fixed intervals – defined criteria – controlled attendance Use sources of authority

Figure 6.7 *Kristoffer Grude's success factors for projects*

Success factor	*Description*
Project mission	Clearly defined goals and direction
Management support	Resources, authority and power for implementation
Schedule and plans	Detailed specification of implementation process
Client consultation	Communication and consultation with stakeholders
Personnel	Recruitment and training of competent personnel
Technical tasks	Ability of the required technology and expertise
Client acceptance	Selling of the final product to the end-users
Monitoring, feedback	Timely and comprehensive control
Communication	Provision of timely data to key players
Troubleshooting	Ability to handle unexpected problems

Figure 6.8 *Jeffrey Pinto and Dennis Slevin's success factors for projects*

CHAPTER **7** *Managing Scope*

We now begin planning how we are going to deliver the desired web space and other supporting changes. The next step is to develop a plan for the project at the strategic level, often called the level one plan. Here we develop an overall framework for coordinating the contribution of different resources to the project, and providing them with a vision for how the web space, and supporting PSO changes, are to be constructed and delivered. Web projects involve diverse people from different departments and perhaps even different sites. We need a tool to:

- set the overall framework
- provide the different resources with a vision for the overall objective and their contribution to it
- apportion the work so people in different departments and different sites know what they have to do, with their work coordinated at this strategic level.

The suggested tool for doing this is a *milestone plan*. We develop a plan that consists of around 20 milestones (12 to 24), which defines a strategy for undertaking the project. The milestone consists of key intermediate deliverables for the project, such as:

- key decision points
- key quality review points
- the delivery of key components or assemblies of the end product
- the completion of life cycle stages.

This chapter describes the milestone plan, and the activity plans which support it. First I give an overview of the milestone plan, then I describe some principles of milestone planning, and finally I suggest how to develop the plan in the start-up workshop. In the second section I describe how to develop lower level plans, milestone scope statements and activity plans.

MILESTONE PLANNING

Figure 7.1 illustrates a milestone plan. This is the suggested milestone plan for implementing the intranet at TriMagi, but is just used as an illustration at the moment. The plan is a strategic level network for the project. It shows key intermediate deliverables, and the logical flow between them. If it were drawn across the page, it would be what is called in the jargon an *activity-on-node*, or *precedence* network (Turner, 1999). The milestones represent the work to be done; the lines the logical flow of the work. We happen to represent the work by the results it will deliver.

There are several reasons for choosing to focus on milestones rather than the work per se, and several for drawing the network down the page rather than across. One reason for representing the work by the result, or milestone, is that it gives a far more flexible and robust plan. The outcomes of a project are often fairly stable. What can change a lot as the project progresses is our understanding of the best way of achieving the results. The work in one stage

TriMagi MILESTONE PLAN

Project:	Intranet Phase 1
Project Champion:	Martin Pacific
Project Manager:	Frances Seeker

Date	P	M	D	H	Milestone name	Short name	End date
18 Aug		M0			When the managing director and personnel manager approve that the project is ready to start	Ready to start	18 Aug
26 Aug		M1			When the overall content and style of the web space has been agreed	Overall content and style agreed	26 Aug
28 Aug				H1	When the current inventory of hardware and data has been identified and logged	Hardware and data inventory	28 Aug
02 Sep		M2			When the content of the home and news pages has been agreed	Home and news pages agreed	02 Sep
02 Sep		M3			When the content of the document processing pages has been agreed	Document processing pages agreed	02 Sep
02 Sep		M4			When the content of the personnel information pages has been agreed	Personnel information pages agreed	02 Sep
03 Sep	P1				When existing procedures have been reviewed and revised procedures written	Procedures rewritten	03 Sep
09 Sep		M5			When the overall content has been agreed ready for design	Ready to design	09 Sep
15 Sep				H2	When the hardware requirements have been defined	Hardware defined	15 Sep
15 Sep	P2				When new jobs required by the revised procedures have been designed	New jobs designed	15 Sep
22 Sep				H3	When the hardware has been designed	Hardware designed	22 Sep
25 Sep			D1		When the home and news pages have been designed and developed	Home and news pages developed	25 Sep
25 Sep			D2		When the document processing pages have been designed and developed	Document processing pages developed	25 Sep
25 Sep			D3		When the personnel information pages have been designed and developed	Personnel information pages developed	25 Sep
29 Sep	P3				When the new procedures have been piloted and adjustments approved	New procedures piloted	29 Sep
07 Oct			D4		When the site has been assembled	Site assembled	07 Oct
14 Oct	P4				When the procedures have been optimized and adjustments made to the web site	Procedures optimized	14 Oct
17 Oct			D5		When the site has been signed off and is ready to be deployed	Site signed off	17 Oct
17 Oct	P5				When the user trial is complete and the operation of the procedures and sites tested and approved	Ready to deploy	17 Oct
11 Nov				H4	When the new hardware has been installed	Hardware installed	11 Nov
11 Nov				H5	When the data for personnel information has been entered or migrated	Data entered and migrated	11 Nov
12 Nov	P6				When the site goes live	Site goes live	12 Nov
14 Nov		M6			When the success of Phase 1 has been reviewed, a report produced and Phase 2 can begin	Ready to proceed to Phase 2	14 Nov

Figure 7.1 *Milestone plan for implementing the intranet at TriMagi*

of the project can change our view of the best way of achieving the next stage. Thus if we plan in terms of the work to be done, the plan can be constantly changing, whereas if we plan in terms of the results, the milestones, the definition of the plan can be much more stable. Further we can find the best way of delivering a given milestone when the work on it is about to begin. This is called rolling-wave planning, which I expand on below.

Another advantage of planning in terms of the deliverable of each work package is work can be more easily overlapped. People using the alternative method of networking, *activity-on-arrow*, often artificially extend projects as they draw logic to show one package of work not starting until the previous one has finished. This is not always necessary; it may be possible to overlap consecutive work packages. Development cannot begin until some design has been done, and cannot end until all design has finished, but we don't have to wait until all design has been done before starting development. However, people drawing arrow networks often show delivery not starting until design is finished. The milestone plan will show completion of delivery dependent on completion of design, but will say nothing about their relative start dates. (Networking is not covered in this book. You can read about it further in Turner [1999] or Turner and Simister [2000].)

It is also iconoclastic to draw the plan down the page; project networks are normally drawn across the page. However, project management is almost unique among management sciences drawing its flow charts across the page. Others draw them down the page. And there are many advantages in doing so:

- You draw the network in one column and write the definition of each node at the side, writing large and clear. If you draw the network across the page, you write the definition of each node in the box, small and difficult to read.
- On a modern computer screen, it is easier to scroll down than across. This is especially the case if your plan is loaded on the web.
- There is consistency with other areas of management science.

Figure 7.1 shows the milestones grouped into columns. These are result paths or areas of work, each delivering a sub-objective of the project. The project in Figure 7.1 has three main project outputs, and there is a result path, or area of work, delivering each output. By drawing the plan in this way you can make sure all the areas of the project are properly addressed, and especially that you haven't forgotten about the PSO work as described in Chapter 3. Experience shows that most web projects that fail do so because the change is not properly managed; this is how you ensure it is all included. You can interrogate the plan to ensure that there is an even balance of milestones in all areas.

A GOOD MILESTONE PLAN

There are several principles that constitute a good milestone plan. It:

- is understandable to everyone
- is controllable, both quantitatively and qualitatively
- focuses on necessary decisions
- is logical, with decisions and work packages in the right order
- gives an overview at the right level.

Understandable: The milestone plan is a tool to build cooperation between the diverse resources working on the delivery of your web space, and commitment to a common vision. It must therefore be understood by all those involved. This requires the milestone descriptions to be written in English, not in technical jargon only understandable to the IS department. Writing milestone names in technical jargon is great for drawing demarcations, and making the technical work the domain of the techies. But it is also great for isolating other people you want to be involved in the project.

Controllable: The plan is a tool for control, and so descriptions must be precise, so you can measure when they have been achieved. Some milestones can have a quantitative measure, such as: 'When one million people have accessed the new web site.' Others must be given a qualitative description, with a measure of quality written in. The milestone 'when the design is finished' is both unmeasurable and unachievable. The milestone 'when the team accepts the design as a basis for starting development' can be measured and achieved. It is measured by taking a decision, and achieved when that decision is taken. The responsibility chart, which we meet in the next chapter, shows who takes the decision.

Decisions: Milestones represent positions en route to the final objective. Often the interesting position is not the production of a design or report. That is not the purpose of the work. It is the taking of a decision, based on the design or report, to allow work to proceed. That is the required deliverable, and provides qualitative control. At the discovery or design stages the milestone plan can be a series of decisions. Most of the milestones in the M column of Figure 7.1 are decision points.

Logical: The milestone plan is a logical plan. It contains a network, which shows the strategy for building through the intermediate products to achieve the final objective.

Single-page overview: The objective is to produce a single-page plan which clearly communicates the project strategy. This is only achieved if the number of milestones and areas of work is limited. I find the ideal number of milestones is somewhere between one and two dozen. With fewer the plan does not give a useful structure, and with more it becomes confusing. Similarly, I recommend three or four areas of work. This is the same for all projects regardless of size. For a small project of about six weeks long, there will be 12 milestones, say, each representing about 5 to 10 days work, and that will be the only level of planning. For a project of 18 months duration, there may be up to 24, each representing a couple of months work. Each milestone will then be broken down into a lower level activity plan, on a rolling wave basis. On a very large project, you might have a plan for each of the discovery stage, design, delivery and deployment. On a very large project, you may also break the plan into several sub-projects running in parallel, with milestones common to several plans to provide links between them.

DEVELOPING THE MILESTONE PLAN

Ideally, the milestone plan should be developed in a start-up workshop, with selected key managers and project personnel present. Developing the plan in a group session builds greater commitment than if the project manager develops it on his or her own and tries to impose it on the team. However, to be effective the workshop should not have more than about twelve people present. The process I recommend for developing the plan has six steps:

1. Start by agreeing the final milestone, the end of the project. This is Question 1 of Francis Hartman's three questions suggested in the last chapter and results from the project definition.
2. Generate ideas for milestones. Brainstorm them on to flip charts. If you have a good session you should generate dozens of ideas. Remember the rules of brainstorming. During this part of the process you should not comment on ideas; *every* idea gets written on the flip chart. If you tell somebody their idea is stupid they will shut up for the rest of the session, and somebody's stupid idea can stimulate a good idea in someone else.
3. Review the milestones and rationalize the list down to one to two dozen. Some will be part of another milestone. Some will be activities, but will generate ideas for new milestones. As you rationalize the list record your decisions, especially where you have decided that one idea is an activity and part of a larger milestone. That needs to be recorded and remembered.

4 Experiment with result paths. Draw them on a flip chart or white board. Write the milestones on Post-It notes and stick them on the paths, in the order they occur down the path. Experiment with different paths, and review them as suggested above. Note this may change the definition of the areas of work.
5 Draw the logical dependencies, starting with the final objective and working back. This may cause you to review the definition of milestones, add new milestones, merge milestones, or change the definition of the result paths.
6 Make a final drawing of the plan.

TriMagi
Project Definition Report

Programme:	Web developments
Project:	Intranet Phase 1
Project Manager:	Frances Seeker

Work areas	**Milestones**
M:	M0: Ready to start
	M1: Overall content and style agreed
	M2: Content of home and news pages agreed
	M3: Content of document processing pages agreed
	M4: Content of personnel pages agreed
	M5: Ready to design
	M6: Ready to proceed to Phase 2
D:	D1: Home and news pages developed
	D2: Document processing pages developed
	D3: Personnel pages developed
	D4: Site assembled
	D5: Site signed off
P:	P1: Procedures written
	P2: New jobs designed
	P3: Procedures piloted
	P4: Procedures optimized
	P5: Ready to deploy
	P6: Site goes live
H:	H1: Hardware and software audit
	H2: Hardware requirements defined
	H3: Hardware designed
	H4: Hardware installed
	H5: Data entered and migrated

Author:	JRT	**Date:**	21 July 2003	**Issue:**	A

Figure 7.2 *Milestones for the intranet at TriMagi*

Figure 7.1 is the milestone plan for the intranet at TriMagi. You might notice that the plan contains the five stage gates in Figures 2.4 and 2.5. Figure 7.2 is the list of milestones. This page can be a contents page for the milestone scope statements which follow.

The project manager should not come to the meeting with the plan ready prepared, and use the meeting to bully the team into accepting it. The team may mouth acceptance, but will have no commitment to the plan. And the team may have some excellent ideas the project manager didn't think about. Hence the workshop must be a group working session where everybody is allowed to be creative and contribute, where they can have a part in developing a plan they can commit to. That is not to say the project manager won't have developed their own plan the

Euro Projex

Milestone Scope Statement

Project:	Intranet Phase 1
Project Champion:	Martin Pacific
Project Manager:	Frances Seeker
Work area:	Design and development
Work area Manager:	Ian Simons
Milestone:	Personnel information pages designed
Milestone Manager:	Ian Simons
Milestone number and name	D3: When the personnel information pages have been designed and developed
Measure of achievement	The personnel manager has approved the pages for content, layout and ease of access The marketing manager has approved the pages as conforming to the desired corporate image Selected users have approved the pages for ease of access and use
Draft activity list	Specify page based on agreed contents Appoint external consultants Manage external consultants Design and develop page Obtain approval from personnel Obtain approval from marketing Obtain approval from selected users Make changes as necessary

Author:	IS	**Date:**	02 Sept 2003	**Issue:**	A

Figure 7.3 *Milestones scope statement for Milestone D3 of the intranet at TriMagi*

night before, and use the steps to slip their own ideas in. They can make sure that all their milestones end up on the flip chart at step 2. But work by trying to influence the team, not telling them the answer.

After the milestone plan has been developed, it can be useful to write a brief note of what is meant by each milestone, in a *Milestone scope statement*. Figure 7.3 is an example of such a statement for milestone D3 from Figure 7.1. The Milestone scope statement fulfils several purposes:

- During milestone planning, as you reduce the list of potential milestones, you may decide one of the ideas is an activity of another milestone. That decision needs to be recorded. The draft activity list achieves that.
- You need to set a quality measure for achievement of the milestone, to provide a qualitative measure for quality control (see above and Chapter 10). The measure of achievement does that.
- The draft list of activities helps with rolling-wave planning and high level estimating. If people have thought about what the milestone entails, they may be more comfortable that they understand the milestone, and can estimate how long it will take and how much it will cost, and that they have not forgotten about any long lead items that need ordering now.
- It helps with risk analysis. If while identifying the draft list of activities, you recognize a significant risk associated with this milestone, you may do detailed planning at an early stage. If the milestone is something that you have done often, and are comfortable with, you can leave detailed planning until late. Where it is completely novel, it is useful to do early detailed planning. The draft activity list helps identify where effort is usefully applied.

ACTIVITY PLANNING

On anything but the smallest of projects, each milestone will be broken down into a lower level plan, a list of activities saying how the milestone is to be delivered. In this section I describe how to do activity planning, but first I consider how different projects can have different levels of breakdown depending on their size and describe the concept of rolling-wave planning and baselining the plan.

LEVELS OF BREAKDOWN

I say anything but the smallest projects. The plan for a project of about two to three months duration may have 12 to 15 milestones, each milestone representing about two weeks work (with the milestones clearly overlapping). The person or team responsible for each milestone may have an understanding of how they will achieve it, but no formal project planning is necessary below the milestone plan. (It is almost quicker to do the work than to plan it.)

A project that is six to nine months long may have a plan of about 18 to 24 milestones, where most milestones represent about two months work. Now it is necessary to break each of those milestones down into a list of activities, where each activity will be of one to two weeks duration. The person or team responsible for each activity may have an understanding of how they will achieve each activity, but no formal project planning is necessary below the activity level. Even so, there may be one or two milestones that only represent about two weeks work. Those milestones don't need to be broken down. There is no need to take the whole project down to the same level of breakdown.

I think that a project of more than 18 months duration should be treated as a programme (see Chapter 16 and Murray-Webster and Thiry, 2000) and divided into several sub-projects. The sub-projects may represent consecutive stages, or work on different elements of the web space running in parallel. You can have a summary milestone plan for the whole programme, supported by operational plans for each sub-project. The sub-project plans will be treated as above.

ROLLING-WAVE PLANNING

I have mentioned rolling-wave planning several times. Under this concept only the next few milestones are planned in detail. Later ones are left until they are about to start, when earlier ones will have finished, giving a rolling wave of planned milestones. In Chapter 1, I used the metaphor of taking a trip to St Tropez in the south of France. The towns we travel through are the milestones; the route map between towns is the activity plan. Rolling-wave planning means we leave planning the route from Aix-en-Provence to St Tropez until we almost reach Aix-en-Provence. Most of us are happy with that. We look at the map, see it is 80 kms say, estimate we will average 80 kph and use 1 litre of petrol per 10 km, and say it will take 1 hour and 8 litres of petrol. We need to be comfortable with that level of planning and estimating, because anything more detailed is a fairy story. Further, the cost of making the detailed plan is far greater than any benefit it gives us.

Making the journey, we know other people have made the same journey before, and we have made other journeys, so we are confident with the estimates. On our projects there are some things we (or others) have done before, so we can be confident with high level estimates. For others, they will be totally novel, and that is why I said above that in areas of high risk or uncertainty it can be worthwhile doing lower level planning early. Our project may be unique and novel, but some of the components may be very familiar and routine. They are just put together in novel ways. These we can plan on a rolling-wave basis, and put our planning effort into those things which are totally new.

BASELINING THE PLAN

At some point, when you are about to start work on the project, it is important to baseline the plan. If you are adopting rolling-wave planning this will be before many of the detailed activity plans have been developed. But it may be after some of them have been done, either early ones, or ones in areas of high risk or uncertainty. The idea behind baselining the plan is you take a snapshot of the plan. You record the work definition, schedule and cost estimate, and freeze it. That becomes the *baseline* against which you judge all future progress. As the project progresses, you may need to adjust the schedule to reflect past delays or changes in scope, or past overspends. But you always track progress against the baseline. If you track progress against the current (updated schedule) you soon lose control. You always appear to be on time and budget, because you have just updated the time and cost plan to reflect actual progress. You might say that you will remember the changes, but people don't. You need to track progress against the baseline to compare progress against the original plan, and keep control. In Chapter 12 I will show how the use of tracked bar charts and milestone tracker diagrams enables you to do this for controlling the schedule, and in Chapter 11 how the use of earned value analysis helps you do this for tracking cost. Microsoft Project™ has a menu item to baseline the plan. When you choose it, the bar chart is converted into a tracked bar chart with bars representing the baseline plan and bars representing the current schedule.

ACTIVITY PLANNING

So now, at long last, we are ready to start the detailed activity planning for each milestone. I suggest a five step process:

1. *Define activities required to reach a milestone:* When selecting activities, the team should choose ones which are controllable; that is they should:
   - *Produce a measurable result:* It must be possible to determine when an activity is finished. It is no good dividing a work-package into five activities each equal to 20 per cent of the work. In those circumstances the last one often takes 80 per cent of the effort!
   - *Have average duration roughly equal to the frequency of review:* However often you meet to review progress should be the rough duration of the activities. I assumed in the discussion above on whether to develop lower level activity plans that you would review progress about once every two weeks. If you meet daily, then a milestone of two weeks duration should be formally broken down into lower level activities.
2. *Ratify the people involved:* The people to do the work were identified in the milestone plan. However, once the activities have been defined it may be necessary to review the team to ensure it contains all the necessary skills.
3. *Define roles and responsibilities:* The involvement of each team member in the activities is then identified. A *responsibility chart* (Chapter 8) can be a useful tool for this.
4. *Estimate work-content and durations:* The work-content and durations are estimated applying the processes used at the work-package level.
5. *Schedule the activities within the work-package:* Finally the activities are scheduled within the work-package to deliver the milestone on time.

Figure 7.4 shows the activity plan for milestone D3 from Figure 7.1.

Who should develop the activity plans? My preference is for the team responsible for delivering this milestone. They must have ownership of and commitment to the milestone, and the activities for delivering it. They will not have that if the plan is imposed on them, especially if by a project manager from another discipline. The team should develop their own plan.

What happens if the schedule as proposed by the team is longer than that estimated at the milestone level? If the schedule they develop at step five fits within the base line at the higher level, that will be fine. If it exceeds the schedule at the higher level by up to 20 per cent, then that should be accommodated. It is within the accuracy of the higher level plan (believe me it is, and to think otherwise is a fairy story – if the project duration is accurate to about ± 5 per cent, the milestone durations will be accurate to about ± 20 per cent, see Chapter 13.) So an extension of up to 20 per cent needs to be accommodated. Perhaps the team can be asked to massage their estimates down a bit. Perhaps their work needs to be run more in parallel with other work. But the extension needs to be absorbed. If the team's schedule is more than 20 per cent longer than the plan at the higher level, the problem needs to be solved. Either they have to be asked to find another way of achieving the milestone, or the higher level plan needs to be delayed.

TriMagi **ACTIVITY PLAN** | **ACTIVITY SCHEDULE**

Project:	Intranet Phase 1
Milestone:	D3: Personnel information pages designed
Manager:	Ian Simons

Period: Day | **Target end:** 25-Sep-03

X	eXecutes the work
D	takes **D**ecisions solely/ultimately
d	takes **d**ecisions jointly
P	manages **P**rogress
T	on the job **T**raining
I	must be **I**nformed
C	must be **C**onsulted
A	may **A**dvise

No	Activity name	Ian Simons	Jan Deptford	Procurement	Contractors	Personnel	Marketing	Selected users	1 (03-Sep)	2 (10-Sep)	3 (11-Sep)	4 (12-Sep)	5 (15-Sep)	6 (16-Sep)	7 (17-Sep)	8 (18-Sep)	9 (19-Sep)	10 (22-Sep)	11 (23-Sep)	12 (24-Sep)	13 (25-Sep)	14	15	d (Duration)	End date
D31	Specify page based on agreed contents	P	X																					7	11-Sep-03
D32	Appoint contractors	Xd		Xd																				2	11-Sep-03
D33	Manage contractors	P																						10	25-Sep-03
D34	Design and develop pages	P			X																			7	22-Sep-03
D35	Obtain approval – personnel	PX	X		X	C																		5	23-Sep-03
D36	Obtain approval – marketing	PX	X		X		C																	2	24-Sep-03
D37	Obtain approval – selected users	PX	X		X			C																2	24-Sep-03
D38	Make necessary changes	PD	X		X	d	d	d																3	25-Sep-03

Figure 7.4 *Activity plan for Milestone D3 from the intranet at TriMagi*

CHAPTER 8 Organizing the Project

Having defined the milestones, we need to identify who will take responsibility for their delivery. Web projects involve a diverse range of people from across the organization. We need to define the skills required, where in the organization people will come from, and what their roles will be. Once people are working on the project team, we need to gain the commitment of those people to their role in the project. Thus we need to organize the project at two levels:

1. *At the interface between the project and the organization* we need to decide the relationship between the project and the parent organization:
   - how the project will be integrated into the parent organization
   - how the parent organization will assign resources to the project
   - which departments or functions will take responsibility for which milestones.
2. *At the project team level* we need to decide the relationship between the people working together on the project:
   - how they will integrate their work
   - who will take responsibility for the activities delivering each milestone
   - what will be the leadership style of the project manager.

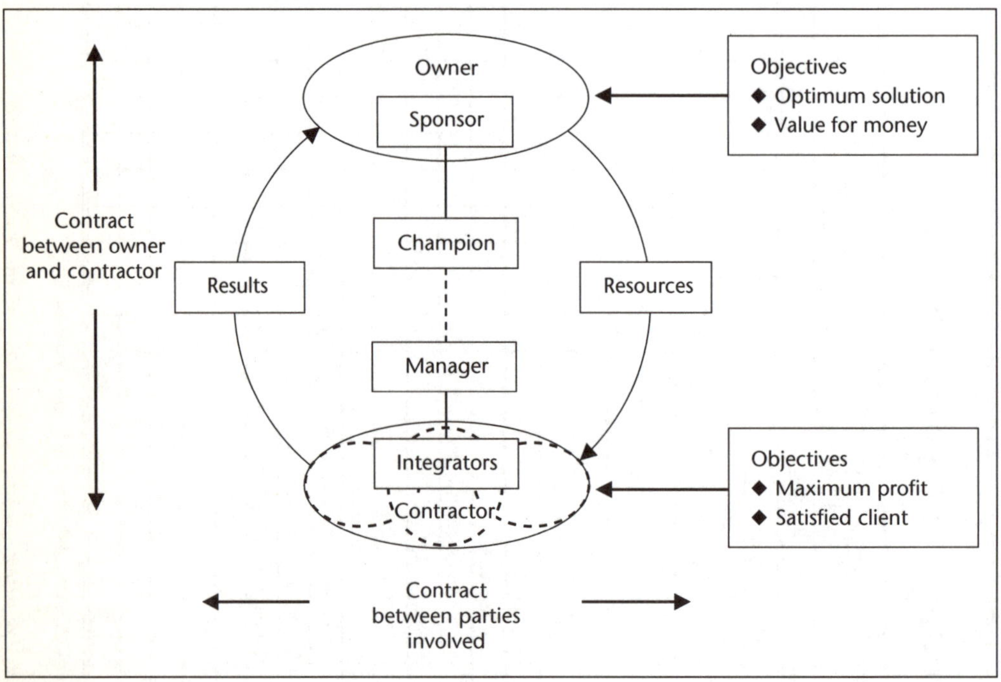

Figure 8.1 *The owner–contractor model (revisited)*

These two levels are illustrated by the owner–contractor model, Figure 8.1 (a modified version of Figure 5.1). It shows the relationship between project and parent organizations as a contract between them: the project promises to deliver a web space, and in return the organization promises to provide resources for it to be able to do that. It shows the relationship between team members as a contract between them, where they agree who is to do what to achieve the results for which they have taken responsibility. This emphasis on planning as a process of forming a contract is key. Like all contracts it needs to be agreed through discussion. It cannot be agreed by the project manager doing the planning, deciding responsibilities, and imposing it on the team. It can only be agreed by the team working together to reach a mutually agreed solution, and is best done through a project start-up workshop. The project start-up workshop determines the contract between project and parent organization. Individual work-package or milestone launch workshops, lasting half a day determine the contract at the team level.

In this chapter, I describe the project organization at the two levels. I then suggest the responsibility chart as a tool to define the structure of the project organization and the roles and responsibilities of the people involved at both levels.

ORGANIZING AT THE PROJECT LEVEL

Figure 8.2 illustrates four options for the relationship between project and parent organization. In choosing an approach, remember the words of the Nobel Laureate in Economics, Harold Coase (1964): '... the choices are between feasible alternatives, all of which are flawed'.

There is no perfect solution to the problem of project organization. It is a matter of choosing one that best meets your needs. But only consider sensible options.

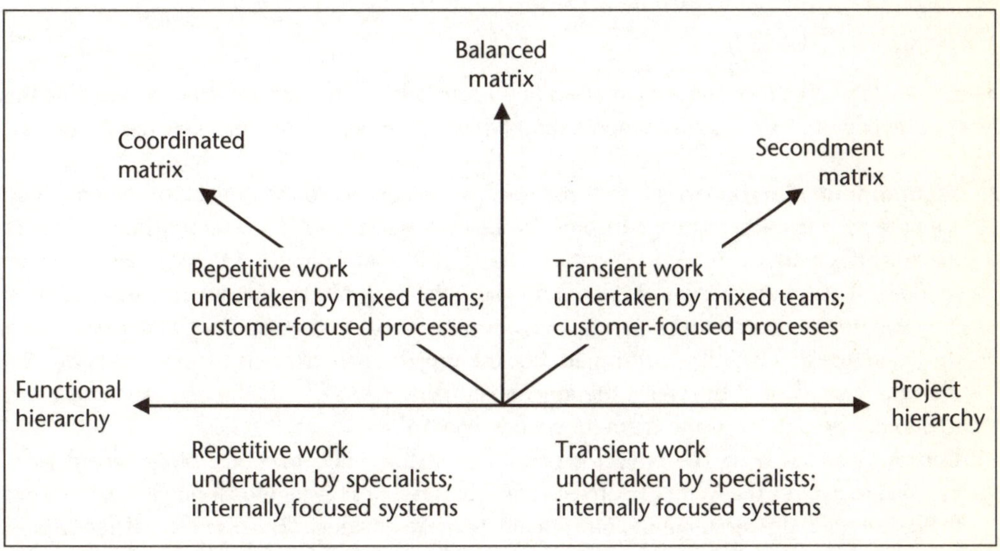

Figure 8.2 *Range of project organization structures*

HIERARCHICAL STRUCTURES

Under the first two extreme options the project is either done in the functional or project hierarchy.

1 **Functional hierarchy:** The project is embedded in the functional organization. This is only appropriate for small web remodelling or maintenance projects, which can be wholly embedded in one function. People from one function work together in a novel way to achieve a novel objective. Web construction projects seldom use people from just one function. It is possible to use the approach for slightly larger projects that need the input of a small number of people from other functions. Their work needs to be agreed by discussion between the functional managers, and it needs to be agreed how much authority the project manager has to determine when the individual will work on the project in preference to their normal functional duties. Of course the problem you meet is that the other person's functional duties always seem to take priority over the project, and the project is never completed for the sake of some small element of work from elsewhere.
2 **Project hierarchy:** Projects are removed from the functional structure. A project department does the organization's web-delivery work, with all the resources it needs, and no input from anybody else – unlikely on web-delivery projects, though this may be the case for the core project team. The problem with this approach is that the project team becomes isolated from the rest of the organization. Given the wide range of stakeholders and user requirements on web projects this is usually not a good idea. Where it can be a good idea is where the adoption of web technology is a totally new idea for the organization which needs to be prototyped. Then it can be useful to set up a totally separate team, free from influence by entrenched positions, which can experiment with new ideas. When it comes to retrofit the new ideas back to the organization, a matrix approach should be adopted.

MATRIX STRUCTURES

Matrix structures are proposed as alternatives to the functional or project hierarchy to overcome the weaknesses of both. Some authors propose three types, but my view is that there are really only two.

1 **Secondment matrix:** Project team members are seconded to the project for the time they are needed, and perhaps only part-time. While they are seconded to the project, the project manager has authority for assigning their time to work. For example, if they are seconded for Monday, Tuesday and Wednesday, on those days, the project manager determines what work they will do. The functional manager remains responsible for the quality of their work, and the standards to which it is performed, but the project manager tells them what to do. On the other two days of the week, the functional manager assigns their work, assigning them to another project, or giving them functional work to do.
2 **Coordinated matrix:** The project is performed in the functions, but a project manager is assigned to oversee the work. The project manager is responsible for monitoring and controlling the delivery of the project, but has no authority to make it happen. The essential difference from the secondment matrix is the team remain under the jurisdiction of their functional manager, who assigns their work day by day, determining what project they will work on, and what work they will do. The project manager must tell the functional manger what needs to be done by when, but the functional manager decides what work will be done on a given day, taking

account of the priority of all the projects and other functional work. A project manager has to have a good working relationship with all functional managers, and must be able to demonstrate priority for their project. This works well where a function has a short input to a project, and the project manager can make the functional manager aware of the need sometime in advance, so he or she can plan for the work to be done. It fails where there are several projects of high priority, requiring extensive inputs from several functions, because then it is left to the functional managers, who do not have a project focus, to determine priority, rather than the project managers working together through the project or programme office.

3 **Balanced matrix:** Some people propose a third type of matrix. The project and functional manager share responsibility and authority for assigning work to individuals, through mutual consent. I think that the balanced matrix is unstable, and will become either a secondment or coordinated matrix depending on the relative strength of the two managers.

CHOOSING AN APPROPRIATE ORGANIZATION

In choosing a project structure, the following issues need to be considered:

- the size of project
- the duration of the project
- the nature of the task
- the type of project according to the goals and methods matrix
- the importance of time, cost and quality
- the competence and availability of personnel.

In reality, most projects use several structures for different areas of the work. For instance, on my standard courses I use a case study of a bank installing an internal network. The project would use all four types of structure for different elements of work.

- project hierarchy for the computer hardware and software
- secondment matrix for writing systems, procedures and job descriptions
- coordinated matrix for marketing, training and redeployment
- functional hierarchy for entering new jobs into the payroll system.

For the intranet at TriMagi, a medium-sized construction project, a coordinated matrix was used.

THE PROJECT MANAGER'S AUTHORITY

Under the matrix structures above, the project manager always has people working on his or her team who do not report directly to them normally. This can raise two related issues:

Sources of authority: What sources of authority can the project manager draw on to encourage people to work on the project the way he or she wishes? There are four possible sources of authority:

- *Position:* The project manager can instruct people they have direct line authority over, including those seconded on to the project team. The project manager can draw on the position authority of the project champion. But beware, that can only be used sparingly, or the project manager loses credibility. It is best to get the champion on side from the start.

- *Control of resources:* The control of money, resources or information gives the project manager authority. But lack of this is often the problem.
- *Credibility:* It is the project manager's job to manage the project. If their plans are credible, and people believe in their management ability, they are more likely to follow.
- *Charisma:* This is the most powerful source of authority if well used.

Managing more senior people: On a web delivery project, with diverse skills, the project manager often has people working on the team who are more senior in strictly organizational terms, and who are more expert in their functional discipline. How does the project manager deal with them? The project manager must be clear in their mind about their role. It is not the project manager's role to instruct technical experts as to how to do their job. To do that is the fast road to lost credibility. It is the reality of web-delivery projects that they will involve a range of skills and disciplines, and so the project manager cannot be expert in all. Indeed, the project manager has been chosen as he or she is expert in managing. The way to manage more senior people is:

- *Lead the development of the plan:* Make sure the plan is the team's idea by developing the plan in a start-up workshop, and following the recommendations in this session and the last for developing the milestone plan and responsibility chart. Do not impose the plan on the experts; lead its development involving the experts in the process.
- *Facilitate the experts in doing their jobs:* It is the job of the experts to perform the work they are good at. Make sure they have all the resources they need on time. On the stage, it is an actor's role to perform their part, not run around looking for props just before they are about to go on. Similarly, the experts should just have to perform their part; it is the project manager's role to find all they need.
- *Coordinate interfaces between the team:* Similarly, the project manager should coordinate the interface between the team members. It is the project manager's role to manage, delegate and motivate, and the expert's role to do the work of the project.

ORGANIZING AT THE TEAM LEVEL

The second decision is about the nature of the team, and the management style adopted. David Frame (1995) suggests four team types, shown in Figure 8.3. The different team types fit best at different stages of the project, with different management styles.

TEAM TYPES

Egoless team: The egoless team, Figure 8.4(a), goes with the laissez-faire style of management. The assumption is the team is a team of equals, and the project manager is *primus inter pares*, first among equals. His or her role is to guide the team of equals, not command them. The team

Stage	*Team type*	*Management style*
Discovery/research	Egoless task force	Laissez-faire
Design	Speciality	Democratic
Delivery	Task hierarchy	Autocratic
Deployment	Surgical task force	Bureaucratic

Figure 8.3 *Team types and management styles through the project life cycle*

members are all experts in their own field, involved in undertaking the task. So, the team must be allowed to go about their task, in which they are the expert, with the manager providing leadership and direction. This type is appropriate on research or development projects, or the discovery stage of a very large project. It was the style used by TriMagi for their intranet, which was a medium-sized development project.

Specialist or Matrix team: In the specialist team, Figure 8.4(b), several professionals work on the project, with several tasks to perform. Each specialist contributes to several tasks. This is sometimes called a matrix approach, because the relationship between the team members and the task is a matrix. It does not imply that matrix management is used. One manager may still be responsible for the whole group. This is used in the design stage of larger projects, or on smaller projects involving knowledge or other professional workers. Democratic management is also usually appropriate in these cases. The manager needs to respect the opinions of the professional team members, but also to provide firm direction to coordinate their inputs.

Task team: In the task team structure, Figure 8.4(c), a multidisciplinary team works on each task. This is the ultimate form of the project hierarchy, because the shape of the team is a hierarchy matching the shape of the task. This is sometimes called an isomorphic structure. It is typically used on large projects in the delivery phase, and autocratic management is used. The design is finished and so there are no decisions to be made. Money is being spent and the project needs to be finished as quickly as possible.

Surgical team: The surgical team, Figure 8.4(d), is another task force, but one in which the manager leads from the front. This is appropriate where there is a focused task to be

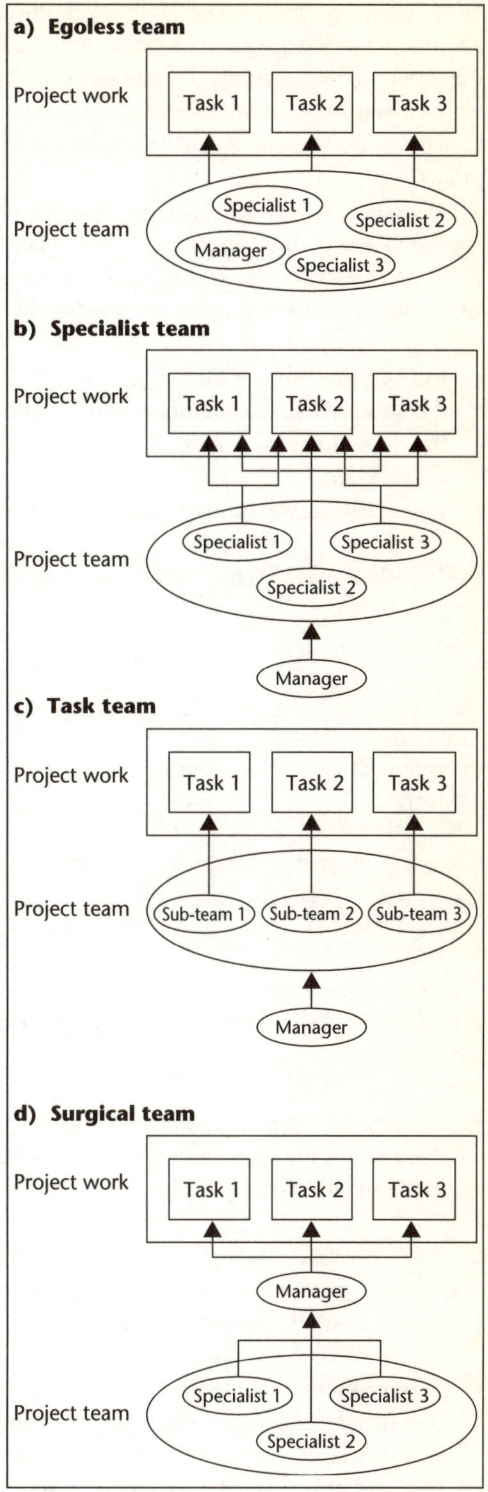

Figure 8.4 *Project team types*

done requiring coordinated input of several specialists. Also there may be some uncertainty about what precisely has to be done, so the team needs to take instruction from the manager as the task proceeds. It is called a surgical team from the medical analogy. It is appropriate on small projects with high uncertainty, or in the deployment stage of large projects. In the latter case, bureaucratic management is appropriate to ensure all testing, commissioning and handover procedures are followed.

All four team types might be used on web-delivery projects. As I have said, the egoless approach was used on the intranet at TriMagi, because it was a smaller, development project. If there had been greater uncertainty, a surgical team might have been more appropriate. On larger web construction projects, what might be appropriate would be to use:

- the egoless structure during discovery
- the speciality structure during design, where coordination between the experts is required
- the task structure during development, where the different teams of experts can work independently
- the surgical team during deployment when it all needs to be pulled together.

MANAGEMENT STYLES

Style	*Flexibility*	*Team involvement in decision-making*	*Team involvement in decision-taking*
Laissez-faire	High	High	High
Democratic	High	High	Low
Autocratic	High	Low	Low
Bureaucratic	Low	Low	Low

Figure 8.5 *Management styles*

Different management styles can also be appropriate on different projects or different stages of a project. Figure 8.5 shows how the four styles in Figure 8.3 are distinguished by three parameters:

- the amount the manager involves the team in the decision-making
- the amount the manager involves the team in the decision-taking
- the flexibility of the manager.

Decision-making is the first five steps of Figure 1.4 where the problem is analysed and possible solutions suggested and evaluated. Decision-taking is the sixth step, where one of the options is chosen for possible implementation.

- **Laissez-faire:** The manager lets the team to decide the best way of doing the task, and leads by example, guiding rather than commanding. This style is appropriate during discovery or concept design, or where the project manager is not the most senior member of the team. This was the style of management adopted by the manager of the intranet delivery at TriMagi. She was the personnel manager, and had experts from many functions on the team.

- **Democratic:** The team are professional experts in their field, and so they are allowed to formulate the content of their work. However, the manager needs to coordinate the overall solution, and so listens to what all the experts have to say, but takes the final decision based on their inputs. The manager takes account of the experts' opinions, but has the final say. This is often the case on web-delivery projects where the team members are highly knowledgeable professionals, but the interfaces between them need to be managed and coordinated. This was the style used by the manager of the el-MBA at Henley Management College. He was the course director of the dl-MBA programme, and needed to have the final say about the nature of the new programme, but needed to listen to experts from many functions, including marketing, administration and course design as well as the IS department.
- **Autocratic:** Time for discussion is over. The project is being implemented, the solution has been chosen, and the team members need to do what they are told. Changes are costly to implement (see Figure 10.7). Real money is being spent; the owner wants the project completed as quickly as possible. The manager tells the team to implement the plan as agreed. However, there may still be some uncertainty, so the manager needs to retain flexibility to deal with that uncertainty. This is appropriate at the delivery stage of large web construction projects.
- **Bureaucratic:** Nobody, not even the project manager, is asked their opinion about what needs to be done. There is a list of tasks to be done, and they must be done without question. This is appropriate at the deployment stage of a large web-delivery project, where there are test procedures to be followed, commissioning sequences to be followed, and handover sequences to be followed. Any checklists of outstanding work also need to be completed.

THE RESPONSIBILITY CHART

Having identified how the project is to be organized at the project and team levels, we need to identify the roles and responsibilities of the people involved in the project. This will be the roles of the functions and departments at the milestone level, to set the contract between the project and the organization, and the roles of the project team members to set the contract of how they are to work together. The responsibility chart is a powerful tool which enables this to be done.

Figure 8.6 illustrates the responsibility chart. At a given level of breakdown, the rows represent the work elements or their deliverables, the columns represent the organizational units, skill types or resources to be used, while the body of the matrix represents the work each resource will do to deliver each work element or deliverable. The

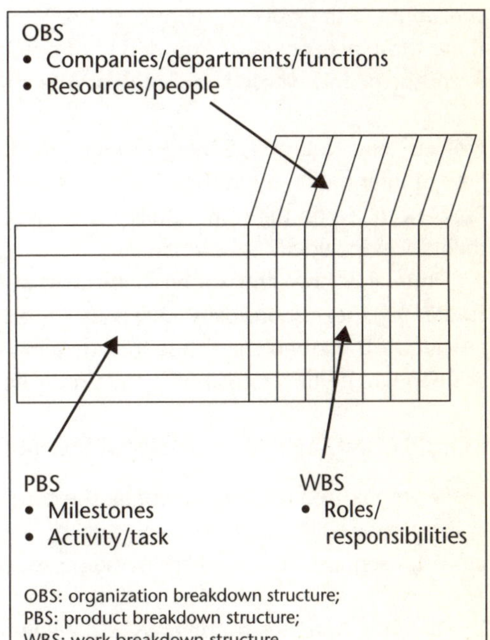

Figure 8.6 *The responsibility chart*

heading of the row names the resource, and then the cells represent the work they are to do, or their roles and responsibilities, for each work element. Symbols are used to represent the roles and responsibilities. Various authors have suggested various symbols (see Cleland and King, 1988). However, I have found that the symbols recommended by Andersen *et al.* (1995), shown in Figure 8.7, meet most needs. The symbols are used as follows:

Letter	*Responsibility*
X	e**X**ecutes the work
D	takes **D**ecision solely or ultimately
d	takes **d**ecision jointly or partly
P	controls **P**rogress
T	provides **T**uition on the job
I	must be **I**nformed
C	must be **C**onsulted
A	available to **A**dvise

Figure 8.7 *Symbols representing roles and responsibilities*

Work roles: The first role defines who is to do the work.
X is the people doing the work.

Management roles: The next four are management roles.
D are the people who ultimately take decisions, or rubber stamp them.
d are the people who close options and advise the ultimate decision-takers
P are the people the project manager delegates responsibility to for managing milestones to, and the people the milestone managers delegate responsibility to for managing activities
T are consultants or trainers hired to guide the project team

Communication roles: The last three roles are for limiting the amount of communication
I are people who must be informed about the outcome of one stage of the project so they contribute to the work of the next stage.
C are those people whose knowledge or opinions must be sought
A are the people whose knowledge or opinions may be sought

Projects tend to be killed by too much information, rather than too little. The idea is limit the flow of information by making it clear who is to receive what, but not to be cloak and dagger. People can see on the responsibility chart who is to be consulted and who informed, and have themselves included.

Figure 8.8 shows the responsibility chart at the milestone level for the intranet at TriMagi, and Figure 8.9 the responsibility charts at the activity level for milestone D3 (and is Figure 7.4 repeated). These two charts also include a bar chart showing when the milestones and activities will happen. I return to planning the timescale in Chapter 12.

COMPLETING THE RESPONSIBILITY CHART

I have emphasized the need to obtain the commitment of the team to the plans, and it is in filling in the responsibility chart that you get the team to take ownership of their contribution to the project. I suggest the following five-step process for completing the chart.

1 Fill in the headings of the rows and columns of a blank chart
2 Project the chart on to a white board
3 Fill in the body of each row

TriMagi PROJECT RESPONSIBILITY CHART

PROJECT SCHEDULE

Project:	Intranet Phase 1
Project Champion:	Martin Pacific
Project Manager:	Frances Seeker

Period: Week ending **Target end:** 30-Jun-02

X	eXecutes the work
D	takes **D**ecisions solely/ultimately
d	takes **d**ecisions jointly
P	manages **P**rogress
T	on the job **T**raining
I	must be **I**nformed
C	must be **C**onsulted
A	may **A**dvise

No	Milestone Name	Manging Director	Board	Personnel Manager	Personnel Department	Marketing Manager	Marketing Department	IS Manager	IS Department	Users	Contractors	Project Manager	Project team	Consultant	Procurement	d (Duration)	End date
M0	Ready to start	D	d	I		I		I				d					18 Aug
M1	Overall content and style agreed		D	d	C	d	C	d	C	C		X	X	T		7	26 Aug
H1	Hardware and data inventory							P	X							9	28 Aug
M2	Home and news pages agreed			D	C	d	C	d	X				X	T		5	02 Sep
M3	Document processing pages agreed			D	C			d	X				X	T		5	02 Sep
M4	Personnel information pages agreed			D	C			d	X				X	T		5	02 Sep
P1	Procedures rewritten			P	X											6	03 Sep
M5	Ready to design		D	d		d		d				d				5	09 Sep
H2	Hardware defined							P	X							12	15 Sep
P2	New jobs designed			P	X											8	15 Sep
H3	Hardware designed							PD	X						Xd	5	22 Sep
D1	Home and news pages developed			d	C	d	C	Pd	X	C	X			A	Xd	12	25 Sep
D2	Document processing pages developed			d	C	d	C	Pd	X	C	X			A	Xd	12	25 Sep
D3	Personnel information pages developed			d	C	d	C	Pd	X	C	X			A	Xd	12	25 Sep
P3	New procedures piloted			I	C					C			X			10	29 Sep
D4	Site assembled							PD	X		X		X			8	07 Oct
P4	Procedures optimized			P	X											5	14 Oct
D5	Site signed off		I	I		I		D	X			d	X			3	17 Oct
P5	Ready to deploy		D	d	X	d		d	X			d	X			3	17 Oct
H4	Hardware installed							Pd			X					17	11 Nov
H5	Data entered and migrated			C	C			Pd			X					17	11 Nov
P6	Site goes live		I	I		I		D	X			d	X			1	12 Nov
M6	Ready to proceed to Phase 2		D	d	X	d		d	X			d	X			2	14 Nov

Schedule weeks: 1 22-Aug, 2 29-Aug, 3 05-Sep, 4 12-Sep, 5 19-Sep, 6 26-Sep, 7 03-Oct, 8 10-Oct, 9 17-Oct, 10 24-Oct, 11 31-Oct, 12 07-Nov, 13 14-Nov, 14 21-Nov, 15 28-Nov

Figure 8.8 *Responsibility chart at the project level for the intranet at TriMagi*

TriMagi ACTIVITY PLAN

Project:	Intranet Phase 1
Milestone:	D3: Personnel information pages designed
Manager:	Ian Simons

X	e**X**ecutes the work
D	takes **D**ecisions solely/ultimately
d	takes **d**ecisions jointly
P	manages **P**rogress
T	on the job **T**raining
I	must be **I**nformed
C	must be **C**onsulted
A	may **A**dvise

No	Activity name	Ian Simons	Jan Deptford	Procurement	Contractors	Personnel	Marketing	Selected users	Duration (d)	End date
D31	Specify page based on agreed contents	P	X						7	11-Sep-03
D32	Appoint contractors	Xd		Xd					2	11-Sep-03
D33	Manage contractors	P							10	25-Sep-03
D34	Design and develop pages	P			X				7	22-Sep-03
D35	Obtain approval – personnel	PX	X		X	C			5	23-Sep-03
D36	Obtain approval – marketing	PX	X		X				2	24-Sep-03
D37	Obtain approval – selected users	PX	X		X			C	2	24-Sep-03
D38	Make necessary changes	PD	X		X	d	d	d	3	25-Sep-03

ACTIVITY SCHEDULE

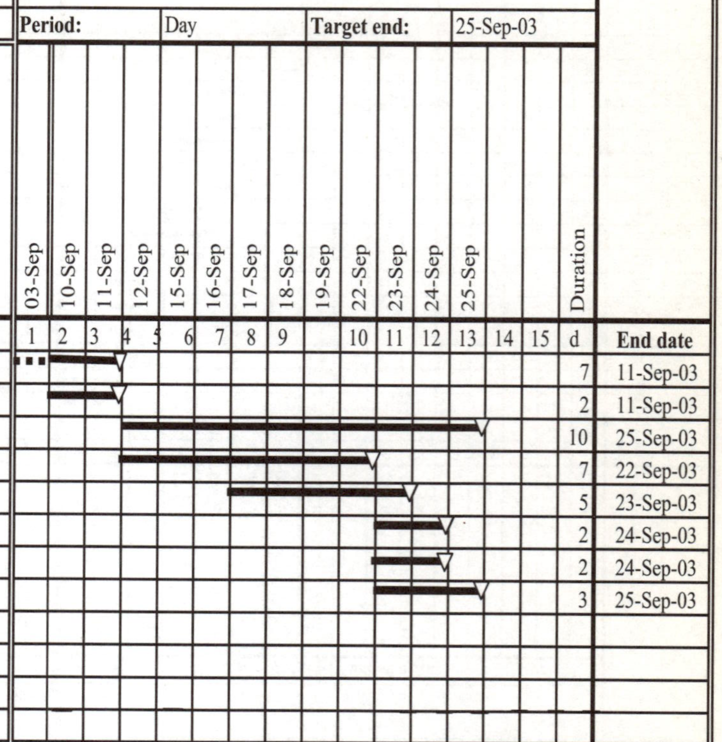

Figure 8.9 *Activity plan for Milestone D3 frm the intranet at TriMagi*

- each row will take up to ten minutes
- the whole chart will take up to 2 hours
- only progress from one row to the next when you have full agreement

4 Calculate the duration of each work element
5 Complete the bar chart.

By going through this process and getting agreement, everyone will leave the project start-up meeting having internalized their contribution to the project. If one or more members of the team will not accept responsibility for work that you and the rest of the team think is theirs, then you can ask them the following questions:

1 Do you think the project is worthwhile? And if yes, then
2 Do you think that milestone or activity is necessary to achieving the project? And if yes, then
3 Do you accept that it is your responsibility? And if no, then
4 Whose is it?

If they answer no to questions 1 or 2 ask them why they are at the meeting.

At the end of the last chapter, I discussed what happens if the schedule shows you require more time than you have available. If it is less than about 20 per cent more than the time available, you can usually massage it down by revisiting the plan. If it is more than about 20 per cent, you need to solve the problem in other ways.

At the end of this process you can almost rub the white board clear as everyone will have internalized their contribution to the project. It is worthwhile copying it down for several reasons:

- The responsibility chart is the best tool for assigning work to people. It shows who has to do what when. The milestone plan is very good for planning the strategy for the project and tracking progress. But the responsibility chart is best for assigning work.
- If someone does renege on their commitments six months down the track, you can get the chart out and show them what they committed to.
- If someone changes jobs, you can show the successor what their predecessor committed to.
- If you find you need to involve people who were not at the meeting, it gives you greater authority if you can show them a group solution rather than your own ideas.

CHAPTER 9 *Managing Stakeholders*

Once, when I was writing an overview of project management, I was asked to say how you should deal with 'irrational people' who resist the implementation of change. But this resistance is not irrational – it is simply another view of the situation that arises from the position in which stakeholders find themselves. Remember that a new project will not optimize the economic position of everyone involved; indeed, some people's position is optimized through the project's failure. Web projects have potentially global reach with a large number of stakeholders, and a diverse team of people working in the project. These people may have objectives, and a view of the project, which may or may not align with the stated project objectives:

- Some people's objectives will be aligned with the project's objectives, and they will be pushing for successful completion of the project.
- Some people's objectives will be aligned with the project's objectives, but they will misinterpret what the project is about, so even though it is beneficial to them they are against it.
- Some people's objectives will be misaligned with the project's objectives, and they will be trying to resist successful completion of the project.
- Some people's objectives will be misaligned with the project's objectives, but they will misinterpret what the project is about, so even though it is disadvantageous to them they are for it.
- Some people's objectives will be misaligned with the project's objectives, but they see that if the project's objectives are changed they can achieve theirs and so will be trying to subvert the project.

We saw in Chapters 2 and 3 that web-delivery projects:

- have global reach with a wide set of stakeholders
- involve many different resources in their delivery
- are managed from outside the IS department
- have a wide range of user requirements
- threaten established ways of working
- may meet with fear and resistance of the unknown.

As a result, web-delivery projects have many stakeholders with differing views and differing requirements from the project. Web-delivery projects are also innovation projects which change the organization's business processes, and result in changes to peoples' working lives. Thus potentially many people can be against the project, even though it is beneficial to the organization, and even though, if they truly understood what the project is about, they would realize it is beneficial to them.

In this chapter I describe a process of managing stakeholders. I describe the process in the next section. Then I describe how you can diagnose the organization's willingness to accept the changes brought about by web-delivery projects, and how you can sell the change to the organization. I discuss how to manage conflict and the role of information. Finally I consider the role of the project champion in the change management process.

THE STAKEHOLDER MANAGEMENT PROCESS

Figure 9.1 shows an eight step stakeholder management process. We can examine each step in turn.

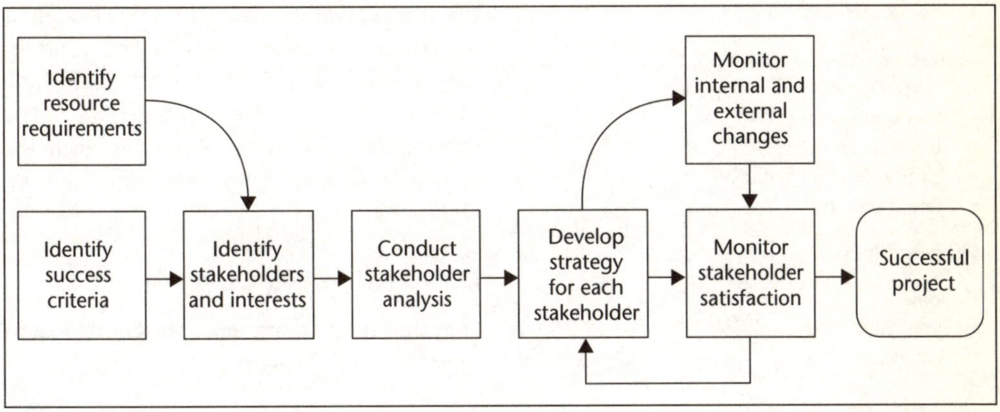

Figure 9.1 *Stakeholder management process*

IDENTIFY RESOURCE REQUIREMENTS

First we must identify the resources we need to draw on to undertake the project. Every resource to a project is a potential stakeholder, and that is not just the people doing work or supplying materials. Figure 9.2 shows a list of potential hard and soft resources. The provider of every one of these is a potential stakeholder. Figure 2.2 listed people involved in a web-delivery project.

Hard resources	*Soft resources*
Finance	Internal support
Materials	External support
Skills	Bureaucratic inertia
Regulatory approval	Emotion
External contacts	Knowledge
Planning approval	Political attention
	Discretion

Figure 9.2 *Hard and soft resources on a project*

IDENTIFY SUCCESS CRITERIA

I said in Chapter 6 that a necessary condition for project success is to agree the success criteria with all the stakeholders before you start. In that chapter I suggested three questions to help you identify the success criteria, and interested stakeholders. The questions are:

Q1: On the last day of the project, what will the project team hand over to operations?

Q2: How will success of the project be judged?

Q3: Who has an opinion on questions 1 and 2?

Possible success criteria and the interested stakeholders were listed in Figure 6.4.

IDENTIFY STAKEHOLDERS AND THEIR INTERESTS

Each one of the resource requirements identifies a potential stakeholder. Every success criterion, both overt and covert, implies a potential stakeholder. Figure 6.4 lists the overt success criteria and associated stakeholders; Figure 9.3 shows the potential stakeholders for a web-delivery project. As I said above, some of the stakeholders may have interests (covert objectives) that are misaligned with the project's objectives. The SWOT analysis – strengths, weaknesses, opportunities, threats – suggested below can help identify those covert objectives. The stakeholders and their objectives form the first two columns of the stakeholder register, Figure 9.4.

Potential stakeholders

Employees
- users
- operators
- bystanders

Management
- resource providers
- user managers
- technical managers
- consumer representatives
- board members

Shareholders

Customers
- internal
- external

Suppliers
- internal
- external

Government
- local
- non-governmental organizations
- national
- continental

Community
- neighbours
- planning authorities
- media

Figure 9.3 *Potential stakeholders for a web-delivery project*

CONDUCT STAKEHOLDER ANALYSIS

The stakeholders are now analysed against three yes/no parameters:

1. Does the stakeholder support the project or not?
2. Can they influence the outcome?
3. Is their stance based on knowledge of the project or ignorance?

The answer to the first of these questions is sometimes presented on a five point scale:

- strongly support the project
- weakly support the project
- ambivalent
- weakly oppose the project
- strongly oppose the project.

Some stakeholders can be ambivalent; they have no interest whether the project is a success or not. Contractors may be in this position. They are paid to do their work, and whether or not the project is a success has no impact on the payment they receive. (Personally I think you should link the contractor's payment to the success of the project, to try to align their objectives with the client's objectives, but that is the topic of another book, [Turner 2003b].)

TriMagi
Stakeholder register

Project:	Intranet Phase 1
Project Champion:	Martin Pacific
Project Manager:	Frances Seeker

Stakeholder name/group	*Objectives*	*Aware Y/N*	*Influence Y/N*	*Support Y/N*	*Strategy for influencing this stakeholder*
Managing Director	Internet banking Communicate better with employees	Y	Y	Y	Keep informed, seek views Try to keep satisfied but uninvolved
Board members	Maintain power base	Y	N	Y and N	Keep informed and uninvolved
Personnel Manager	Online processing of forms Online personnel information	Y	Y	Y	Managing the project. Needs to communicate vision, and stop scope creep
IS Manager	Influence web presence and policy				
Production Manager	Internet banking, online application for products				
Staff	Some welcome it Some resist it	N N	Block	Y N	Keep informed. Consult early. Form focus groups

Author:	JRT	**Date:**	21 July 2003	**Issue:**	A

Figure 9.4 *Stakeholder register for the intranet at TriMagi*

The first two parameters give four groups of stakeholders:

1 Those who can support the project and can influence the outcome are our main friends. We want to maintain and strengthen their support. But be careful; there are some people whose support we may be glad of, but we don't want them interfering. Those people we need to move carefully into the next category, without ruffling their feathers.
2 Those who support the project but can't influence the outcome are also good friends. We will try to maintain their support and may even try to find ways of involving them in the project.
3 Those who oppose the project but can't influence the outcome are annoying. We may try to change their position. If not we try to ensure they remain powerless.
4 Those who oppose the project but can influence the outcome are our real enemies. We must either try to find a way to change their views (see Figure 9.5), or find a way to isolate them from the project (see below).

> I worked on a computer system development project where the chief user representative was due to be made redundant by the project. He was aged 63 and due to retire in two years time. He also had a temporary promotion from management grade 1 to management grade 2. Under the company's rules at the time, if he got made redundant, he would be demoted back to grade 1 and be made redundant on that. If he retired he would retire on grade 2. His pension would be higher for the rest of his life if he could retire rather than be made redundant. He was positively against this project and it showed. Since this man wanted to retire early, I suggested to the project manager he should either try to obtain a special dispensation, or get his grade 2 made substantive. Then he would be in favour of the project.

Figure 9.5 *Changing a stakeholder's view*

The influence strategy is mainly based on the first and third parameters, as discussed below.

Conducting a SWOT analysis on each project can help answer the three questions and also identify any covert objectives the stakeholders may hold. Actually for our proponents it is more of an OTSW analysis, and for our opponents a TOWS analysis:

Proponents

- *Opportunities:* We want to understand why this stakeholder supports the project. Hopefully it is because their objectives are aligned with the project objectives; that is they share the project objectives, or if the project is successful that will enable them to achieve their objectives in a way that is beneficial to the project. It may be, as I said above, that they have a different agenda – that if the project is successful, it will enable them to achieve a bunch of objectives that conflicts with the project's true purpose. You need to be aware of that type of covert objective.
- *Threats:* It is possible there are elements of this project that are a threat to this stakeholder. It might even be that they are unaware of the true nature of this project, and if they did understand it, they would view the project more as a threat than an opportunity. If the project is more of an opportunity than a threat to the stakeholder, then you ought to be open about the threats, and work with the stakeholder to minimize them. If you try to hide the

potential threats and the stakeholder finds out about them, that may turn them against you. If the project is more of a threat than an opportunity, then you may be working hard to sell the benefits of the project, and downplay the potential threats.

- *Strengths:* You will also want to understand what strengths this stakeholder has that will enable them to support you; how can they influence the outcome. You will want to reinforce their strengths.
- *Weaknesses:* You will want to understand their weaknesses. How will your opponents try to undermine them?

Opponents

- *Threats:* Why do your opponents view the project as a threat? What is it about the project that they don't like? What covert objectives do they have for undermining the project?
- *Opportunities:* The project may offer the stakeholder some benefit. In fact it is even possible that the project is more of a benefit to them than a threat. Unfortunately, psychologically, people find it very difficult to change their opinion once formed. Thus if they already view the project as a threat, it may be too late to sell the benefits to them. I discussed this in Chapter 3, when discussing Figure 3.5. I also think that if people find out about the project on the grapevine they are going to be against it. They will assume that if they heard about it on the grapevine, management are keeping it secret, and if management are keeping it secret it must be bad. So you want to identify the benefits of the project to the various stakeholders early and sell them the project before they find about it in other ways.
- *Strengths:* And you want to be aware of their strengths so you can protect yourself from them.
- *Weaknesses:* Now you want to know the stakeholder's weaknesses to stop them undermining you and your supporters.

The analysis of opportunities and threats helps you identify whether the stakeholder is for you or against you and what their overt and covert objectives may be, and the analysis of the strengths and weaknesses helps you identify whether they can influence the outcome or not.

DEVELOP A STRATEGY FOR EACH STAKEHOLDER

Now we are ready to develop a strategy for influencing each stakeholder. The influence strategy is mainly based on the first and third parameters. First we should be aware people are now far better educated than they were forty years ago, and they have been educated to value their own opinions, even if they are derived from a position of ignorance. Further, it is well known that, psychologically, human beings find it very difficult to change their opinions, once formed. If people form an opinion based on incomplete information, they find it difficult to change even when new information is available that proves their position wrong. I will discuss this again under quality assurance in the next chapter. This means that you should start your information campaign and influence strategy early, because once people are against the project, it may be impossible to win them over.

So there are four potential strategies for stakeholder influence:

1. *Aware-support:* For those who support the project from a position of awareness, try to maintain their support and keep them informed. Don't be complacent; work at keeping them informed and on board.

2 *Ignorant-support:* For those who support you from a position of ignorance you will try to:
   - maintain their support
   - protect them from the influence of those who are against the project
   - inform them about the project to try to reinforce their support further.
3 *Ignorant-against:* These people you will try to win over to the project by informing them of what it is about. But beware that it is very difficult to change people's opinions, and so it is best to start the influence campaign very early on. You should work out early those people who may be against the project, especially if they get an incorrect idea of what the project is about, and you should try to inform them very early on about the benefits of the project. Also try to involve them in the project decision-making to make them feel part of what is going on. You also must inform people in layman's language. I said in Chapter 7 that it is important to express the milestones in inclusive terms. It is also important to sell the project's benefits in terms people can understand (see Figure 9.6).
4 *Aware-against:* First you should try to find a way to win these people over (Figure 9.5). If that is impossible, they need to be isolated.These are the four main categories of stakeholder – but there may be others (Figure 9.7).

Figure 9.4 is the stakeholder register for the intranet at TriMagi.

> A British mining company was developing a uranium mine in Canada. At the public enquiry, one of their engineers was on the witness stand, and a mischievous barrister acting for the environmental lobby asked him what would be the level of radioactivity of waste water leaving the site. The engineer gave a precise answer, so many becquerels. Immediately that was in the local press. The waste water was going to be radioactive; children would be born with two heads; all the local community would die of cancer. The correct answer was 'half the level of rainwater'. The waste water would have half the level of radioactivity of naturally occurring water. But it was too late, the genie was out of the bottle, Pandora's box was opened, there was no putting the furies back in.

Figure 9.6 *Speaking in terms the laity understand*

> Ralf Müller once told me that he was working on the development of a system and trying to recover a project that had previously gone wrong, undertaking a pilot to develop a new application. He was reporting progress to the Product Manager, who in turn was reporting to senior management. Progress was not good, but he wondered why he was not receiving comments from the senior management. By chance he found out that for political reasons the Product Manager was embellishing the reports before forwarding them to senior management, making it look as though the project was on schedule, and the new application would shortly be ready for release to market. For his own purposes, and in the hope that the project could still be turned around, this stakeholder was misreporting progress.

Figure 9.7 *Ensure that the right information gets through*

Monitor progress to achieve a successful outcome

As the project progresses, you should monitor the impact of your influence strategy on each stakeholder. Hopefully it will be successful and lead to a successful project. If not, you may want to go back and adjust your influence strategy. Further, changes in the environment may also lead you to revisit your influence strategy.

I said that agreeing the success criteria with your stakeholders at the start is a necessary condition of project success. Agreeing the success criteria with them throughout at predefined review points is also a necessary condition, and I will discuss that further under configuration management in the next chapter.

DIAGNOSING WILLINGNESS TO ACCEPT CHANGE

We saw in Chapter 3 that web-delivery projects entail considerable change. We need to ask ourselves whether the organization is ready and able to accept those changes. First we consider what may cause people to have a different view to the required changes by considering barriers to effective problem-solving. Then I present a check list to help determine the readiness of the organization to accept the changes required to support the new web space.

BARRIERS TO PROBLEM-SOLVING

Some people may resist the implementation of the new web space because they just cannot see the solutions and opportunities that it offers. Figure 9.8 contains a list of barriers to problem-solving based on the work of J.L. Adams (2001). Some of these blocks may arise because people are deliberately resisting the change, some because they are subconsciously resisting it, and some may be completely unintentional, arising because of the culture of the organization or the people working in it. I have also identified five idols of modern management which stop people thinking laterally to derive novel, innovative solutions to their problems. These are:

1 *The Idol of the Cave:* Based on the metaphor of the cave used by Plato in Book VII of *The Republic*, what we see is not reality, but a reflection of reality. We cannot find the most effective solutions to our problems, because through our limited experience we cannot see what our problems truly are. We only see a reflection of our problems, and only find an ephemeral solution to that reflection.

2 *The Idol of the Tribe:* This is group think. The group applies peer pressure on individuals to fall in with the group's opinion. The group's solution may not be the best, and even wrong, but nobody dares challenge the group's solution. There was a global example of this with the celebration of the new millennium. Most people wanted to celebrate 1 January 2000. If any one dared suggest that the start of the millennium was actually a year later they were labelled a pedant and ridiculed. They weren't told they were wrong because everyone knew they were right, but they were ostracized. The tribe wanted to celebrate 1 January 2000, and peer pressure was used to stop anyone saying otherwise. The same can happen in organizations, but this is worse because it matters rather than just being a bit of fun. It is particularly prevalent where the managing director surrounds him or herself with a bunch of yes-men, and then nobody dares challenge the perceived wisdom. Organizations sleepwalk into disaster.

   I said in Chapter 3 that all new ideas go through three stages: first people think they are stupid, then they think they are dangerous, then they say it is obvious and they believed it all along. The first two steps are the tribe trying to block the new idea.

Barrier	*Comment*
Perceptual blocks	
1 Stereotyping	We see what we expect to see
2 Problem isolation	We solve the wrong problem
3 Tunnel vision	Too narrow a focus
4 Blinkered vision	Constrained by our professional teaching
5 Data overload	Can't see the wood for the trees
6 Data underload	Insufficient information
Emotional blocks	
1 Loss aversion	Fear of failure
2 Ambiguity aversion	Fear of uncertainty
3 Urgency	Fear of wasting time, or being seen to waste time
4 Closing options	Preference for the known and certainty rather than the creative
Cultural blocks	
1 Taboos	Some ideas cannot be countenanced
2 Lack of fantasy	Logical left-brained rather than creative right-brained thinking
3 Lack of humour	Business is serious
4 Tradition	'We have always done it this way'
Environmental blocks	
1 Lack of support	Making people feel isolated and undervalued
2 Aversion to criticism	In a blame culture
3 Boss knows best	Surrounded by yes-men
Cognitive blocks	
1 Use of language	Language can block problem-solving
– Jargon	Can be excluding
– Local terminology	'That's not the way we do it here'
– Cultural diversity	Stereotyping is boorish and can be excluding
2 Use of models	Can aid understanding but also limit creativity
3 Use of information	Information is power

Figure 9.8 *Barriers to problem-solving*

3 *The Idol of the Marketplace:* As people gather in the forum to discuss ideas they often adopt jargon, a vocabulary to be able to talk succinctly about concepts central to the discipline. But the use of jargon seems to lead inevitably to people trying to use the jargon to block new ideas, and also to vacuous argument and empty controversies. An example of the latter is meaningless discussions over the difference in meaning between vision and mission, and between goals, aims and objectives (Figure 1.8). Further people can forget the concept to which the word applies, or different authors can put different interpretations on words, and with time, incorrect meanings can attach to words. In the project management arena the words 'sponsor' and 'budget' have changed their meaning over the last twenty years, and in management in general, the words 'vision' and 'mission' have swapped meaning. But of particular concern in the organizational context is the use of jargon to block creativity, to block new ways of doing things, to label new ideas as either stupid or dangerous. Also jargon can be used to isolate people who might contribute to the project, in one of two ways:

- they feel isolated because they don't understand the jargon
- they are labelled as being wrong because they don't use the jargon.

4 *The Idol of the Soap Opera:* This is where people fail to differentiate between fiction and reality. Whatever is proposed becomes accepted as being almost more important than reality. In the tabloid press it is sometimes difficult to draw the line between the reporting of the storylines in the soap operas on television, the lives of the stars of the soap operas, and world news. A few years ago, the Prime Minister of the UK was asked to intercede with the Home Secretary to secure the release from jail of one character in a famous soap opera. In an organizational context, models can be proposed, and they take on a validity that is divorced from reality. The project plan is treated as being more correct than what everyone knows to be true progress. It is said the computer system must be right.

5 *The Idol of the Fool on the Hill:* The fifth Idol arises when the Tribe makes a fawning acceptance of the Guru's pronouncement. We have seen it over the last two decades. All it takes is some guru to pronounce, and managers are slavishly following the latest fad:
   - upsizing, downsizing, rightsizing, leftsizing
   - SPC, TQM, BPR and all manner of other TLAs
   - ISO 9000, and certificates awarded to factories making concrete life jackets.

   The problem is we adopt the latest fad as a one-size-fits-all solution to all our problems, and when it doesn't work in every case (as it won't), we reject the idea as being totally wrong; rather than accepting that it was only ever appropriate in certain circumstances, and retaining it as being the best solution for those circumstances. In the Wild West of the nineteenth century, quacks would travel around selling their elixir as a universal panacea. When that didn't work, people would buy the elixir off the next quack to come along. People never change; human nature is like a stick of Brighton Rock.

To achieve a creative solution to the project's purpose, and develop a web space that meets the real need, project team members must learn to:

- identify the real problem
- challenge perceived wisdom
- use language to aid communication not constrain creativity
- use models to aid understanding not cloud reality
- avoid the fads, recognizing there are no one-size-fits-all solutions, but different concepts have their strengths and weaknesses.

Effect	*Behaviour*
Encouraging	Remain fluid until rigour is needed Protect new ideas from criticism Acknowledge good ideas, listen, show approval Eliminate status or rank Be optimistic Support confusion and uncertainty Value learning from mistakes Focus on the good aspects of an idea Share the risks Suspend disbelief Build on ideas Do not evaluate too early
Discouraging	Interrupt, criticize, disagree, argue, challenge Be confrontational Mock Be dominant Be pessimistic React negatively and point out flaws Be inattentive and use silence against people Insist on having 'the facts' Give no feedback Pull rank Become angry Be distant

Figure 9.9 *Encouraging and discouraging involvement*

There are also behaviours that the project manager can adopt which will encourage or discourage team members from engaging in the work of the project team, and from being creative, (Figure 9.9). Adopting the discouraging behaviours can be isolating and create enemies.

DIAGNOSING THE READINESS TO CHANGE

You can also attempt to diagnose how ready and willing the organization as a whole is to accept change. Figure 9.10 contains a checklist of items you can use to work out how ready and willing people in the organization are to accept the web space, and the new ways of working involved. Having identified potential problems there are things that can be done to alleviate them:

Question/answer

1 In the past, new policies or systems introduced by management have been:
- seen as meeting employees' needs
- not well understood
- greeted with some resistance
- vigorously resisted

2 Employees may be best described as:
- innovative
- independent
- apathetic
- conservative or resistant to change

3 The most recent and widely known change in the organization was viewed as:
- a success
- moderately successful
- had no obvious impact
- conservative or resistant to change

4 Expectations of the changes resulting from the new web space are:
- consistent throughout the organization
- consistent amongst senior management but not otherwise
- not at all consistent
- unclear

5 What can people directly affected by the new web space tell you about the organization's business or strategic plan?
- a full decription
- a description of where it affects their own department or activity
- a general idea
- nothing

6 The desired outcomes for the web space have been:
- specified in detail
- outlined in general terms
- poorly defined
- not defined

7 Present work procedures to be affected by the new web application are seen as needing:
- major change
- significant alteration
- minor improvement
- no change

8 The problems to be dealt with by the new web application were first raised by:
- the people directly involved
- first-line management and supervision

continued

- senior management
- outside management

9 The proposed web application is viewed by end users as:
- crucial to the organization's future
- generally beneficial to the organization
- beneficial only to part of the organization
- largely a matter of procedure

10 Top management support for the proposed web application is:
- enthusiastic
- limited
- minimal
- unclear

11 Top management has:
- committed significant resources to the adoption of web technology
- expects the web space to be implemented from existing sources
- has withheld resources
- has not planned the resources needed

12 The management performance appraisal and review process is:
- an important part of management development
- a helpful problem-solving process
- routine
- an obstacle to improvement

13 The proposed web space deals with issues of relevance to the business:
- directly
- partly
- only indirectly
- not at all

14 The proposed web space:
- makes jobs more rewarding financially and otherwise
- makes jobs easier and more satisfying
- replaces old tasks and skills with new ones

15 The proposed web space is technically:
- similar to others undertaken in recent past
- novel
- unclear technically

16 Are employees adaptable?
- very adaptable
- adaptable
- reluctant to change
- inflexible

17 Are employees used to working in teams?
- yes, in clearly defined teams
- only occasionally, when certain projects arise
- very occasionally
- never

18 In the past employees have:
- been strongly committed to the adoption of web technology
- only been committed if they benefited personally
- not been particularly committed to web technology
- not been prepared to accept web technology

Figure 9.10 *Diagnosing the organization's readiness to change*

Questions 1 to 3 deal with implementing change:

- Has there been unsuccessful past experience of change?
- Do we have a risk-averse culture?
- Are there communication problems?
  - Keep everyone informed by making information available; explaining plans clearly; allowing access to management for questions and clarification.
  - Ensure the benefits of the new web space are sold realistically by making a practical case for change; explain change in terms which the employee will see as relevant and acceptable; show how it fits business needs and plans; spend time and effort on presentations.
  - Prepare carefully by making a full organizational diagnosis; spend time with people and groups, building trust, understanding and support.
  - Involve people by getting feedback on proposals; get people to fill out the checklists; discuss the data from these checklists.
  - Start small and successful by piloting a receptive group of employees, and in departments with a successful track record; implement changes in clear phases.
  - Plan for success by starting with elements of the new web space that can give a quick and positive pay-off; publicize early success; provide positive feedback to those involved in success.

Questions 4 to 6 deal with the effects of change:

- What are people's expectations of change?
- What are the objectives of change?
  - Clarify benefits of the new web space by emphasizing benefits to those involved and to the business.
  - Emphasize where the new systems utilize existing knowledge and skills.
  - Minimize surprises by specifying assumptions; focus on outcomes; identify potential problems.
  - Communicate plans by being specific in terms familiar to the different groups of employees; communicate periodically and through various media; ask for feedback; do not suppress negative views but listen to them carefully and deal with them openly.

Questions 7 to 9 deal with ownership of the new web space:

- Are procedures, systems, departments, products and services seen as a problem?
- Who planned the changes – top management or a staff department?
  - Plan visible outcomes from change.
  - Clarify views by exploring concerns about the change and examining impact on the day-to-day routines.
  - Specify who wants change and why; explain longer term advantages; identify common benefits; present potential of change.

Questions 10 to 12 deal with ensuring top management support:

- Will top management support web technology openly?
- Will top management promote the necessary resources?
- Is the management performance appraisal process an obstacle to change?
  - Build a power base by becoming the expert in the problems involved; understand top management's concerns; develop information and formal support; develop a strong and polished presentation in top management language.
  - Specify who wants change and why; explain longer term advantages; identify common benefits; present the potential of this change.

Questions 13 to 15 deal with acceptance of the new web space:

- Does the planned web space fit other business plans?
- Is there a clear sense of direction?
- Does the proposed web space place greater demands on people?
- Does the web space involve new technology or expertise?
  - Identify relevance of the proposed web space to the organization and its business objectives by reviewing plans and specifying how it fits; incorporate consequent changes into ongoing developments; if possible, frame changes in terms of the organization's style.
  - Implement the new web space using flexible or adaptable people, who are familiar with some or all of the change; in a part of the business where there are strong supporters for web technology; recognise why people support it (career, rewards, company politics).
  - Do not oversell web technology. Be clear about conflicts with present practices; encourage discussion of them.

Questions 16 to 18 deal with building an effective team to implement change:

- Will team members be inflexible in dealing with web technology?
- Will managers need to work hard to ensure commitment to web technology?
  - Ensure that teams have clear and agreed goals.
  - Involve all members of the team in ways they each see as relevant and using their own skills/expertise.
  - Be prepared to face and deal with conflict.
  - Encourage constructive feedback.

SELLING THE CHANGE

Having diagnosed the organization's willingness to accept the new web space, and the associated technology and changes, you now need to think about how you are going to sell the ideas to the people in the organization. Above all the stakeholder influence strategies are related to how we were going to inform the different types of stakeholders about the work and results of the project. In this section I give a few pointers about how to keep the team informed about the project, how to inform the organization and the type of information that needs to be given.

INFORMING THE TEAM

The team need to be briefed about the project at the start, and that will be done in the project start-up workshop (Chapter 4). However, throughout the project you need to build and maintain the commitment of the project team members. There are several things that can help achieve that:

- *Maintain a team charter:* the team charter will be closely allied with the project mandate (Chapter 5), but it can also deal with such issues as how the team will work together, setting standards that team members can expect from each other. It will be developed as part of the norming process (Chapter 4) where the team begin to feel closer attachment to the project team than they do to the department they have come from.
- *Establish a team identity:* choose a name for the project and the team, with a logo.
- *Maintain a team home page:* share news and information about the project and about the team members. To develop psychological attachment between the team members, especially if they are working on remote sites, they must feel they are working with other people, with lives, and families, and homes and a social life. So attach a page about each team member to the home page, with information that they are happy to share with the others. On the team home page maintain a project notice board, with information about the project, and cartoons to liven the project up and aid creativity.
- *Identify the team's ambassador:* identify somebody whose job it is to act as ambassador for the team, keeping the team informed about the project, keeping the organization informed, and winning the resources (both hard and soft, see Figure 9.1) that the team needs. Merideth Belbin called this role the 'resource investigator' (see Turner *et al.*, 1996).

INFORMING THE ORGANIZATION

When I worked as a consultant with Coopers and Lybrand, we clearly differentiated between education and training as part of the project process. Avoiding politically incorrect jokes:

- Training is giving people new skills in order for them to be able to use and operate the products of the project, in this case the new web page, and attendant operating procedures.
- Education is brainwashing them that the project is a good idea.

Neither is going to happen on its own. Both must be planned and managed as part of the project. Both above and in Chapter 3 I emphasized the need to inform people early. Tell them about the project before they hear about it on the grapevine, so you can win their support before they decide they don't like it. Engage people in the project process and make them feel as though they are contributing, and that their ideas are being listened to and taken account of. I get accused of being manipulative here. What is important is people feel they are contributing and being listened to – it doesn't matter whether they actually are. There are several things you can do to sell the project to the organization:

1. *Identify the team's ambassador:* as just described.
2. *Develop a marketing plan for the project:* plan how you will sell the project to the organization. Perform the stakeholder analysis, and identify the benefits of the project to the organization and the people in it. Think not just about what you are going to tell people, but how and when and where. And think about the benefits to individuals that will make them more accepting of the project. In marketing products and services the marketing literature talks about the 4Ps: product, price, promotion and place of sale. You need to think about those for the project:

- What will the project deliver to the organization and what benefit will it be?
- What commitment are you asking for from people, hard and soft resources (Figure 9.1)?
- How are you going to sell the idea to them?
- Where are you going to sell it to them?

3 *Plan the education programme:* based on the marketing plan, develop a plan for a series of seminars and other events to inform people about the project.

4 *Arrange focus groups:* these are very topical, and perhaps you might even think they belong to the Idol of the Soap Opera, that they are more theatre than substance. But they can be very useful for making people feel as though they are contributing to the project; that their ideas are being heard and taken account of. If you feel I am being manipulative, then perhaps they are more theatre than substance, but useful for that purpose all the same.

THE RIGHT INFORMATION

Bob Graham (2003) emphasizes the need to give people the right information. Traditional project managers give people the information produced by the project management information system (PMIS). That is usually a network and a schedule, but it's not what people want to know. Bob Graham also says it is problematic asking people what information they need as many people do not think that way. He therefore suggests that you should look upon the information you provide people with as answering a series of questions that are likely to be useful to them. He suggests typical questions.

Questions of outcome

People want to know what the end result of the project will be. These were answered by Hartman's three questions proposed in Chapter 6 and repeated at the start of this chapter. They include:

- *Questions of functionality:* What will the web space developed by the project do? What will be its configuration, what will be the functionality and purpose of its various elements? What will it do?
- *Questions of success:* How will the success of the project and the new web space be judged?
- *Questions of market:* What market segment will the new web space be aimed at? The identification of the stakeholders will help answer this question. Remember from Chapter 2 that the products of web projects can have much wider reach than conventional projects, so it is important to be clear about the intended market of the web space developed. It is particularly important on web projects to be clear about all the market segments the project is aimed at, so that you can be culturally sensitive to all the people in those different markets. Managing culture is beyond the scope of this book. To read more, see David Rees's work (2003).

Questions of performance

People want to know that the time, cost and quality targets will be met. Ralf Müller and I have shown that when the client takes an interest in performance, it leads to the best project outcomes.

Questions of moral hazard

The client wants to know that the project manager and project team are taking decisions in the owner's best interests.

MANAGING CONFLICT

With the large number of stakeholders, with diverse requirements, there is a good chance that conflict will occur. There are three strategies for resolving conflict:

CONFRONTATION

Confrontation seeks to deal directly with the sources of the conflict, requiring the conflicting parties to discuss their differences openly. A typical solution is to conduct a problem-solving workshop, managed by a facilitator, where the conflicting parties try to identify the causes of the conflict and possible solutions. This can involve high emotions and solidify the conflict if not handled well. On the other hand I have known situations where it has lead to excellent solutions. In one case a contractor put in a ridiculously high claim for a delay. At the workshop it turned out that the contractor knew the claim was ridiculously high, but they had felt they were being ignored by the client. There was something the client had to do to help them minimize the impact of the variation, and putting in the high claim was the only way of making the client pay attention. The issue was resolved in the workshop to the benefit of all parties, including subcontractors.

DIFFUSION

Diffusion tries to defuse the conflict for long enough for the conflicting parties to resolve their differences. One technique is to emphasize the common goal and mutual benefit of the project. That is where the workshop just described went to. Another approach is to negotiate a mutually beneficial outcome with some give and take. The emphasis is on trying to find the mutually beneficial compromise without necessarily identifying the trigger event for the conflict.

AVOIDANCE

When explaining this, I have had people misinterpret what is meant by avoidance, and say that it is cowardly, and ostrich like. It is not evasion. It is not pretending the conflict is not happening. Avoidance methods directly address the conflict, without necessarily trying to resolve the conflict itself. One technique is for the project manager to send signals that the conflict is not a good idea, that it is not beneficial for the project or the team members. Another is enforced separation, giving the team members tasks that keep them separate. Another is forced togetherness where they are given a task to work on together, which hopefully they can agree on, and forget their former differences.

When discussing innovation in Chapter 3, I said differences can be a source of creativity. Marketing people and engineers are notorious for having differences of opinion, but getting them to work together can help them to respect their mutual contributions.

THE ROLE OF THE PROJECT CHAMPION

I used to think that the project manager was responsible for the project holistically, and complained that traditional project managers were almost tunnel visioned in their focus on delivering the project, to time, cost and functionality, while ignoring the business context. Sometimes they don't even question whether the time, cost and functionality targets are correct, they just do as they are told. I have changed my view now. It is the project manager's role just to focus on the project, to deliver the project's time, cost and functionality role. Part of that role is to ensure that the project is properly integrated as a whole: that the team members know what they have to do, and that they have the equipment and support to do it. But it is the project champion's role to ensure that the project is properly integrated into the business. With a good champion in support, the project manager can focus on the project unimpeded, while the champion sorts out the relationship with the project's external stakeholders. The champion's roles include the following:

ACCOUNTABLE FOR THE INVESTMENT IN THE PROJECT

The most significant role for the champion is that they (and not the project manager) are responsible to the business for the investment in the project. They initiate the discovery phase of the project on behalf of the organization. It is common for the champion to manage the feasibility stage of the project before the project manager is appointed. They will determine the business objectives and set the constraints for the project manager and the users.

The champion will manage the business case for the project, setting the success criteria, and helping to obtain approval at each one of the project toll gates (Figures 2.4 and 2.5). It will be the champion who will be responsible for the business element of the decision at each toll gate. That will include, most significantly, being responsible for preparing the financial case at the appraisal stage. The champion will obtain the funding for the project, and manage the relationship with the project's sponsor or financier during delivery.

Once the project is completed, the champion and not the project manager will be responsible for ensuring that the business benefit is obtained. This is the last step in the project control process, and is discussed further in Chapter 15. The champion must ensure that the web space is being used to generate the revenues expected, at the costs expected, and that it is therefore making the profit expected. The champion will also be responsible for generating increased revenues into the future.

FIRST POINT OF CONTACT WITH THE ORGANIZATION

The champion will be the first point of contact between the parent organization and the project. He or she will represent the organization in the project control process. The champion will agree the milestone plan with the project team, and monitor progress against the milestone plan. He or she will also be the first call for approval for major changes.

MONITOR THE PROJECT'S ENVIRONMENT

The champion also has a key role in monitoring the project's environment and the relationship with key external stakeholders. This will enable to project manager to focus on the project and the internal stakeholders (users, resource providers, key line managers). The champion will manage the relationship with the external stakeholders, watch for any major changes in the external context, and work with the project manager to incorporate any such changes into the project. That will enable the project manager to focus on the project, to work with the internal stakeholders to deliver the project to time, cost and functionality.

CHAPTER

10 *Managing Quality and Configuration*

The nature of web-delivery projects, as described in Chapter 2, makes the achievement of the desired quality and functionality more problematic than on traditional IS projects:

1 *Shorter timescales:* means corners are cut to achieve the duration, impacting on quality and functionality
2 *Global reach with many stakeholders:* means that there is a wide range of views to be incorporated and balanced with each other
3 *Managed from outside the IS department:* means that the people implementing the project are less familiar with delivering quality and functionality on projects
4 *Multidisciplinary teams:* means that there is a wide range of skills to be incorporated into the end product with perhaps different views on how that should be achieved
5 *Wide range of user requirements:* means these all have to be balanced and incorporated into the final design
6 *Technological challenges:* means that the technology can impact on quality, and the need to achieve FRAMES can itself be a quality requirement, but one that also impacts on overall quality and functionality
7 *Skill shortages:* can create pressures on quality
8 *Lack of integrative methodologies:* means quality, functionality and configuration may suffer at the interface between design and project management
9 *Fast changes in the industry:* means the technology can change faster than your ability to deliver the system, and you are not able to backtrack to recover a previous configuration if the current prototype doesn't work
10 *Greater risk:* is thereby created by all of the above.

In this chapter, I describe the management of quality and configuration on web-delivery projects. First I consider what we understand by quality in the context of the project. I then introduce a five-element model for the management of quality, and describe each of the elements. Finally I describe the use of configuration management as a tool of quality management. In fact, configuration management is more a tool for achieving the right functionality of the project's end product. However, as we shall see in the next section, that is quite a significant element of the definition of quality. When people talk about the so-called 'triple constraint', they describe it variously as:

- time, cost and quality
- time, cost and functionality
- time, cost and specification
- time, cost and performance
- and so on.

Functionality, specification and performance are all elements of quality. Configuration management is a tool to manage the delivery of all of them.

QUALITY IN THE CONTEXT OF PROJECTS

There are several definitions of what we mean by good quality on projects:

- meets customer requirements
- meets the specification
- solves the problem
- fit for its purpose
- satisfies or delights the customer.

The customer will have an idea of the problem they are trying to solve, and will formulate a solution. That will become their requirement. They will attempt to enunciate their requirement, and a designer will try to capture that in a specification. When the web space is delivered, it should be delivered in accordance with the specification. If there have been no mistakes in the preceding steps, the web space delivered will solve the problem, that is it will be fit for purpose, and it will delight the customer.

Are these definitions the same thing? Well hopefully yes, but of course the phrase 'If there have been no mistakes in the preceding steps', says it all. The chance is small that each step is performed perfectly. There is a chain of gaps:

Gap 1: Between the actual problem (and the correct solution) and what the customer derives

Gap 2: Between the customer's solution and their mental picture of it

Gap 3: Between the customer's mental picture and what they enunciate

Gap 4: Between what they enunciate and what the person writing the specification hears

Gap 5: Between what they hear and what they write down in the specification.

With these gaps, the chance that the specification represents a solution to the customer's problem, meets their requirements and will delight them is small. Thus, the standard definition of quality is taken at the end of the project, the web space is fit for purpose, it solves the problem required of it, and (hopefully) thereby satisfies the customer. This requires the project team to accept that the specification may be imperfect, and therefore requires some refinement. This gives us a dilemma. Traditional project managers think that the specification is sacrosanct, and therefore must not be changed. However, if it is imperfect, then the web space may not solve the problem, and so may need to be refined as the project progresses. On the other hand, if the specification is changed constantly, the project will never finish. Thus it must be changed, but changed sparingly, using the techniques of configuration management described below.

There are three additional questions to be considered about quality in the context of projects:

WHO IS THE CUSTOMER?

Whom do we mean by 'the customer' (above)?

- The owner of the web space, who pays for it and receives the income stream from its operation?
- The operators of the web space, or users of the services it provides?
- The consumers of the eventual product it produces?
- The media, or local community, or politicians?

The answer is they are all the customer, and all their requirements must be satisfied. They will usually have different requirements and to satisfy them all will be a difficult juggling act. The owners must be willing to pay for it. The operators must believe it will work; they can make failure a self-fulfilling prophecy. The consumers must want to buy the product. Configuration management can also be used to try to gain agreement from the various parties (warring factions) as the project progresses. (These are all stakeholders as considered below, but not all the stakeholders.)

DO YOU GIVE THE CUSTOMER WHAT THEY WANT OR WHAT THEY NEED?

In the 1970s the attitude was to give the customer what they needed, not what they wanted, because all-knowing, sagacious engineers knew better than their customers what their requirements were. This arrogant attitude led to the demise of many industries. It is arrogant to think you know better than your customers; it is arrogant to think you are unfailingly correct. By the 1980s this had changed. It did not matter what trivial whim the customer had, 'the customer is king, give them whatever they ask for'. It doesn't matter how much it costs, and whether it is right or wrong for their actual need, they asked for it, give it to them. On the one hand you give the customer what you think they need. They look at the product, say 'that's not what we asked for', and refuse it. On the other you give them what they say they want. When it does not work, you say 'the customer is king', and they say 'but you should have advised me it wouldn't work'. The way out of this dilemma is to use configuration management so that by the end of the project what the multiheaded customer now thinks they want, what they actually need, and what you think they need are all the same.

WHAT IS THE DIFFERENCE BETWEEN GOOD QUALITY AND HIGH QUALITY?

To consider the difference between good and high quality, consider the question: *Is a Rolls-Royce a good quality motor car?* A Rolls-Royce is a high quality, well-engineered car. But it satisfies almost no specification you can draw up for a motor car, or need you might have. If you want a car that is economical, easy to manoeuvre and park, is a Rolls-Royce a good quality car? If you want a car that can drive off-road, across farmland, and survive a collision with a kangaroo, is a Rolls-Royce a good quality car? If you want a car that represents your status as a successful manager, is a Rolls-Royce a good quality car? The answers are no, no and no. It is important not to over-engineer the product, but to produce something that satisfies, even delights, the customer, but is good value for money to achieve the goals. Often something over-engineered will not delight the customer because it will not work.

FIVE-ELEMENT MODEL FOR QUALITY

Figure 10.1 shows a five-element model for delivering good quality. The components are:

- the quality of what? The product or the management processes?
- quality assurance and quality control
- attitudes.

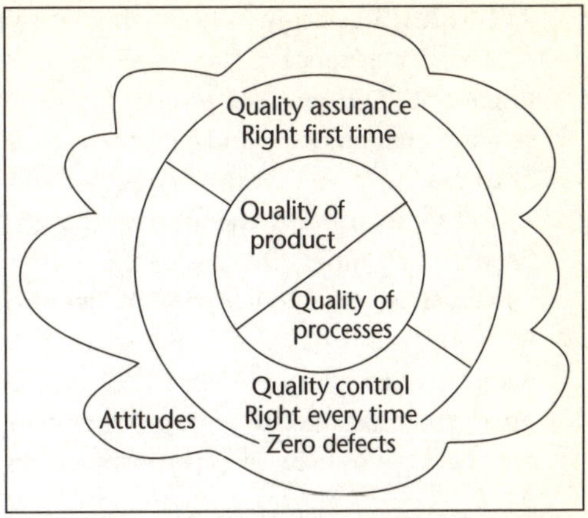

Figure 10.1 *A five-element model for quality in the context of projects*

1 **Quality of the product:** It is the web space delivered that meets the criteria of the previous section. It is the web space that provides the functionality, solves the problem and generates revenue. It is the quality of this product that is the ultimate arbiter of the quality of the project.
2 **Quality of the management process:** There is no doubt that following well-defined, previously proven successful ways of delivering the project increases the chance of successful outcome. Part of quality assurance of the product is following standard procedures for its delivery. However, the procedures must not be rigid rules, slavishly followed as more important than the quality of the product. What is important is that for this project, you design a process or procedure that converts inputs into desired customer outputs that meet their needs. That means taking the firm's standard procedures, which are flexible guidelines to best practice, and tailoring them to the needs of this project. Then at the end of the project, you should audit the process to determine how you did, and change the firm's standard procedures to encompass new learning.
3 **Quality assurance:** Quality assurance is about taking steps to ensure that the product as delivered, and the management process are both 'right first time'. The best result, in terms of time, cost and quality, will be obtained if the product is delivered correctly at the first attempt.
4 **Quality control:** However, human beings are fallible, and a last line of defence needs to be built in to check the product as it is delivered, and the management process as it is implemented. This is necessary to ensure that the product the project produced is 'right every time' with 'zero defects'.

   There is a major difference between projects and routine production in the balance between quality assurance and quality control. In the latter, millions of products are produced. The output can be sampled, every hundredth item destructively tested, and using the techniques of statistical process control you can determine when production is going off specification. With a project, you cannot destructively test every hundredth product. You only produce one. Wrong once means wrong every time. Destructively testing the one, is 100 per cent of production. This pushes the emphasis back on to quality assurance, making sure the one is right first time, right the only time, not relying on quality control. It also pushes the emphasis of quality control on to ensuring that the process is correct at the early stages, on to making sure the early components produced are right. If you get it right from the start, you find that a momentum of quality builds up.

5 **Attitudes:** Having the right attitude towards achieving success is an important element of achieving that success. Having all the stakeholders believe in the project from the start is an important contributor to project success. These attitudes are not solely the responsibility of senior management, middle management or junior management. They are the responsibility of all management, working together and doing their part for project success.

You sometimes get the attitude that 99.9 per cent correct is good enough. But when you have that attitude, 99.9 per cent becomes a target. But 99.9 per cent is not good enough, you must aim for 100 per cent. At Heathrow Airport, 99.9 per cent correct is one crash a day. For your heart, 99.9 per cent correct is it stops beating for one and a half minutes a day. I used to tell the story in Figure 10.2 as a joke, but one of my clients said it happened to them once. You must aim for your product being 100 per cent correct, to have **zero** defects. And it is the responsibility of everybody on the project team to achieve that.

A company ordered 10 000 electronic components from a Japanese supplier, and specified that there should be no more than 0.5 per cent faulty items. When the consignment arrived they opened the package and found a small box on top. They started testing the components, and found that they all seemed to be OK. They then wondered what was in the small box, and found there were more components – so they started testing those, and found that they were all faulty. They then realized the small box contained 0.5 per cent of the total consignment. The Japanese supplier had very carefully put the 0.5 per cent of faulty items they asked for in a separate box.

Figure 10.2 *Having the attitude that you will get it right and give the customer what they ask for*

ACHIEVING GOOD QUALITY

There are four processes of quality management resulting from combining the first four elements of the model:

Quality assurance of the product

Quality assurance is about preventative medicine. It is about trying to do things that increase the chance of a successful outcome, and that often means maximizing previous experience used in the delivery of the project's product. I cannot stress enough that the more you use previous experience, standards and qualified personnel, the more you increase the chance of success. The more you start with a blank sheet of paper, the more you increase the chance of failure. Ways of assuring the quality of the product are using:

A clear specification: The specification may not be perfect, but it should be clear. The diverse stakeholders, users, and project team must clearly understand what is intended so:

- they can buy into it
- there are no surprises
- the team know what to deliver.

Company standards: where the company has standards for this new, rapidly changing technology, they should be used. Company standards represent tried and tested ways of doing things, things that are known to work.

Historical lessons: as I have just said, maximizing previous experience increases the chance of success.

Experienced team: This keeps on appearing. It was a success factor (Chapter 5) and it will appear as a risk factor (Chapter 13). Using experienced team members increases the chance of success. This is problematic with projects managed from outside the IS department, in a climate of shortages of skilled people. If your team are not experienced, perhaps you need to ask them to thoroughly research what they are doing.

Design reviews: It is common in many industries to have an independent team conduct a high-level review of the design. You might say, 'What, don't you trust the team to do it right?' It is not about trust, but human psychology. It is known that people find it very difficult to recognize their own mistakes. Once people have formed a wrong diagnosis, perhaps based on faulty or incomplete information, they find it very difficult to change, even when there is now more than enough information to show the diagnosis is faulty. Recognize that you need to conduct independent reviews of the design; but these independent reviews should not be a line for line check of the design, that is failing to trust the design team to do their job well. It should just be a high-level overview of the design. This is another dilemma. Too little is wrong, too much is wrong.

Change control: Without change control you have no control. The specification may not be perfect, but it should be frozen between configuration reviews (see below). If it needs to be changed at a review, that should be subject to strict change control. Otherwise you will get scope creep. With the diverse numbers and types of stakeholders, users and project team members, everyone will be trying to make the web space reflect their wishes and needs. You must strictly control the changes, get them defined, agreed and get everyone to buy into them.

Quality control of the product

There is a standard four step process for quality control (Figure 10.3). As you do work to produce results, you:

1 plan what you want to achieve
2 monitor what you are achieving
3 compare that to your plan, and
4 take action to recover progress.

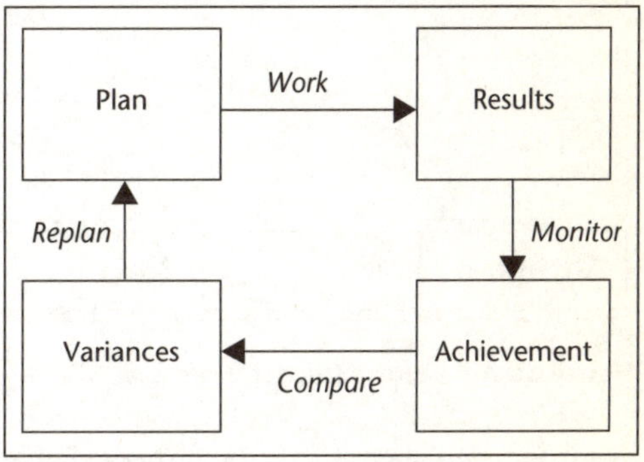

Figure 10.3 *Four step control cycle*

For a project this means you must have a clear idea of what will be delivered at each milestone, and the quality of that deliverable. You must also have an idea of what will be delivered at each activity and the quality of that. You also must know how these components will be configured into the final product. As you deliver each milestone or activity, you check the quality of the deliverable, as you configure the components, you check their quality, and you check the quality of the overall web space against the specification. You do not wait until you deliver the web space and then check it. You build up a momentum of quality from the first

Euro Projex

Milestone Scope Statement

Project:	Intranet Phase 1
Project Champion:	Martin Pacific
Project Manager:	Frances Seeker
Work area:	Design and development
Work area Manager:	Ian Simons
Milestone:	Personnel information pages designed
Milestone Manager:	Ian Simons
Milestone number and name	D3: When the personnel information pages have been designed and developed
Measure of achievement	The personnel manager has approved the pages for content, layout and ease of access The marketing manager has approved the pages as conforming to the desired corporate image Selected users have approved the pages for ease of access and use
Draft activity list	Specify page based on agreed contents Appoint external consultants Manage external consultants Design and develop page Obtain approval from personnel Obtain approval from marketing Obtain approval from selected users Make changes as necessary

Author:	IS	**Date:**	02 Sept 2003	**Issue:**	A

Figure 10.4 *Milestone scope statement for Milestone D3 of the intranet at TriMagi*

milestone, and even the first activity of the first milestone, to carry you through. That is a good attitude. The milestone scope statement, Figure 7.3, had a space for entering the quality measure for each Milestone. Figure 10.4 is the scope statement for Milestone D3 for the intranet at TriMagi, showing the quality measure for the milestones entered.

Quality assurance of the management process

I suggested above when discussing quality assurance of the product that you should have company standard processes for project management, perhaps based on Prince 2 (OGC, 2002) or ISO 10 006, tailored to the needs of this project and the web space it produces. The procedures also need to be configured as an integrated approved whole. (To read more about procedures for project management see Pharro, 2000.)

Quality control of the management process

This can be achieved through the application of health checks and audits (Wateridge, 2000), but they are beyond the scope of this book.

CONFIGURATION MANAGEMENT

We saw in Chapter 6 that a project is ultimately judged successful if it satisfies the purpose for which it was undertaken, it solves the problem (or exploits the opportunity) intended, and thereby delivers value to the owner and sponsor. To achieve this, the project's output, the web space delivered, needs to perform required functions, the functionality, as set out in the specification. Configuration management is the process by which the project team ensures the web space (and supporting PSO changes) has the required functionality. There may also be some uncertainty about the optimum process to deliver the desired output. In a development project, the main point of the project is to find the best method of delivering the output. In other projects, uncertainty in the design of the output can feed into uncertainty in the method of delivery. And in yet other projects, uncertainties in the background information, which can only be resolved as the project progresses, create uncertainty in the methods of project delivery. Configuration management is the process used to manage the resolution of these uncertainties. In my view, configuration management is one of the three or four core methodologies of project management. People talk about the triangle of time, cost and quality/functionality, the 'triple constraint' (see above). Well:

- Critical path analysis, bar charts and milestone tracker diagrams (Chapter 12) are the methods for managing the timescale.
- Earned value analysis (Chapter 11) is the method for managing the cost (and time on average).
- Configuration management is the method for managing quality and functionality (and, en passant, uncertainty in the process of delivery).
- The fourth core methodology is resource histograms and smoothing, to manage people and organization which Harold Kerzner (1999) puts at the centre of the triangle.

In this section, I describe configuration management. I describe four steps in the process, and give a simple example of its application. I then show the different emphasis of configuration management at the design and development stages. In the final section I give a brief overview of document management that various project management standards say should be used to support the process.

THE CONFIGURATION MANAGEMENT PROCESS

There are four steps in the configuration management process:

1 identify the configuration
2 review the configuration
3 control the configuration
4 record the configuration and changes.

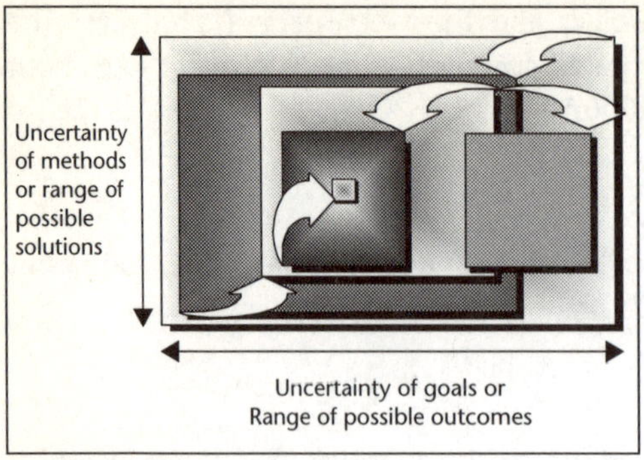

Figure 10.5 *The configuration management process*

I describe each step in the process below, but first I give an overview (Figure 10.5). The horizontal dimension represents the uncertainty in the project outcomes. The vertical dimension represents the uncertainty in the project delivery methods. At the start of the project, the team define both as well as they can. This is known as configuration identification. The configuration, as defined, is then agreed with all the stakeholders. (I said in Chapter 6 that it is important to agree success criteria with the stakeholders before the project starts, and then at all the configuration review points throughout. This is where it begins.) The configuration at its current level of definition is frozen (baselined), and work on the project discovery and design begins.

Through the discovery and design stages, understanding of project outcomes and work methods improves; uncertainty is reduced. At regular intervals, the team hold configuration reviews with the stakeholders, to agree the revised configuration. Note this is hopefully a process of reducing uncertainty, narrowing the range of potential outcomes and work methods. The new configuration lies within the scope of the old. The configuration should not need to change. However, it is necessary to agree the refined configuration with the stakeholders, to agree the options taken in narrowing the range. In this way, not only does the team agree the success criteria with the stakeholders before they start, they continue to agree them throughout the project.

The process is repeated, and (hopefully) the configuration narrowed to the eventual outcome. In the process, the team massage the expectations of the stakeholders, so that at the end they get what they are expecting, and expect what they get. However, the team also massage their own understanding of the requirements, so that what is delivered is what the stakeholders actually need (it is fit for purpose), not what the project team think they need. The final configuration should also incorporate the stakeholders' desires (wants) as much as possible, so that they are delighted with what they get.

At one review one of the stakeholders may say the configuration is not what they are expecting. If this happens, either the previous specification was wrong, or the work to reach this specification was wrong. Either the specification needs to be changed or the work needs to be repeated. Both are anathema to traditional project managers, but the team need to know whether it is more important that the outcomes should be fit for purpose, or delivered on time and cost. (This should have been decided before the project started.) Hopefully, if the mistake is discovered early enough it will cost very little (in time and money), to rectify. This step is known as configuration control.

Finally, if a mistake is discovered, the team need to be able to cycle back to a previous configuration, and start again from there. This will not be possible if the team have lost all memory of previous configurations. At each review, the team should record the current configuration, and the changes made since the last one, so that at any time they can go back and start again from there – this is known as status accounting. This last step is problematic on web-delivery projects. The technology is changing so fast, and the web design so dependent on the technology, that it may not be possible to cycle back to pick up a previous configuration, because that was dependent on now outdated technology. All I can say is that you need to do the best you can.

A case

East Lauderdale Management School (ELMS), is producing new course materials for its distance learning MBA. The materials are being converted from paper based to CD-ROM based, and revised in the process. Half the course materials are being written and published by a sister organization, East Lauderdale Academic Publishers (ELAP). For one course, Managing People, ELMS gives ELAP a specification, and ELAP goes off for nine months to produce a prototype for the course. They derive a contents list, and identify authors for each session. Each author writes a synopsis of their session, including text, and audio and video support. ELAP check and agree that. The authors write their text, which ELAP edits and publishes. They also produce the support audio and video material. They produce a prototype CD-ROM. They then show ELMS their handiwork and ELMS say 'No! That is not what we were expecting the course to look like.'

What has happened is that ELAP has interpreted Managing People as Personnel Management. The course is about industrial relations, employment law, selection and recruitment, appraisal and counselling. ELMS wanted about one-third of the course to be about that, but about a third on leadership and team building, and about a third on organization and work design. There is only one session on each of these latter two subjects. But too late! The money has been spent, and it would be too expensive to go back and rewrite the course. ELMS have to use an inappropriate course for five years until the next edition is published (not wrong, just the wrong balance).

But it would have been so easy to avoid. All ELAP had to do was produce a contents page with word count, and sign that off with ELMS. At that stage, with almost no money spent the mistake would have been found. Then, ELAP could have also asked ELMS to approve the synopsis for each session. For this simple project only two or three reviews would have been required. (Reviews do not serve the same purpose once design is finished and delivery stage of the project starts, see below.)

The process

So the steps in configuration management process are:

Identify the configuration: The configuration is identified through the breakdown structures. The outcomes are defined through a product breakdown structure (PBS), and the work methods through a work breakdown structure (WBS). We refine our understanding by breaking the PBS or WBS down to lower levels, and putting a clearer definition on the elements of the breakdown structures. Figure 10.6 shows how it would work for the course. ELMS tells ELAP that they want a course on Managing People, to cover personnel management, work and organizational design, and management, leadership and team building. ELMS and ELAP write an overall specification showing the broad content and structure of the course. ELAP now develop a contents page, showing that the course has three parts:

- personnel management
- work and organizational design
- management, leadership and team building.

They agree that with ELMS. ELAP then break each part into several sessions. Personnel management includes sessions on employment law, contracts of employment, recruitment and selection, appraisal, and so on. Work and organizational design has sessions on management theory, Taylor and work study, Fayol and organizational structures, the theory of the firm, and so

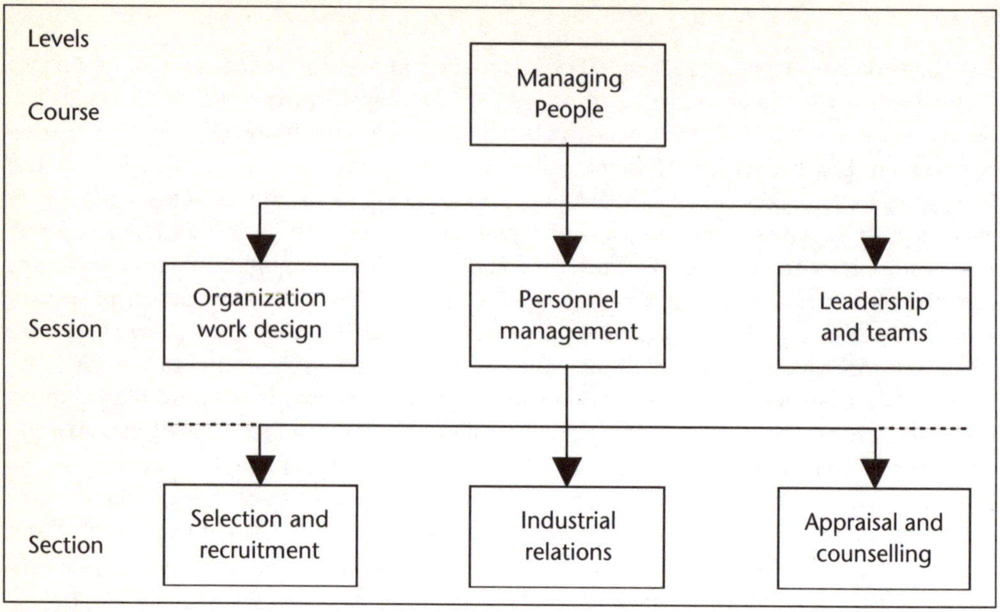

Figure 10.6 *Configuration identification for a course*

on. Management, leadership and team building has sessions on the role of the manager, leadership versus management, motivation, personal development, and so on. ELAP propose how many words each session should have. Perhaps the initial word count suggests a split between the three parts of 70 per cent, 15 per cent and 15 per cent respectively. ELMS and ELAP work together to redefine the balance as 50 per cent, 20 per cent and 30 per cent respectively. ELAP now commission authors, and ask them to write a synopsis of their sessions, including a list of the sections, indicating how the words will be split between them. ELMS now agree that.

At this point writing commences. The emphasis of configuration management changes, and the configuration should now become the baseline against which delivery of the course is judged. Once work starts the team should avoid any further changes as they are very expensive from this point on. The configuration is the baseline against which delivery of each section is judged, and then delivery of each session, and then delivery of the parts and the course.

This is not an ideal example of the development of the work breakdown structure. Writing words is writing words. However, what you can say is each author will have their own style of writing and their own approach to the session they are commissioned to do – and their own view of the sections in their session. Thus the PBS is not resolved until the WBS is resolved, and the WBS is not resolved until the project resources are assigned. In this simple example, the responsibility chart at each level defines the WBS and OBS, and so identifies the configuration of both.

Review the configuration: We saw above that ELMS and ELAP met three times to agree the current baseline:

1 they agreed the broad specification of the course
2 they agreed the specification, contents page and word count of each part
3 they agreed the sysnopsis, section titles and word division of each session.

ELMS needs to involve several stakeholders in these decisions. By agreeing each decision point, all are involved in agreeing the final configuration. There can be no surprises. The stakeholders include:

- the faculty who must approve content from a pedagogical perspective
- the course director who has to run the course, and who must approve use as a studying aid
- the marketing department, and perhaps people involved in developing company programmes, who must approve content from a client needs perspective
- the finance department who have to agree to the budget.

Control the configuration: As we have seen, it is possible that at one review, one or more of the stakeholders says that the revised configuration is not what they were expecting. In that case, one of two things has happened. Either the previous configuration was wrong, or the work to go from the previous configuration to this one was wrong.

With ELMS's distance learning course, at the second review the word count was unbalanced. ELAP had proposed that the split of words between the three parts be 70:15:15. This was an inappropriate interpretation of the specification as agreed at the first review, and after further work a split of 50:20:30 is agreed. Perhaps, at the second review, one of the authors who has been given 5000 words for her session says she needs 10000. Either the author needs to be told to go back to revise their design, or if her argument is persuasive, the previous specification needs to be changed and 10 000 words accepted, or perhaps 8000. We see that perhaps the work needs to be redone, or the specification changed, or perhaps some mixture of both.

Record the configuration and changes: At each review a record should be made of the current components of the breakdown structure, and the specification of each, and work methods to deliver them. This is the baseline against which to judge the configuration at the next review. Does the new configuration lie within the range of uncertainty at the previous review, in which case it can be accepted. Or has it fallen outside, in which case the specification needs to be changed or the work redone to pull it inside. If at a review the team find they cannot make the new configuration work, they may need to go back to the previous configuration and restart from there. Sometimes they need to cycle back two or three reviews. Thus a record needs to be kept of the configuration at each review. If the team get to a subsequent review and find they can't make the configuration work, but have lost the memory of previous configurations, then they are stuck up the creek without a paddle. It is very difficult to unpick the previous changes. Thus it's essential that the team record the configuration at each review, keeping careful account of the status. This is also the case if the team is developing several prototypes. They then need to record the configuration of each prototype, and how they relate.

CONFIGURATION MANAGEMENT AND THE PROJECT LIFE CYCLE

We began to see above that the emphasis of configuration management changes throughout the life cycle (Figure 10.7). This figure shows the four project stages:

1. discover
2. design
3. develop
4. deploy.

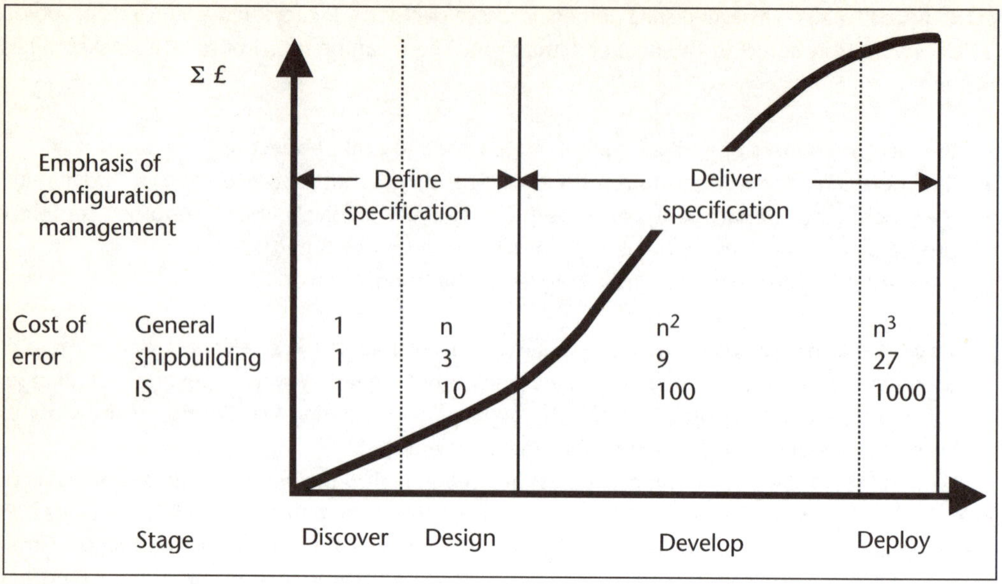

Figure 10.7 *Configuration management throughout the life cycle*

There is a rule of thumb in many industries, that for every £1 it costs to correct a mistake during the discovery stage, it costs £n in design, £n^2 in delivery and £n^3 in deployment. In shipbuilding the ratios are £1:£3:£9:£27. In IS/IT/ICT and web delivery the ratios are £1:£10:£100:£1000. The reason changes become more expensive is that the design becomes more integrated and changes in one area lead to changes in another. Once work begins, changes require increasing amounts of rework elsewhere and lead to delays in delivery, increasing costs further and reducing benefits. The consequence is that the project team should aim to make all the changes during discovery and design. Once delivery begins, as much as possible the design should be frozen and no more changes made. Certainly during delivery and deployment the team should no longer consider changes which are 'nice to have'. They may be improvements on the current configuration, but they should have been identified during discovery or design. Even if they are improvements, during delivery and deployment the cost of the changes cannot possibly be justified by the benefit from the improvement (if they are nice to have). This is especially the case on web projects, since, as identified in Chapter 2, the dynamic nature of HTML enabled post-completion changes to be made so easily as remodelling and maintenance work. Get it installed and working, reviewed, and then make the nice-to-have changes. The only changes that should be countenanced during delivery and deployment are show-stoppers, for example, the system will not work without this change. Then the benefit is infinite.

This means the emphasis of configuration management changes as the project moves from design to delivery. During discovery and design, when little money is being spent, the emphasis is on trying to agree the configuration with the stakeholders, and to come up with the optimum design. It is worthwhile during these stages to spend a bit longer getting the right answer.

During delivery and deployment, the emphasis is on using the configuration as agreed as a baseline to measure the delivery of the components of the system and then the overall system. Once the team start spending real money, they need to deliver the solution as quickly as possible to get the revenue stream to repay the money invested. I said above that once authors start writing words on ELMS's distance learning course, then the configuration should be used to judge the sections, sessions and parts produced. See also Figure 10.8.

> A Mediterranean country was developing its air traffic control system. The government wanted the new system in 18 months, so they gave the team writing the functional specification 2 weeks to complete their work. As a result, the people writing the specification could only do a desktop exercise. They had no time to talk to air traffic controllers, pilots, the airlines ... Because of flaws in the specification, delivery of the system took 5 years, incurring 3.5 years' extra interest charges before benefit was obtained. Better to have spent 2 months writing the functional specification and completed in 18 months from then.

Figure 10.8 *Spending more time on discovery to save time and cost later*

CONCLUDING REMARKS

Configuration management is one of the three or four core methodologies of project management. It is my view that it should be used on almost every project, unlike the other three – critical path analysis, earned value analysis and resource scheduling – which only need to be used on more complex projects.

Configuration management can be turned into a bureaucratic nightmare. However, on simple projects, the four steps can be applied in a simple fashion, providing powerful control of the project outcomes, refining understanding of the outcomes, and avoiding mistakes at an early stage, when they cost next to nothing to rectify. It is therefore one of the core methodologies that does so much to ensure that the project delivers its purpose and provides value to the sponsor, and yet it is so simple to apply.

CHAPTER

11 *Managing Cost*

In this chapter and the next, I deal with cost and time. I have deliberately placed the three chapters on quality, cost and time in that order. I think you need to know the quality of the product you will deliver, then you can work out how much it will cost to achieve that quality, then work out how long it will take from the rate at which you can consume resources. Many writers on project management, and project practitioners, talk about them in the reverse order, as if time is some inherent property of the project, and that determines the cost, and from that we can work out what quality we can achieve. In fact some authors even treat the management of cost and time as wholly separate subjects, quite separated in their books. Cost and time are two of the most significant resources. The other two are labour and materials, but these can be viewed as two components of cost, and will be treated as such here.

In this chapter I describe how to estimate the cost of a project, and forecast cost to complete during project delivery. First I describe the types of costs on a project. I reinforce the message that the estimate is not point-wise accurate, and how it increases in accuracy at successive stages of a project. Then I show how spreadsheets can be used to compile the cost estimate for a project, and briefly describe estimating methods and sources of data. I end by describing how to control costs by forecasting cost to completion using *earned value analysis*.

ESTIMATING COSTS

WHAT TO ESTIMATE

There are two main resources used on a project which generate cost, labour and materials, but there are others (Figure 11.1). These resources are commonly divided into direct and indirect, but a better way of viewing them is as work dependent and time dependent (although neither categorization is totally accurate). Figure 9.2 lists hard and soft resources. Figure 11.1 gives variants of the hard resources. The soft resources don't generate cost. But remember, all the people who provide resources are stakeholders. Most of these resources are self-explanatory, but some do need mentioning:

Type	*Resource*
Direct	Labour
Work dependent	Material
	Subcontract
	Plant and equipment
Indirect	Management
Time dependent	Temporary services
	Overhead
	Administration
	Fees
	Taxation
	Inflation
	Working capital
	Contingency

Figure 11.1 *Resources generating costs on a project*

- *Finance:* This is not on the list. It is a significant resource involving substantial cost and appears in Figure 9.2. However, it tends not to be estimated as a cost. It is allowed for in the discount factor when doing investment appraisal. (Investment appraisal is beyond the scope of this book. For further information on it see Turner, 1995, or Lock, 2000b.)

- *Subcontract:* Labour brought in from outside.
- *Plant and equipment:* Material used but not consumed in the project. It is things such as temporary computer facilities for programming, and so on, necessary to do the work, but left over at the end, available for use on other projects.
- *Inflation:* May or may not be included. Sometimes it too is included in the discount factor during investment appraisal. If you use real interest rates, then you should estimate both cost and revenue inclusive of inflation. However, if you estimate in terms of money in one year, exclusive of inflation, you should use interest rates net of inflation. Contractors bidding for a job either in the future, or which is expected to take several years, should either:
  (a) include inflation in their estimates, and then put a time limit on the validity of their bid, or
  (b) make their bid subject to an escalation clause.
- *Working capital:* There may be materials you need not for the creation of the web space, but for supporting its ongoing operation. The web space can be commissioned without that material, but can't be operated without it, or can't be operated for very long. That type of material is called working capital. It may be maintenance equipment or spare parts for computer equipment and peripherals. Or if the web space is to be used to advertise a product for sale, it will be an initial charge of the product for sale. For working capital you will typically allow three months operating and maintenance costs.
- *Contingency:* You may think contingency is an admission of failure. But it is essential to allow for the natural variability in our estimates. I want to discuss this important topic in more detail.

CONTINGENCY: ALLOWING FOR UNCERTAINTY

Figure 11.2 illustrates that natural variability in estimates leads to the need for contingency. It assumes a project comprising ten identical work packages. Each has an estimated out-turn of 100 units, so the project has an estimated out-turn of 1000 units. This is called the raw estimate for the project. Because of natural variability, each work package has a minimum possible out-turn of 70 units and a maximum of 150. Estimates are usually skewed to the worse like this. The amount an activity can turn out better is limited by the laws of physics, whereas the amount it

Work pack	*Minimum value*		*Likely*	*Expected*			*Maximum value*
Estimate	70		100	105			150
Likelihood	P00		P40	P60			P99
Project	*Theoretical Min*	*Min*	*Raw*	*Expected*	*Budget*	*Max*	*Theoretical Max*
Estimate	700	950	1000	1050	1100	1200	1500
Likelihood	P00	P01	P05	P60	P80	P99	P100

Figure 11.2 *The need for contingency*

can turn out worse is almost unlimited. But there is usually some maximum likely out-turn beyond which a greater figure would be viewed as an insurable risk rather than a business risk (Chapter 13). The estimate for each work package is:

$$100 \text{ units} \quad \begin{matrix} +50\% \\ -30\% \end{matrix}$$

Because the distribution is skewed, the chance of achieving the estimate is less than half. For a typical distribution, the chance of achieving the estimate may be say 40 per cent (indicated as the 'P40 estimate'). The estimate is the most likely out-turn, but there is only a 40 per cent chance of coming in less than that. For the ten packages of work, we expect four to have an out-turn between 70 and 100, and six between 100 and 150. Adding over the ten packages, this means the theoretical minimum out-turn for the project is 700 units and the theoretical maximum out-turn is 1500 units. But if you perform the Monte Carlo analysis (Chapter 13) you may find that for all intents and purposes, the minimum is say around 950 units and the maximum around 1200. The chance of a smaller or larger amount respectively is virtually zero. Also if you perform the Monte Carlo analysis, you will find the chance of achieving the raw estimate for the project is very small; I have suggested 5 per cent here.

Now if we are doing ten identical packages of work, and at the end we add up the out-turn across all ten and divide by ten, we get the average out-turn of the packages. Our prediction of what that average will be is the expected out-turn for each package. For the values I have suggested here, that expected value is likely to be around 105 units. It can be calculated using the 1:4:1 formula:

$$\text{Expected out-turn} = \frac{\text{minimum} + 4{*}\text{estimate} + \text{maximum}}{6}$$

I have also suggested that typically we have a 60 per cent chance of achieving the expected value. (Two of the ten packages will have an out-turn between 100 and 105, and four worse than 105.) Now, if the expected out-turn for each package is 105, the expected out-turn for the project is not 1000, but 1050. The expected out-turn is the sum of the expected out-turn for each work package. The difference between the raw estimate and the expected out-turn is contingency:

contingency = expected out-turn – raw estimate

We need contingency not for failure, but just because of the natural variability of the work. For this project the contingency is 5 per cent. It is normal to allow between 5 per cent and 10 per cent, depending on the risk.

I have also suggested that the chance of achieving the expected outcome for the project is 60 per cent. That means there is still a 40 per cent chance the project will do worse than this. What do we tell the owner we expect to spend? I have suggested the 80 per cent figure, which I have called the budget. The difference between the expected out-turn and the budget is project manager's reserve:

project manager's reserve = budget – expected out-turn

For this project the project manager's reserve is also 5 per cent. The project has an expected out-turn of 1050, with a likely minimum of 950 and a likely maximum of 1200. The predicted project cost is:

$$1050 \text{ units} \quad {}^{+15\%}_{-10\%}$$

You will notice that the expected out-turn for the project has less variability than the packages of work. If E is the error of the project estimates and e of the work package estimates, and there are N work packages, it can be shown that:

$$e/E = \sqrt{N}$$

The figures in Figure 11.2 conform to this.

Project estimate	*Project success rate*	*Rough calculation*	*Sum of activity estimates*	*Activity success rate*
Estimated	P05		Estimated	P40
Contingency	P60–P05	5–10 per cent of P05		
Expected	P60		Expected	P60
Project Manager's Reserve	P80–P60	5–10 per cent of P05		
Budget	P80			

Figure 11.3 *Estimates and contingencies*

Figure 11.3 summarizes the three different estimates for the project, and the two types of contingency. My view (and I am sometimes criticized for this), is that you should give the team doing the work the estimate for their package of work. Tell the teams above that the estimate for each package of work is 100. As project manager you expect the project to cost 1050 and tell the owner the maximum budgeted cost is 1100. People tell me that I should be 'honest' with the team and tell them the expected cost of their package of work is 105. But if you give the team that to work to, that will become the P40 value; the expected cost of each work package will now become 110 and of the project 1100, and you will need to increase the budget to 1150. I don't think it is being dishonest to say to the team that the estimate for their package is 100, that you expect them to come in under it some of the time, and over it some of the time, but that there is some contingency should they need it. You must also be clear with the owner about the difference between the raw estimate, the expected cost and the budget. Figure 11.4 describes the

A subsidiary of a larger company was developing a new system. This was a repeat of an implementation in another plant that had cost £10 million. The subsidiary thought they could do the repeat system 30 per cent cheaper, so set a tight target of £7 million. In the event it cost £8 million. The managing director of the subsidiary was sacked for being £1 million overspent, rather than praised for saving £2 million. It was right to set the team a tight target of £7 million to work to, but the MD should have expected the project to cost £7.7 million, and told the parent company to expect a cost of £8.5 million. Then he would have been praised when it came in at £8 million.

Figure 11.4 *Owner's expected out-turn versus raw estimate*

Stage	*Level of estimating*	*Accuracy at that level (%)*	*Accuracy of project (%)*	*Cost as % of project*	*Use of estimate*
Pre-project	Project	± 40	± 40	0.05	Budget
Discover	Work area	± 40	± 20	0.25	Proposal
Design	Milestone	± 40	± 10	1	Sanction
Develop	Activity	± 40	± 05	5	Control

Figure 11.5 *Estimating through the life cycle*

case of the managing director of a subsidiary company who lost his job because he didn't make the parent company understand the difference between the raw estimate and the budget.

ACCURACY OF THE ESTIMATE THROUGH THE LIFE CYCLE

We saw that the more work elements there are in our work breakdown structure, the more accurate is the estimate at the project level. Since you tend to break the project into greater and greater detail as you work through the project life cycle, the estimate at the project level becomes more and more accurate. Figure 11.5 gives typical examples of accuracy of the project estimates at successive stages of the project. This was the basis of the accuracy figures given in the fourth column of Figure 1.3. However, there is a price to pay. The cost of preparing the estimates becomes increasingly greater. Because the accuracy is proportional to the square root of the number of work elements, to double the accuracy requires four times as much planning effort as has been expended so far. This is captured in the fifth column of Figure 11.5. Thus as we progress through the project and get more information about it, our estimates become more accurate. It means we should not rush from having a germ of an idea to a detailed implementation plan in one step. We should work through the stages of discover, design and develop, committing resources to the next stage based on the estimates at this stage, but only committing resources to full implementation once we have properly appraised the project.

As a simple example, at the start of discovery you might estimate the project will cost £100 and give a return of £50 per year – two year payback. But at the levels of accuracy, the cost can range from £50 to £150, and the benefit from £25 to £75. Best case to best case (£50: £75) gives payback of about 8 months – wonderful business. Why are we waiting? Worst and worst (£150: £25) gives payback of 6 years – terrible business. Why do we even consider it?

But the mid case allows us to proceed to discovery. At the end of discovery our estimates have changed to £120 and £40 respectively; a three year payback which is still good business. The £120 now ranges from £100 to £140 and the £40 from £30 to £50. Best and best is still good business, and worst and worst still marginal.

But we are able to proceed to design based on the mid case. In design we confirm the £120 and the £40, but narrow the estimates further so that the cost is £110 to £130 and the return £35 to £45. Even the worst and worst (£130, £35) is just acceptable business, so we approve the project, get finance and proceed to development.

I want to reinforce the point that at the early stages you are not able to proceed directly to development, but you are able to commit resources to the next stage.

Figure 11.6 *Accuracy of the estimate through the life cycle*

> A pharmaceutical company was building a new plant. They asked a design and construction contractor to do design studies and write an invitation to tender (ITT) for the detailed design and construction of the plant, subject to a fixed-price, lump sum contract. The client said they would pay £0.5 million for the studies. The contractor said that to do them properly they needed £1 million, but the client was only willing to pay £0.5 million. The contractor did the studies and wrote the ITT which went to six companies, including themselves, for bidding. The original contractor won with a bid of £60 million. The plant cost £90 million, and the contractor claimed £25 million for things not properly specified in the ITT. The client said 'How can this be? You wrote the ITT.' The contractor replied that they had wanted twice as much time to do the design studies properly, but the client had not been willing to pay. So they had listed in the ITT all the things they had not been able to properly specify, and had repeated those in their bid. The client somewhat reluctantly paid up, but probably never used the contractor again.
>
> It is because of this sort of conflict of interest that the World Bank will not let the company that did the design studies bid for the final job on contracts they are paying for.

Figure 11.7 *Understanding the accuracy of your estimates*

There are several messages from this:

1 You cannot rush from initial estimates straight into development. You start with a coarse initial estimate which justifies assigning a very small number of resources to a discovery. That gives a more accurate estimate which you use to justify assigning more resources to design. That gives an even more accurate estimate, which you use to raise finance for the project and commit resources to development and then deployment (see Figure 11.6).
2 You need to understand that the estimates are not point-wise correct, but that they become more accurate the more effort you put into them, and the closer you get to development.
3 You pays your money and you takes your choice. Understand the level of accuracy of your early estimates (Figure 11.7). As a manager you also need to massage the expectations of more senior management. Unfortunately, initial estimates have a terrible habit of taking hold, and being treated as point-wise correct. So an early estimate of £60 million in a project like Figure 11.7 is treated as meaning £60.0 ± 0.1 million, and management is angry when it ends up costing £75 million, even though that is well within the initial accuracy.

METHODS OF ESTMATING

Estimating methods are either top-down, or bottom-up:

Bottom-up methods of estimating break the project down into its component parts, and work out the cost of each part from first principles. People who are used to estimating in a production engineering environment will often use this approach, because it is what is used there. However, this is a very expensive approach. You can afford this sort of estimating costs in production engineering because you are going to make the product millions of times, and so it is well worth shaving pennies from the cost, and spending pounds to do it. On a project you cannot afford it, because you are only going to make the product once. You can only afford to spend pennies to save pennies. You just have to be comfortable with the top-down methods of estimating, and to manage the residual risk that it leaves.

Top-down methods of estimating follow the pattern shown in Figure 11.5. As you work through the project, you break it down into lower and lower levels of breakdown, and in the process improve your understanding of the project and its product. We met this idea earlier when we discussed configuration management (Figure 10.7).

So how do you work out how much each element of work will cost? The main way is by comparison with similar projects. This requires you and your firm to keep a record of how much projects cost, to build up a record of typical costs. That is how it works; to be able to estimate future projects, you need to keep a record of how much projects cost in the past. But every project is unique, you say. Yes, but every project is made up of components, many of which are similar to things you have done before. If the project really is completely unique (a stranger or alien), and you have never done anything like it before, you are thrown back to using expensive, bottom-up estimating. For things which are repeats of projects done in the past, your estimating costs can be cheaper. (In Figure 11.7, the plant was novel, and so more time should have been spent on the design studies.) Similarly one work element may be totally novel, requiring bottom-up estimating, while the rest of the project is a repeat, and can be estimated top-down. That is why, in Chapter 7, I suggested that repeat work could be planned using rolling-wave planning, while novel work needed to be planned early on, and carried high residual risk.

The type of work element used in estimating varies depending on the type of project (Figure 1.12). In Chapter 1, I said type 1 and 2 projects would be planned using milestones representing components of the product, whereas type 3 and 4 projects would be planned using milestones that represent completion of life cycle stages. Thus you find that the former are estimated more through a product breakdown structure (Bill of materials), whereas the latter are planned using

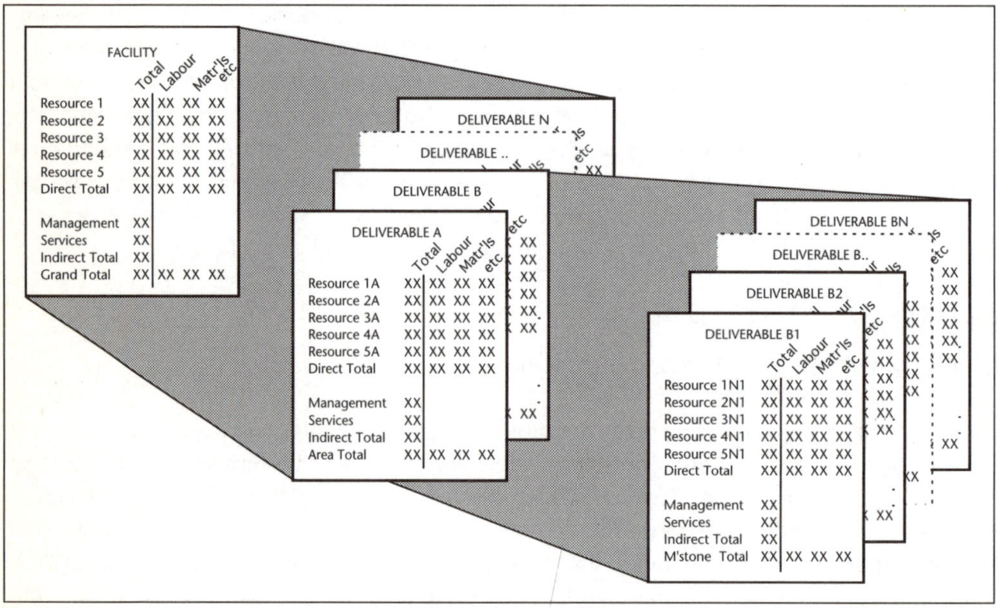

Figure 11.8 *The use of spreadsheets for estimating*

a work breakdown structure, representing life cycle stages. Web-delivery projects will have some components which are type 2, while others will be type 3 or 4.

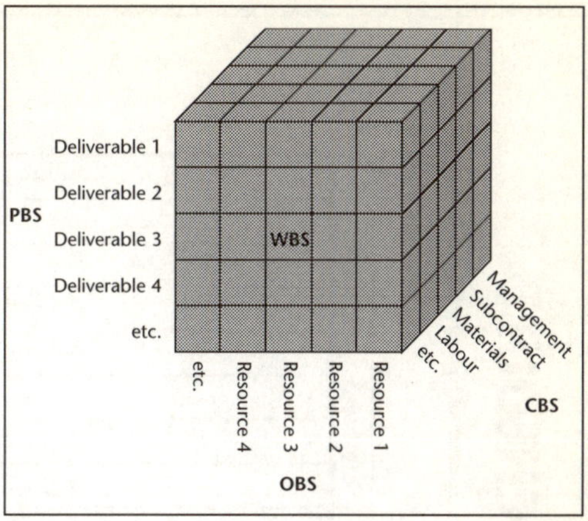

Figure 11.9 *The cost control cube*

THE USE OF SPREADSHEETS

Spreadsheets are very useful for building up the estimate. As you develop the estimate through the levels of breakdown, you can develop worksheets at lower levels to expand on the work elements in worksheets at higher levels previously developed (Figure 11.8). Using three-dimensional spreadsheets in this way, we build up what is commonly called the *cost control cube*, shown in Figure 11.9. The cost control cube is a three dimensional matrix made up of the cells in the responsibility chart, Figure 8.8 and the cost types in Figure 11.1. Each cell in the responsibility chart represents an element of work, and associated with each element is each cost type. Thus the total cost for the project can be built up as this three dimensional matrix of costs, through a cascade of spreadsheets as illustrated in Figure 11.8. On simple projects, this may be quite straightforward. The milestones may be the lowest level of breakdown, and associated with each milestone there may be only two cost types, labour and materials. On more complex projects there will be many more components in each dimension. But quite complex spreadsheet models can be built up with care. In 1985, I built up a model for a petrochemical plant costing £60 million, and in those days spreadsheets were not as refined as they are today. (In Figure 11.9, PBS is product breakdown structure, OBS is organization breakdown structure, CBS is cost breakdown structure, and WBS=PBSxOBS is work breakdown structure). The cost control cube becomes the tool to help control costs, as we shall see next.

Figure 11.10 is an estimate at activity level for Milestone D3 for the intranet at TriMagi, and Figure 11.11 is the estimate against the milestones at the project level.

CONTROLLING COST – EARNED VALUE ANALYSIS

As the project progresses, we need to monitor our performance, comparing what we are doing against what we planned. There is a very simple way of doing that by forecasting the cost at completion, and comparing that against the original estimate.

Forecast cost at completion = actual cost to date + forecast cost remaining

I will show you in Chapter 14 how to gather the data needed to calculate actual cost to date. For work completed there is no cost remaining. For work in progress, you need to estimate the percentage completion, and then extrapolate the forecast cost to complete that work. For work yet to start, you can either accept the original estimate, or consider whether you have new information that might make you change your mind. This can be done very easily by adding a few extra columns to your estimating spreadsheet, shown at the right in Figures 11.10 and 11.11.

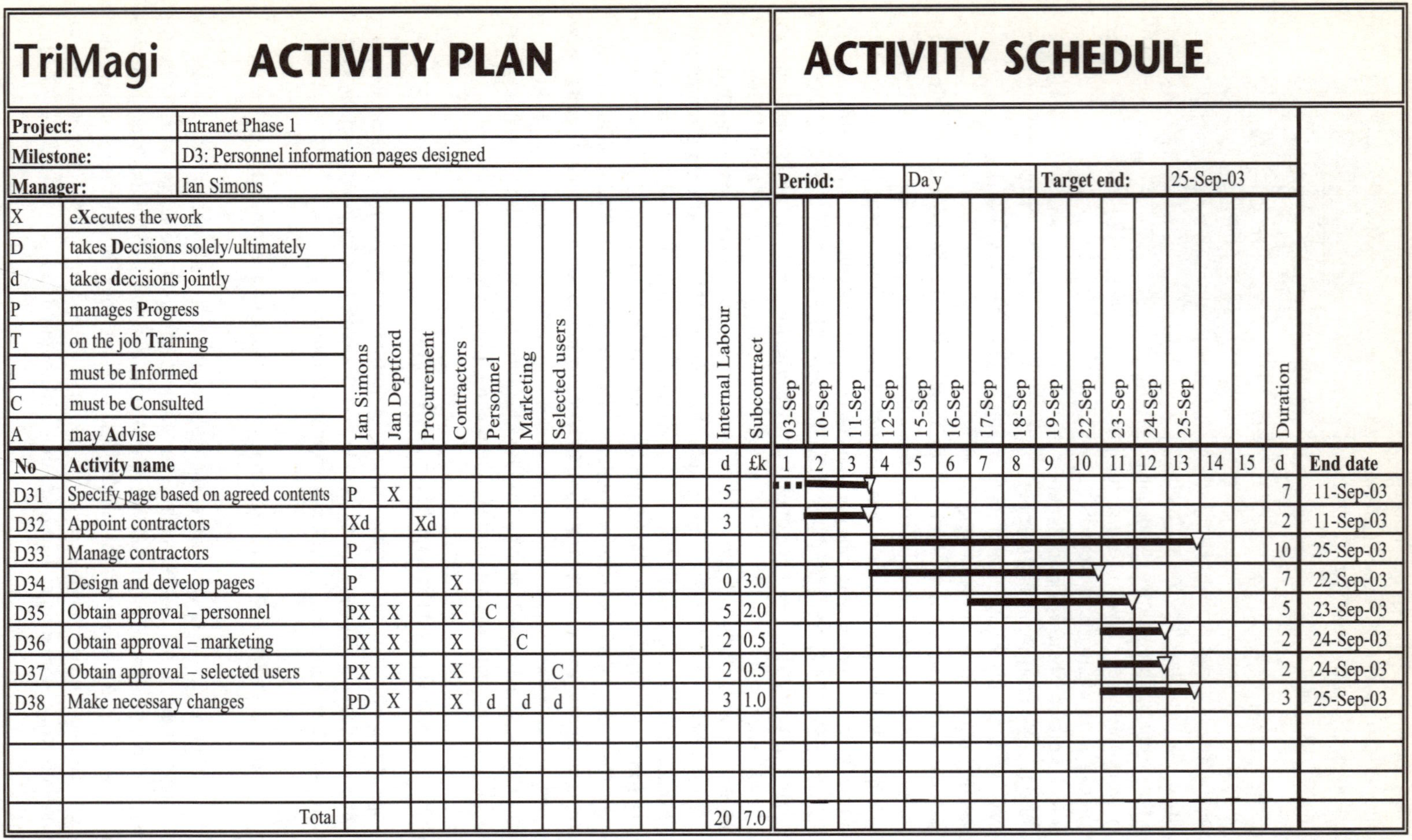

TriMagi **ACTIVITY PLAN** | **ACTIVITY SCHEDULE**

Project: Intranet Phase 1
Milestone: D3: Personnel information pages designed
Manager: Ian Simons

Period: Da y | **Target end:** 25-Sep-03

X	eXecutes the work
D	takes **D**ecisions solely/ultimately
d	takes **d**ecisions jointly
P	manages **P**rogress
T	on the job **T**raining
I	must be **I**nformed
C	must be **C**onsulted
A	may **A**dvise

No	Activity name	Ian Simons	Jan Deptford	Procurement	Contractors	Personnel	Marketing	Selected users	Internal Labour (d)	Subcontract (£k)	Duration (d)	End date
D31	Specify page based on agreed contents	P	X						5		7	11-Sep-03
D32	Appoint contractors	Xd		Xd					3		2	11-Sep-03
D33	Manage contractors	P									10	25-Sep-03
D34	Design and develop pages	P			X				0	3.0	7	22-Sep-03
D35	Obtain approval – personnel	PX	X		X	C			5	2.0	5	23-Sep-03
D36	Obtain approval – marketing	PX	X		X		C		2	0.5	2	24-Sep-03
D37	Obtain approval – selected users	PX	X		X			C	2	0.5	2	24-Sep-03
D38	Make necessary changes	PD	X		X	d	d	d	3	1.0	3	25-Sep-03
	Total								20	7.0		

Schedule days: 1 03-Sep, 2 10-Sep, 3 11-Sep, 4 12-Sep, 5 15-Sep, 6 16-Sep, 7 17-Sep, 8 18-Sep, 9 19-Sep, 10 22-Sep, 11 23-Sep, 12 24-Sep, 13 25-Sep, 14, 15

Figure 11.10 *Estimates at the activity level for Milestone D3 for the intranet at TriMagi*

TriMagi PROJECT ESTIMATES

Project: Intranet Phase 1
Project Champion: Martin Pacific
Project Manager: Frances Seeker

No	Milestone Name	Personnel Department	Marketing Department	IS Department	Users	Contractors	Project Manager	Project Team	Consultant	Procurement	0	0	Subcontract	Materials	Plant and equipment	Duration
		d	d	d	d	d	d	d	d	d	d	d	£k	£k	£k	d
M0	Ready to start															0
M1	Overall content and style agreed	2	2	2	2		2	7					1.5			7
H1	Hardware and data inventory			9									0.0			9
M2	Home and news pages agreed	2	2	5				5					1.0			5
M3	Document processing pages agreed	2	2	5				5					1.0			5
M4	Personnel information pages agreed	2	2	5				5					1.0			5
P1	Procedures rewritten	6											0.0			6
M5	Ready to design												0.0			5
H2	Hardware defined			12									0.0			12
P2	New jobs designed	8											0.0			8
H3	Hardware designed			5						2			0.0			5
D1	Home and news pages developed	2	2	14	2					1			7.0			12
D2	Document processing pages developed	2	2	14	2					1			7.0			12
D3	Personnel information pages developed	2	2	14	2					1			7.0			12
P3	New procedures piloted	5			5			10					0.0			10
D4	Site assembled			8				8					4.0		2.0	8
P4	Procedures optimized	5											0.0			5
D5	Site signed off			2				3					0.0			3
P5	Ready to deploy	1		1				3					0.0			3
H4	Hardware installed												8.5	5.0		17
H5	Data entered and migrated	8											8.5			17
P6	Site goes live			1				1					0.0			1
M6	Ready to proceed to Phase 2	2		2				2					0.0			2
Sum		49	14	99	13	0	2	49	0	5	0	0	46.5	5.0	2.0	169

PROGRESS REPORT

No	Milestone Name	Labour: Labour estimate	Labour: Actual	Labour: Estimated remaining	Labour: % Complete	Labour: Earned value	Labour: Calculated remaining	Costs: Cost total	Costs: Actual	Costs: Estimated remaining	Costs: % Complete	Costs: Earned value	Costs: Calculated remaining
		hrs	hrs	hrs	%	hrs	hrs	£	£	£	%	£	£
M0	Ready to start	0	0	0	1.0	0	0	0.0	0.0	0.0	1.0	0.0	0.0
M1	Overall content and style agreed	17	20	0	1.0	17	0	1.5	1.5	0.0	1.0	1.5	0.0
H1	Hardware and data inventory	9	8	0	1.0	9	0	0.0	0.0	0.0	1.0	0.0	0.0
M2	Home and news pages agreed	14	15	0	1.0	14	0	1.0	1.0	0.0	1.0	1.0	0.0
M3	Document processing pages agreed	14	15	0	1.0	14	0	1.0	1.0	0.0	1.0	1.0	0.0
M4	Personnel information pages agreed	14	15	0	1.0	14	0	1.0	1.0	0.0	1.0	1.0	0.0
P1	Procedures rewritten	6	10	0	1.0	6	0	0.0	0.0	0.0	1.0	0.0	0.0
M5	Ready to design	0	0	0	1.0	0	0	0.0	0.0	0.0	1.0	0.0	0.0
H2	Hardware defined	12	10	0	1.0	12	0	0.0	0.0	0.0	1.0	0.0	0.0
P2	New jobs designed	8	10	0	1.0	8	0	0.0	0.0	0.0	1.0	0.0	0.0
H3	Hardware designed	7	6	0	1.0	7	0	0.0	0.0	0.0	1.0	0.0	0.0
D1	Home and news pages developed	21	14	8	0.6	13	8	7.0	4.5	3.0	0.6	4.2	2.8
D2	Document processing pages developed	21	14	8	0.6	13	8	7.0	4.5	3.0	0.6	4.2	2.8
D3	Personnel information pages developed	21	14	8	0.6	13	8	7.0	4.5	3.0	0.6	4.2	2.8
P3	New procedures piloted	20	8	12	0.4	8	12	0.0	0.0	0.0	0.4	0.0	0.0
D4	Site assembled	16	0	16	0.0	0	16	6.0	0.0	6.0	0.0	0.0	6.0
P4	Procedures optimized	5	0	5	0.0	0	5	0.0	0.0	0.0	0.0	0.0	0.0
D5	Site signed off	5	0	5	0.0	0	5	0.0	0.0	0.0	0.0	0.0	0.0
P5	Ready to deploy	5	0	5	0.0	0	5	0.0	0.0	0.0	0.0	0.0	0.0
H4	Hardware installed	0	0	0	0.0	0	0	13.5	0.0	13.5	0.0	0.0	13.5
H5	Data entered and migrated	8	0	8	0.0	0	8	8.5	0.0	8.5	0.0	0.0	8.5
P6	Site goes live	2	0	2	0.0	0	2	0.0	0.0	0.0	0.0	0.0	0.0
M6	Ready to proceed to Phase 2	6		6	0.0	0	6	0.0	0.0	0.0	0.0	0.0	0.0
Sum		231	159	83		147	84	53.5	18.0	37.0		17.1	36.4
	Forecast Cost at Completion	242				231		55.0				53.5	

Figure 11.11: *Estimate and cost report at the milestone level for the intranet at TriMagi*

I worked with a contractor making electronic equipment for the military, where senior managers wanted to see just one number for cost control purposes in the monthly project reports, the forecast margin. At the start of the project the margin is calculated as

$$\text{margin} = \frac{\text{fixed price bid} - \text{estimate}}{\text{estimate}}$$

At any monthly report the forecast margin is calculated as:

$$\text{forecast margin} = \frac{\text{fixed price bid} - \text{forecast cost at completion}}{\text{forecast cost at completion}}$$

where the forecast cost at completion was calculated as above. Just one number for cost control. If that one number stayed within certain bands, the senior managers were happy.

This technique has been formalized into a system of project cost control called *earned value analysis* (Fleming and Kippleman, 2000). Most web projects are simple enough to apply the approach above, but I do briefly describe the more formal approach. Figure 10.3 shows a simple, four step control cycle. To control progress we need to:

- have a plan
- monitor the results we are achieving
- compare them to the plan to calculate variances
- take action to recover progress, or change the plan.

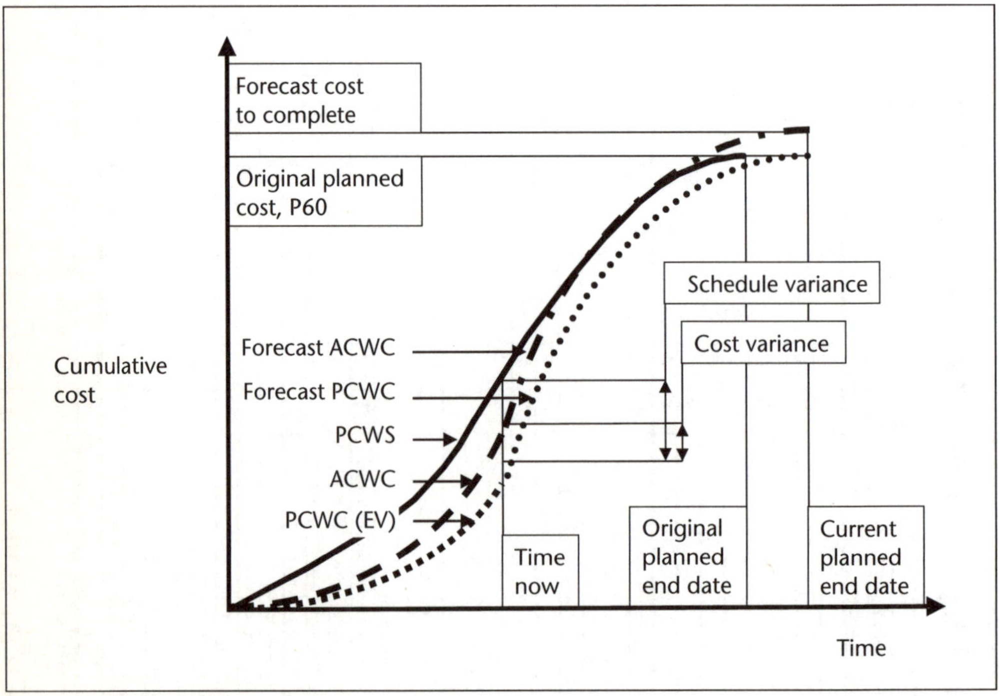

Figure 11.12 *Earned value analysis*

> I audited a company that had overspent disastrously on a contract overseas. The contract had been forecast to cost US$ 20 million: to hedge currency fluctuation, the company bought forward that amount at the start of the project. The Finance Director was monitoring spend of the US dollars against the forecast. The spend of dollars was following just behind the forecast spend so the Finance Director was happy – until about 90 per cent of the dollars were spent. At this stage the forecast showed the rate of spend trailing off (following an S-curve), but the actual spend continued at the previous rate. So the Finance Director asked the project manager how much work was left to do, and the project manager said he was HALF finished! The project ended up being 100 per cent overspent, and 100 per cent late.

Figure 11.13 *Misleading cost control*

A common mistake people make when monitoring cost is that they estimate the costs, as above. They then schedule the work, and so work out when they expect the money to be spent. This is known as the planned cost of work scheduled (PCWS), the solid line in Figure 11.12. They then monitor how much they are actually spending. This is called the actual cost of work complete (ACWC), the dashed line in Figure 11.12. If ACWC is less than PCWS (the dashed line is below the solid line), they assume they are under budget. However, this is a fallacy. The comparison of ACWC and PCWS tells us nothing (see Figure 11.13). If the dashed line is below the solid line we don't know whether the project is:

- ahead of schedule and very underspent
- behind schedule and slightly underspent or slightly overspent
- way behind schedule and very overspent.

To control cost properly we need a measure of progress compared to the plan. This is called the planned cost of work complete (PCWC), the dotted line in Figure 11.12. It is how much we had planned to spend on the work we have actually done, and is sometimes called the *earned value.* The comparison of PCWC and ACWC tells us if we are over- or underspent on the work we have done. The comparison of PCWC and PCWS tells us if we are ahead or behind schedule. Both ACWC and PCWC can be calculated easily using the cost control cube or spreadsheets suggested above. In the cost model, all you need to do is mark up how much has been spent against each element of work, and the percentage completion of each element of work and the spreadsheet will automatically calculate both ACWC and PCWC. By marking up the planned percentage completion of each element of work you can calculate PCWS. From PCWS, ACWC and PCWC, we can calculate the following:

Cost variance:	CV	=	ACWC – PCWC
Cost variance per cent:	CV%	=	CV/PCWC
Schedule variance:	SV	=	PCWS – PCWC
Schedule variance per cent:	SV%	=	SV/PCWS
Forecast cost at completion:	FCC	=	P60 + CV
or	FCC	=	P60 * (1 + CV%)

In Figure 11.12 and the equations above, I have shown the planned cost at completion as the P60 value. If that is the case both PCWS and PCWC should be calculated inclusive of contingency. You may be giving the team the values exclusive of contingency (P40 at the work package level) to work to, but you should be monitoring costs using the values inclusive of contingency. This is what you as project manager expect to spend. You could do the calculations based on the figures exclusive of contingency, the raw estimates, in which case you would change the estimate in the figure and equations to P05.

In many books you will see PCWC and PCWS defined as the budgeted cost of work scheduled (BCWS), and budgeted cost of work complete (BCWC). In that case you should do the calculation based on the P80 values. My view is this is wrong, and BCWS and BCWP are used by people who do not understand the difference between estimated, expected and budgeted cost, which unfortunately is a very large number of (influential) people. (In the 1980s, the B in BCWS and BCWC stood for 'baselined', ie the expected or P60 value. It was mistakenly changed to 'budgeted' in an influential publication in the 1990s.)

Some people calculate PCWC differently. Rather than adding up the planned cost of work complete, they add up the planned cost of work not complete (PCWNC), and subtract that from the estimate. So:

PCWC = P60 – PCWNC

You might (correctly) say that gives you the same answer as above. However, we are now able to adjust PCWNC, taking account of any known variances, and savings we hope we might make. This is called 'forward-looking control' (see Chapter 14). It is the future we can control, not the past. There is nothing we can do to change PCWC, but there is something we can do to change PCWNC, so we focus on that. That takes us back to the formula I started this section with.

Forecast cost at completion:	FCC	=	P60 + CV
			P60 + ACWC – PCWC
			P60 +ACWC – P60 + PCWNC
			ACWC + PCWNC

Figure 11.14 contains a simple example of the application of earned value analysis. The project consists of five work packages, each expected to cost 100 units. On the middle day of the project, A and B are expected to be finished, C half finished, and D and E not started. The actual amounts spent are shown in the third column. That tells you nothing until you know the percentage completion of each work package. A is clearly overspent, but by how much? B is underspent so far, but is it finished or still in progress? D shouldn't have started, but what has been achieved for the 20 units spent? We need to know the percentage completion for each package of work. Note that this could be calculated by repeating the process at the next level of work breakdown based on the activities making up the work package (except for A and B which are finished). In Figure 11.14, I first calculate forecast cost at completion (FCC) using percentage complete to calculate PCWC. I then use percentages not complete to calculate PCWNC. I then re-estimate PCWNC by extrapolating progress to date on C and D and by assuming E is the same as D.

Figure 11.11 contains a cost report for the intranet at TriMagi made on the 19 September, calculating the forecast of labour and cost to complete using both methods just described.

Work pack	*Original estimate*	*PCWS*	*ACWC*	*% complete*	*PCWC*	*% not complete*	*PCWNC*	*PCWNC re-estimated*
A	100	100	120	100	100	0	0	0
B	100	100	90	100	100	0	0	0
C	100	50	60	40	40	60	60	90
D	100	0	20	30	30	70	70	50
E	100	0	0	0	0	100	100	70
Sum	500	250	290		270		230	210

Cost variance	=	290	–	270	=	20 (UF)	Note 1
Cost variance %	=	20	/	270	=	7.5%	
Schedule variance	=	250	–	270	=	20 (F)	Note 1
Schedule variance %	=	20	/	250	=	8%	
Forecast cost to complete 1	=	500	+	20	=	520	Note 2
Forecast cost to complete 2	=	500	*	(1 + 7.5%)	=	537	
Forecast cost to complete 3	=	290	+	230	=	520	Note 2
Forecast cost to complete 4	=	290	+	210	=	500	Note 3

Notes:

1 UF means unfavourable, we are 20 units overspent. F means favourable, we are 8 per cent ahead of schedule (if that is favourable).

2 It is necessarily the case that calculations 1 and 3 give the same answer. Calculation 4 would give the same answer as 2 if we applied the same percentage overspend throughout.

3. Using the information we have we find we can recover the original expected cost.

Figure 11.14 *Worked example of earned value analysis*

CONCLUDING REMARKS

There is a lot of discussion in the project management press about the place of earned value analysis. I get the impression that a lot of project managers are innumerate. I also think that a lot of project managers and project planners overcomplicate things. There is also a tendency to use too much jargon. To that end above I was nervous about using the terms PCWS, and so on. and considered using simpler symbols. But I decided to stick with the normal terminology. If kept simple, as suggested above, earned value analysis is a powerful technique which can give a concise view of the time and schedule progress on the project. If plotted as in Figure 11.12, it is highly visual; and if presented as a single figure, as the predicted percentage profit as with the contracting company mentioned above, it can be tracked very easily. There are columns in Figures 11.10 to 11.11 to perform the calculations.

CHAPTER **12** *Managing Time*

Web projects are delivered against short time horizons. Seemingly small delays can be significant in terms of the total duration of the project and managing the time is critical. I introduce two simple tools for doing that:

1 The bar chart, which is a very visual way of telling the team when you want them to do the work and can also be used for tracking progress
2 The milestone tracker diagram, a tool just for tracking progress, but one which makes progress glaringly obvious.

To schedule the project, we need to determine how long each milestone will take. Some may view that as a mathematical exercise. However, in the next section I try to show it is a heuristic exercise, relying on judgement rather than mathematics. I assume most web-delivery projects are simple enough to determine the schedule manually, by drawing the bar chart, first at the milestone level and then at the activity level. It is only in complex engineering construction projects that you need to use computer-based analysis to determine the schedule. You may well use a computer system to draw the schedule, but you do not need to use network analysis to calculate it. Thus network analysis is not considered in this book. If you want to read about it you can read Turner (1999) or Lock (2000a).

ESTIMATING DURATIONS

In order to schedule the project we need to work out the expected duration of each activity. There is a simple formula for estimating the duration of a work element:

$$\text{Duration} = \frac{\text{Effort}}{\text{Number of people involved}}$$

So if the job is 100 days effort, 1 person takes 100 days, 2 people 50 days, and so on. That was what we were taught in primary school. However, there are a number of problems with this formula:

Interference: The first is a problem of interference. Five people may take 20 days, but 10 people take 12 days and 20 people take 7 days. As you try to load the job, people interfere with each other, and the total amount of effort begins to increase.

Internal logic: The job may well be 100 days effort, 20 days for an analyst, 50 days for a programmer and 30 days for a tester, and you may have three people, an analyst, a programmer and a tester. But they have to work in sequence, and so the job takes 100 days, not 33.

Waiting time: The job may be 100 days of effort, and there is one person to do it. But half way through, he or she has to wait for another 100 days to watch the paint dry or the grass grow.

Lost time: This is time spent away from the coal face. How many hours work do you think a person does a year? Fifty-two weeks x 5 days per week x 8 hours per day is 2040 hours per year? But people do not work for 52 by 5 by 8. There is lost time through holidays, sickness, courses, and group meetings, and so on. And on a given day, you can expect at most 6 hours work out of somebody. Typically somebody works between 180 and 220 days per year. Thus we expect about 1200 hours out of a person in a year.

You need to be aware of this when estimating duration, and whether you allow for it depends on what time scale you are estimating. If you talk about hours work, you probably mean time at the coal face working. So 1200 hours is one year's work for one person, whereas 12 months work will also mean one year's work for one person. In the middle, if you are talking about days or weeks of work, you need to be aware of whether you are talking about time at the coal face, or elapsed time assuming normal working patterns. If you are talking about time at the coal face, one year is 200 days or 40 weeks. If you are talking about elapsed time, one year is 260 days or 52 weeks.

A related problem is that most of the work on web-delivery projects is professional or knowledge work. On a building site, if the bricklayer you had yesterday is ill, you expect the contractor providing bricklayers to provide another bricklayer today, and the replacement will carry on from where the other left off. But that is not possible with knowledge work, a replacement cannot continue with the work being done yesterday. Professional or knowledge work is far more exposed to absences.

Communication: Finally there is loss through communication between team members. It is widely accepted that the optimum team size is about three people. Three people seem to support and motivate each other, and so work at a higher rate than one or two people on their own. But as the team grows, there is loss through communication between team members. The work done is proportional to the number of team members, whereas the number of communication channels is proportional to the number of team members squared. The complexity increases as the number of people increases, and the amount of work produced per team member reduces. The maximum amount of work is done with a team of about 12 people. Beyond that, new team members do negative work, reducing the output of the team. (If a thirteenth person joins the team the increase in the amount of communication is greater than the work done by the new person.) Thus you get the highest productivity with three people, and the most work with 12 people. If your team is bigger, it is best to break it into hunting packs of three, with central coordination.

All of this means that estimating duration is not a comfortable, mathematical exercise, but a heuristic, qualitative assessment taking account of a number of factors. Project management is not a mathematical science, but a human management exercise, a social science.

MANAGING TIME WITH BAR CHARTS

The simplest way of representing the schedule is through a list of activities, with start and finish dates listed against each. This can be simply used for assigning work to people. It is sometimes called a work-to list. A team member is given a list of activities to complete with:

- the expected start date
- the expected finish date
- the expected work effort.

A very visual way of representing the schedule is the use of bar charts. A bar is drawn to represent the planned start and finish of each work element and its duration. The responsibility chart, Figure 8.8, has space to draw the schedule as a bar chart, at the milestone level and activity level respectively. Figure 12.1a shows a stylized bar chart. It shows some activities as being critical and some as non-critical. Critical activities are ones, which if delayed, will delay the project. With a critical activity, it cannot start any earlier because it is dependent on other activities being completed, some of which are themselves critical. And if it starts any later, it will delay activities which are dependent on it, some of which are also critical, and so will delay the project. Every critical activity is dependent on at least one critical activity, and has at least one critical activity dependent on it (except the start and finish activities on the so-called critical path, obviously). This sequence of critical activities is called the critical path. The bar chart represents it visually. The default colours used by Microsoft Project™ are red for critical activities and blue for non-critical activities.

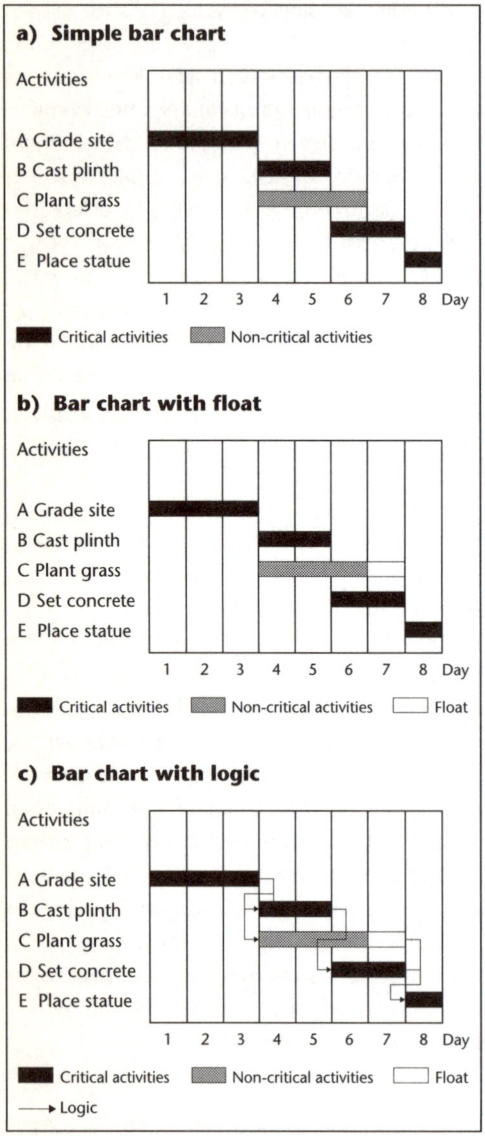

Figure 12.1 *The use of bar charts*

It can be valuable to show the critical path, to show where management effort must be focused. There is however a slight danger. There are usually other paths in a project that are just subcritical. The risk is that you may focus on THE critical path, but it is another, almost critical path that delays the project. Monte Carlo analysis, mentioned in Chapter 13, can help identify the near critical paths.

All non-critical activities have float, the amount they can be delayed before delaying the project. Figure 12.1b shows float. I don't believe in showing float to the team, for the same reason that I don't believe in telling them the expected cost of work (Chapter 11), and I get criticized for the same reason. I believe work expands to fill the time available, so if you tell the team they should start on Day A and finish on Day B, but by the way they can go as late as Day C, they will finish on

Day C. You should tell them to start on Day A and finish on Day B, but also tell them the activity is non-critical so if they need extra time they can negotiate it, especially if they have a priority problem with a critical activity. Microsoft Project™ does not show float in the default view.

Figure 12.1c is the bar chart with logic overlaid. If I don't believe in float being shown, I certainly don't believe in logic being shown. Microsoft Project™ has two views. The view without float is to show to the team when to start and finish their work. The view with logic is for the project manager and project controllers to use during planning and control, to conduct 'what-if' analysis. As they try to massage the project to reduce the initial duration, or recover delays later, they need to know what is and is not possible. The logic is an invaluable guidance. But when the work is given to the team to do, you just tell them when you would like them to start and finish each activity.

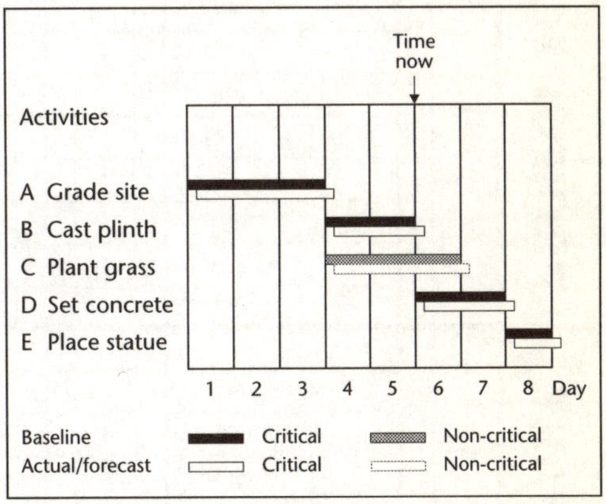

Figure 12.2 *Tracked bar chart*

Figure 12.2 shows a tracked bar chart. Actual progress and revised dates are drawn under the original bar chart. Time now is the date of the report. The original plan is retained as the baseline, against which progress is tracked, and is shown as solid bars. The outline bars are actual and predicted dates. Dates in the past are actual, dates in the future are predicted based on progress to date. Some people draw actual dates in one colour and the predicted dates in another. Microsoft Project™ with irrefutable logic, says dates in the past are actual and those in the future are forecast, so uses the same colour for each. In the default view, it draws them both as outline bars, with red for critical and blue for non-critical. A previous critical activity may have become non-critical, and vice versa, as other activities are delayed or speed up. Their current status is shown, not the baseline status. It is important to track progress against the baseline. If you just draw the actual and predicted dates, you lose control, as you are not judging progress against the original plan, but against what you drew the last time you slipped the plan. The original plan gives you the baseline against which to track progress. But equally you should not hold the team to the original plan if it is now unachievable. To say to team members they should start late (because an earlier activity is finishing late) but you want them to finish on time, can be demotivating. Tight targets are motivating, impossible targets demotivating. Tracked bar charts are a powerful control tool, but not quite as powerful as milestone tracker diagrams, described next.

DETERMINING THE SCHEDULE

How do you determine the schedule? The complex way is to use critical path analysis, but I don't think that is necessary on most web projects, and so it is not covered in this book. If you are interested in reading about it, it is described elsewhere by me (Turner, 1999) and Dennis Lock (2000a).

But on the vast majority of projects, anything but the most complex engineering construction projects, the schedule can be drawn by hand. The schedule is drawn first at the milestone level,

TriMagi PROJECT RESPONSIBILITY CHART

Project:	Intranet Phase 1
Project Champion:	Martin Pacific
Project Manager:	Frances Seeker

X	eXecutes the work
D	takes **D**ecisions solely/ultimately
d	takes **d**ecisions jointly
P	manages **P**rogress
T	on the job **T**raining
I	must be **I**nformed
C	must be **C**onsulted
A	may **A**dvise

No	**Milestone Name**	Manging Director	Board	Personnel Manager	Personnel Department	Marketing Manager	Marketing Department	IS Manager	IS Department	Users	Contractors	Project Manager	Project team	Consultant	Procurement		
M0	Ready to start	D	d	I		I		I				d					
M1	Overall content and style agreed		D	d	C	d	C	d	C	C		X	X	T			
H1	Hardware and data inventory							P	X								
M2	Home and news pages agreed			D	C	d	C	d	X				X	T			
M3	Document processing pages agreed			D	C			d	X				X	T			
M4	Personnel information pages agreed			D	C			d	X				X	T			
P1	Procedures rewritten			P	X												
M5	Ready to design		D	d		d		d				d					
H2	Hardware defined							P	X								
P2	New jobs designed			P	X												
H3	Hardware designed							PD	X						Xd		
D1	Home and news pages developed			d	C	d	C	Pd	X	C	X			A	Xd		
D2	Document processing pages developed			d	C	d	C	Pd	X	C	X			A	Xd		
D3	Personnel information pages developed			d	C	d	C	Pd	X	C	X			A	Xd		
P3	New procedures piloted			I	C					C			X				
D4	Site assembled							PD	X		X		X				
P4	Procedures optimized			P	X												
D5	Site signed off		I	I		I		D	X			d	X				
P5	Ready to deploy		D	d	X	d		d	X			d	X				
H4	Hardware installed							Pd			X						
H5	Data entered and migrated			C	C			Pd			X						
P6	Site goes live		I	I		I		D	X			d	X				
M6	Ready to proceed to Phase 2		D	d	X	d		d	X			d	X				

PROJECT SCHEDULE

Period:	Week ending	**Target end:**	30-Jun-02

No	22-Aug	29-Aug	05-Sep	12-Sep	19-Sep	26-Sep	03-Oct	10-Oct	17-Oct	24-Oct	31-Oct	07-Nov	14-Nov	21-Nov	28-Nov	Duration	
	1	2	3	4	5	6	7	8	9	10	11	12	13	14	15	d	**End date**
M0																	18 Aug
M1																7	26 Aug
H1																9	28 Aug
M2																5	02 Sep
M3																5	02 Sep
M4																5	02 Sep
P1																6	03 Sep
M5																5	09 Sep
H2																12	15 Sep
P2																8	15 Sep
H3																5	22 Sep
D1																12	25 Sep
D2																12	25 Sep
D3																12	25 Sep
P3																10	29 Sep
D4																8	07 Oct
P4																5	14 Oct
D5																3	17 Oct
P5																3	17 Oct
H4																17	11 Nov
H5																17	11 Nov
P6																1	12 Nov
M6																2	14 Nov

Time now

Figure 12.3 *Responsibility chart at the project level for the intranet at TriMagi with report up to 19 September*

TriMagi ACTIVITY PLAN

Project:	Intranet Phase 1
Milestone:	D3: Personnel information pages designed
Manager:	Ian Simons

X	eXecutes the work
D	takes **D**ecisions solely/ultimately
d	takes **d**ecisions jointly
P	manages **P**rogress
T	on the job **T**raining
I	must be **I**nformed
C	must be **C**onsulted
A	may **A**dvise

No	Activity name	Ian Simons	Jan Deptford	Procurement	Contractors	Personnel	Marketing	Selected users	Internal labour	Subcontract
									d	£k
D31	Specify page based on agreed contents	P	X						5	
D32	Appoint contractors	Xd		Xd					3	
D33	Manage contractors	P								
D34	Design and develop pages	P			X				0	3.0
D35	Obtain approval – personnel	PX	X		X	C			5	2.0
D36	Obtain approval – marketing	PX	X		X		C		2	0.5
D37	Obtain approval – selected users	PX	X		X			C	2	0.5
D38	Make necessary changes	PD	X		X	d	d	d	3	1.0
	Total								20	7.0

ACTIVITY SCHEDULE

Period:	Da y	**Target end:**	25-Sep-03

No	03-Sep	10-Sep	11-Sep	12-Sep	15-Sep	16-Sep	17-Sep	18-Sep	19-Sep	22-Sep	23-Sep	24-Sep	25-Sep			Duration	
	1	2	3	4	5	6	7	8	9	10	11	12	13	14	15	d	**End date**
D31																7	11-Sep-03
D32																2	11-Sep-03
D33																10	25-Sep-03
D34																7	22-Sep-03
D35																5	23-Sep-03
D36																2	24-Sep-03
D37																2	24-Sep-03
D38																3	25-Sep-03

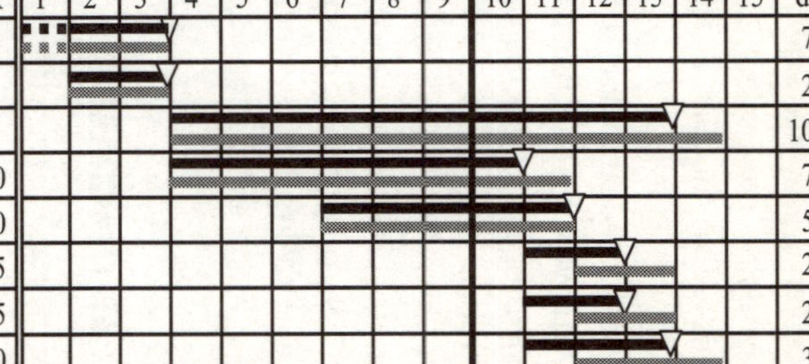

Time now

Figure 12.4 *Activity plan for Milestone D3 from the intranet at TriMagi with report up to 19 September* against the 20 or so milestones. You know the start date, today. You usually know the end date; that is imposed by external factors or market conditions. You calculate the duration of each work package as described above. Then you just draw the bars in the time available. Your first attempt may show the project taking longer than you have. But if it the overrun is less than about 20 per cent of the duration you can usually massage the project down. If the overrun is greater you need to find another way of doing the project. Next you repeat the process at the activity level, scheduling the activities within the plan at the milestone level. This may happen on a rolling-wave basis.

Figure 12.3 is Figure 8.8 repeated and shows the responsibility chart at the milestone level for the intranet at TriMagi with the bar charts drawn. Figure 12.4 is Figure 8.9 repeated showing the activity plan for Milestone D3 with the bar charts drawn. Both also have progress reports made on the 19 September.

Sometimes (usually), you will see bar charts called *Gantt charts*, named after Henry Gantt who pioneered their use for production planning in the early twentieth century. It is amusing that project managers who hate production managers name one of their key tools after a production manager. But I think that calling bar charts Gantt charts is needless jargon, adopted in a vain attempt to make project management sound like rocket science, so I stick with calling them bar charts here.

MILESTONE TRACKER DIAGRAMS

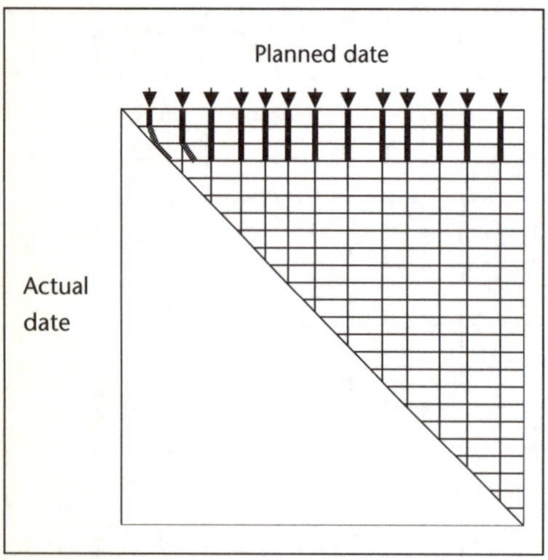

Figure 12.5 *Milestone tracker diagram*

Milestone tracker diagrams, Figure 12.5, are another powerful tool for monitoring time. You will often hear them called milestone slip diagrams. I think this is a negative attitude – you assume the milestones are going to slip. Milestone tracker diagrams make it almost impossible to lie. What you are trying to avoid is the common syndrome where the team track the last milestone only, and for the first 11 months of a 12 month project it is on time, and then suddenly, two weeks from the end, it is 12 months late.

In the diagram the horizontal dimension represents the planned date. The vertical dimension is the date of the report. Along the top abscissa, the milestones are lined at their original planned date. At each subsequent reporting date, their current planned date is shown. If the project goes exactly to schedule, the milestone planned dates will appear as vertical lines going down until they cut the diagonal, when they will stop. However, if things are not going according to plan, it becomes almost impossible to lie about actual progress.

- Say the first milestone starts to slip. You will ask the team, or the project manager, why aren't subsequent milestones slipping. If they say the first milestone is non-critical, asked to be convinced, and ask why it was chosen. Not all milestones are critical, but ask to be convinced.

- When the first milestone almost hits the diagonal, and then starts being shown at every report as slipping down the diagonal and being 99 per cent complete, you will be asking just how complete is it.
- If at every report all the milestones are shown as having slipped a week since the last report two weeks ago, you will tell the team to stop lying, and just tell you when they actually will finish. You don't want to see milestones slipped every report. You want to see them slipped once and that date then held.

The milestone tracker diagram can use a colour scheme developed by the Lockheed aircraft corporation in the US:

- Green means going according to plan
- Amber means not going according to plan, but containable
- Red means not going according to plan, with serious impact on the project.

CHAPTER

13 *Managing Risk*

Web projects are risky (see Figure 2.3), and that risk needs to be managed. One way to reduce the risk is to do more planning and design, but that costs time and money. We reach a point where we put more effort into the planning process than the quality of the data we get out. At some point, we have to stop planning and manage the residual risk. There is now ample evidence that effective risk management can improve project performance (Cooke Davies, 2002). Further, it can improve the pay off from planning and design in reducing uncertainty, by focusing effort on those areas where the uncertainty exists. Christensen and Rydberg (2001) show how that was achieved on the fixed link between Copenhagen and Malmö to achieve an opening date which at the outset had a 10 per cent chance of being achieved. I want to reinforce this point. There are two ways you can use risk analysis. You can:

- frighten yourself out of doing the project
- identify areas which create uncertainty and put management effort into reducing them.

In an earlier work (Turner, 1999) I quoted the managing director of one of Britain's top 100 companies, who, when shown a highly detailed quantitative risk analysis about why his pet project wouldn't work, said:

> Don't confuse me with the facts: tell me how I am going to do it.

What he was saying was don't try to frighten me out of the project, tell me how you will to use the risk analysis to make the project a success. They didn't do that project; they did frighten themselves out of it, but that was the right outcome. In the case of the fixed link between Copenhagen and Malmö they had to do the project, so they were left to identifying areas of uncertainty, and eliminating them.

In this chapter, I describe risk management. In the next section, I introduce the concept of risk management as a process, and list several standard processes. I then step through the five steps of a generic process: identify the risk; do qualitative assessment of the risks; do quantitative analysis of the risks; develop a strategy for mitigating the risk; and control the risk through the project life cycle.

THE RISK MANAGEMENT PROCESS

To manage all areas of a project, it is essential to follow a methodology or process, and risk management is no different. Many professional and standards institutions around the world have suggested various risk management processes. Figure 13.1 summarizes the processes proposed by:

- The Project Management Institute, *A Guide to the Project Management Body of Knowledge*, Chapter 11 (PMI, 2000)
- The UK's Association for Project Management (APM 1997)
- The British Standards Institute, BS6079.

Generic	*PMI*	*APM*	*BS6079 Part 3*
Context	Planning	Define, focus	Context
Identify	Identify	Identify	Identify
Assess	Assess	Estimate	Analysis
Quantify	Quantify	Evaluate	Evaluation
Mitigate	Mitigate	Plan	Treatment
Control	Control	Manage	

Figure 13.1 *Risk analysis and management processes*

These risk management processes share six essential steps:

1 Set the context for risk analysis and management
2 Identify the risks
3 Do qualitative assessment of the risks
4 Do quantitative analysis of the risks
5 Develop a strategy for mitigating the risks
6 Manage and control the risks.

The processes in Figure 13.1 all include qualitative assessment and quantitative analysis of the risks. They all start with the qualitative assessment. This is essential:

- to structure the project plan for risk analysis
- to identify the risks
- to assess the impact of the risks and prioritize them for further analysis and management.

It is then possible, but not necessary, to follow up the qualitative assessment with quantitative analysis to gain greater understanding of the risks. So there are two essential messages:

- start with the qualitative assessment – this is necessary
- the quantitative analysis is optional, but can provide useful additional information.

There are of course many people who launch straight into highly complex, quantitative analysis, developing highly complex models, with levels of sophistication finer than the level of uncertainty (see Figure 13.2). These sophisticated models consume a lot of effort in the creation, but provide little value. Further you do not know what to focus on in the quantitative model until you have done the qualitative analysis.

> I once saw someone estimating a project, comprising 100 packages of work with total cost of £400 million, working out costs to the nearest pound, but throwing in contingencies of £100 000. Figures 11.3 and 11.5 would suggest that we can expect the project estimate to be accurate to ± £20 million, and the estimate for each £4 million work package to be accurate to ± £1.6 million. So this is about the right level of contingency, but totally the wrong level of sophistication in the model. It takes a lot of effort to estimate at the level of the nearest pound, but that effort contributes no value.

Figure 13.2 *Excessive sophistication*

In this chapter I follow the PMI process. I assume step 1 has already been done. The chapters up to this point of the book have set the context for risk analysis and management. So I start with identifying the risks.

IDENTIFYING RISK

The first step in the risk management process (after creation of the risk management context) is to identify and classify potential risks.

IDENTIFY

There are organic and structured ways of identifying risks.

Organic approach

The organic approach involves creative methods of group working, such as brainstorming, to identify potential risks. I gave a brief overview of brainstorming when discussing milestone planning in Chapter 7. It is a two stage process. In the first phase the group shouts out ideas, and the project manager records every one, *without comment*. In the second phase, all the ideas are reviewed, and useful ones identified, and taken forward for further assessment. Remember, during the creative phase, do not pass judgement on peoples' ideas. One person's stupid idea can generate a good idea in someone else, and if you tell someone their ideas are stupid they will withdraw from the creative process. Value judgements of the ideas suggested are reserved for the second phase.

Structured approach

Using the structured approach, you work through the project plan, and at each stage ask yourself:

1 What can go wrong here?
2 What can cause it to go wrong?
3 If it does go wrong, what impact will it have?

In this way you identify potential risks and their impacts. I talk below about how to mitigate both. Figures 2.1 and 2.3 also suggested features of web projects, and associated risks, which could be used to stimulate ideas for potential risks.

CLASSIFY

There are two ways of classifying risks:

- by the impact of the risk on the project
- by where control of the risk lies, with three subclassifications.

Risks by impact on the project

We consider first risks by their impact on the project. There are two types:

1 business risks
2 insurable risks.

Some people call business risks 'uncertainty', and reserve the word 'risk' just to cover insurable risks. However, risk management processes apply to both, and it is reducing the spread of business risks that delivers much of the performance improvement from risk analysis and management.

Business risks: I explored this in Figure 11.2. Every estimate we make is a mid-range value, but in the event, the outcome can be better or worse. It is a grand self delusion of projects that people somehow imagine that their estimates are point-wise correct. When they say an element of work will cost £10 000, they mean that and not £9 999, nor £10 001. But nothing is that predictable, even something we have done before. Everything can work out better or worse than the estimate. This is business risk. If things go better than we estimate, we will make a greater profit; if things go worse, we will make less profit. The spread of possible out-turns will depend on a number of factors:

- the uniqueness or novelty of the element of work
- the impact of external influences (such as weather or the work of others)
- the inherent uncertainty of the work.

So some estimates have a low spread, say ± 1 per cent, so an estimate of £10 000 means somewhere between £9 950 and £10 100. (I have shown this as skewed to the worse, as most estimates are.) Or other risks may have a high spread, say ± 50 per cent, so an estimate of £10 000 means somewhere between £7000 and £15 000. If a risk has low spread and low impact on the project, there is little point in putting much effort into reducing that risk. On the other hand, if it has high spread and high impact on the project, there is considerable value in spending time understanding what is creating the spread and trying to reduce it. I showed in Figure 11.2 how this leads to a need for contingency. Figure 13.3 illustrates this diagrammatically and Figure 13.4 gives a simple example of it in practice.

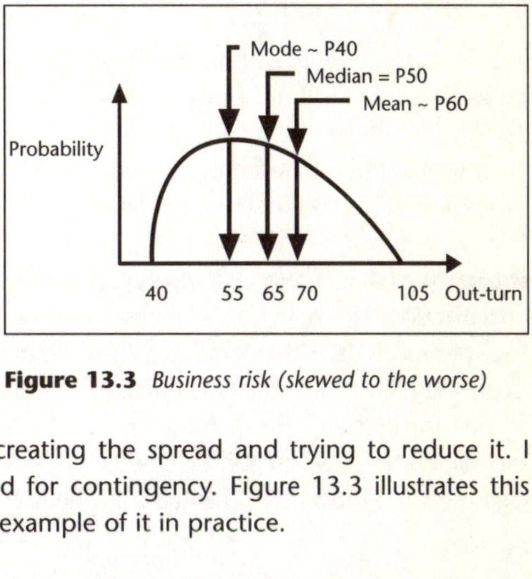

Figure 13.3 *Business risk (skewed to the worse)*

Insurable risks: Insurable risks are one-sided risks, usually to the worse. Something can happen that causes our project to go wrong (or perhaps better). There may be a fire, earthquake, war damage, traffic accident. These will all result in a loss only. Some people like to emphasize the positive and say there may be insurable risks which result in an outcome better than expected. I find it very difficult to think of examples that are not the upside of business risk, for example our technology may work better than expected, but I guess there are some.

As the name implies, it is possible to insure against insurable risks. An insurance company works out the probability the risk will occur, and the estimated cost impact if it does, multiplies the two together, and we pay that amount to the insurance company as a premium. However, I show later that we don't always want to protect against insurable risks in that way. Often we pay the premium in another way.

I use the example of driving to Henley Management College, where I work occasionally. The distance from my home is 40 miles, and I find my most likely journey time to be 55 minutes. If I drive at the speed limit the whole way, which I have done once or twice, late at night with no traffic, I can do the journey in 40 minutes. That is the irreducible minimum (without exceeding the speed limit). However, if I travel in the main rush hour in the morning, the journey can take up to 105 minutes. If I am teaching at 09.00 in the morning, I need leave home before 07.15. (In fact I usually leave home at 06.30, when the journey takes me closer to the 55 minutes. That is risk mitigation.) The average journey time is about 65 minutes, and the median (P50 value) about 60 minutes. These journey times are shown in Figure 13.3.

The 1:4:1 formula given in Chapter 11 would suggest a mean journey time of about 58 minutes. Here it is worse than that because it is actually a bimodal distribution – there is a set of light traffic outcomes and a set of heavy traffic outcomes. The distribution is therefore skewed more heavily than the formula assumes.

Figure 13.4 *Driving to Henley Management College*

Risks by where control lies

The second way of categorizing risks is where the control lies. There are two subcategories, each broken into two further subcategories:

1 internal risks: technical or non-technical
2 external risks: business or insurable.

Internal risks: These are risks within the control of the project manager or his or her organization. They can be technical or non-technical. The non-technical (people) risks often have larger impact than the technical risks. Figure 13.5 shows the top ten risks identified on the Copenhagen to Malmö link (Christensen and Rydberg, 2001). Some of these are internal to the owner and some to the contractor. One is external to both. Of the internal risks, six are non-technical and three technical. One of the internal, non-technical risks is also a contractual risk (see below). I found that this table supported my preconceptions. Twice as many risks are non-

Risk	*Impact (%)*	*Impact 1*	*Impact 2*
Interface management	18	Internal	Non-technical
Element fabrication	17	Internal	Technical
Owner's organization	14	Internal	Non-technical
Joint venture	12	Internal	Non-technical
Bridge accidents	4	Internal	Non-technical
Tunnel accidents	3	Internal	Non-technical
Tunnel design	3	Internal	Technical
Labour and materials	3	Internal	Both
Weather	2	External	Business
Road test	2	External	Insurable

Figure 13.5 *Top ten risks on the Copenhagen to Malmö (Øresund) link*

technical as technical. Of the six risks identified by James Jiang, Gary Klein and Selwyn Ellis (2002) (see Figure 2.3), all are internal, and all but the first are non-technical.

External risks: These are risks beyond the control of the project manager, or his or her organization. They are business or insurable risks. When it comes to a mitigation strategy, all the project manager can do is allow a contingency, or pass them on to someone else to manage, either through the contract or by taking out an insurance policy.

A common mistake, made under normal contracting practice, is to take what is an internal risk that the project manager can control and pass it on to a contractor, where it becomes an external risk to both the owner and the contractor. Then all the contractor can do is allow a contingency, and add a profit margin, and pass the cost back to the owner. Whereas if the owner retained ownership of the risk, they might be able to manage and reduce the risk and save money. Worse, under compulsory competitive tendering, the owner gets potential contractors to bid for the work, and awards the contract to the contractor that has bid the least. That is they award the contract to the contractor that has allowed the least for the risk and is therefore the most likely to fail. Modern practice, especially on high risk contracts, using a technique called partnering, is for the client and contractor to share all the risk (Bower and Skountzos, 2003). They work together to reduce risk that is internal to one of them or the other (or both), and to reduce the impact of external risk. Empirical evidence is that this approach is leading to substantially reduced project costs (Scott, 2001).

QUALITATIVE ASSESSMENT OF RISK

Having identified the risks, we need to assess their impact. We do this by assessing their impact on their own, and then prioritizing the risks for further study, and assessing their joint impact.

INDIVIDUAL IMPACT

There is a simple relationship for assessing the impact of risks individually:

Impact = Likelihood x Consequence

A simple way of illustrating this is by considering whether buildings in the UK are designed to withstand earthquake. By and large, no! Multi-storey office blocks in London are not designed to withstand earthquake. If there were an earthquake of force 6 on the Richter scale in London, most buildings would collapse, with massive loss of life. But the chance is so small, there is no protection. Are there any buildings with earthquake protection? Yes! Reactors of nuclear power stations. The likelihood is unchanged, but the consequence is now enormous, or it is thought to be enormous.

The last statement illustrates another point. The assessment of risk can be extraordinarily irrational. People give huge emphasis to a trivial risk, while ignoring substantial ones. At the height of the BSE scare in Britain, people who smoked and/or drank too much alcohol and/or talked on their mobile phones while driving said they were not eating beef because it was too dangerous. Since the outbreak of the new form of brain disease possibly (and only possibly) caused by eating beef, there have been 10 deaths per year. There are 100 000 deaths a year from smoking related diseases and 50 000 a year from alcohol related diseases, and 3000 a year on the country's roads. There is no comparison of the comparative risks, and yet still people did not eat beef (though we shall see a possible explanation for this behaviour later). We can add an extra dimension to the formula above to allow for this:

Impact = Likelihood x Consequence x Perception

This initial assessment is qualitative. Working out likelihood and consequence to two significant figures, and differentiating risks at the fourth figure, is silly. You don't know the likelihood or consequence to even one significant figure, but you can probably estimate the order of magnitude. So you can rate the likelihood and consequence (and perception and any other relevant parameters) on a scale of 0 to 3 (Figure 13.6). Then adding figures associated with the parameters gives an indication of the relative impact of the risks. (Adding the figures is the appropriate thing to do, treating the numbers we have associated with the parameters as logarithms of the order of magnitude.) Thus a risk of high likelihood and medium consequence would rate 5, as would one of medium likelihood and high consequence (ignoring perception). (In the fourth column of Figure 13.6, C is the cost of the project.)

Parameter	*Size*	*Likelihood (%)*	*Consequence (% of cost of project)*	*Perception*
High	3	10	10	National impact
Medium	2	1	1	Company impact
Low	1	0.1	0.1	Team impact
Negligible	0	Nil	Nil	No impact

Figure 13.6 *Parameters associated with risk assessment*

However, even this simple analysis can be misleading. We might say a risk of high likelihood and low impact is equivalent to a risk of low likelihood and high impact. Both rate 4. But that is not the case. The reason is the risk with high likelihood has a much lower spread of possible outcomes than one with low likelihood. The latter is a more insidious risk. They both have the same expected out-turn, but the low likelihood risk has a wider spread. This explains the reaction to BSE. The probability of catching the disease is low, but we don't know what it actually is. Estimates of the total number of people dying from the disease in the UK range from 200 to 200 000 depending on quite small changes in parameters. With smoking we know quite predictably that 100 000 people will die a year, and life expectancy is shortened by six years. Human beings seem to have built in a mistrust of low likelihood, high consequence risk, especially if there is also associated high ambiguity.

With business risks, it is the spread of outcomes that determines the impact of the risk. If there is a low spread, that is the outcome is very predictable, there is little uncertainty or risk. If there is a high spread, there is high uncertainty. With insurable risks, the likelihood by the consequence is more significant, especially when it comes to choosing a mitigation strategy.

Sometimes, a risk will be described by several parameters, some describing the likelihood, some the consequence, some perception, some political fall-out. Adding the parameters together, as suggested above, can lead to rather spurious outcomes. For instance, if there were seven parameters, all rated on a scale of 0 to 3, adding them would give an overall scale of 0 to 21, and could we then differentiate between a risk of 15 say from one of 18? What is suggested is a refined qualitative approach. Each risk is assessed against each of the parameters (on a scale

Risk	*P1*	*P2*	*P3*	*P4*	*P5*	*P6*	*P7*	*Impact*
R1	High	High	Low	High	Med	High	High	High
R2	Medium	Medium	Low	High	Medium	Medium	Low	Medium
R3	Low	High	Low	Medium	Low	Low	Medium	Low

P: parameter

Figure 13.7 *Qualitative risk assessment*

of 0 to 3 say, or as high, medium, low or negligible) and the data presented in a table (Figure 13.7). The team then assess the risks against the same scale, by interrogating the table. This is the key thing. Rather than ending up with a spuriously fine scale, they are rated in the same way, high, medium, low or negligible, on a scale of 0 to 3. Clearly, this requires subjective decisions to be taken, but the team can err on the side of caution.

PRIORITIZING RISK

I worked with a client in the public sector who were doing a major refurbishment for about £10 million. They asked a consultant to help them with the risk analysis and the consultant identified about 100 risks. A Risk Item Tracking Form, Figure 13.8, was developed for each risk, as was a risk register. The organization didn't know where to begin managing the risks, and so the consultant's report became a doorstop. The Øresund link, a project 100 times as big, had just ten key risks (Figure 13.5).

In Chapter 6, I said that if you have 125 key performance indicators, at least 119 of them are not key. It's the same with risks – focus on the significant few. Once you have eliminated those, focus on the next most significant few. On the Øresund link, the significant few were the top four; the next most significant few were the next six.

Figure 13.8 *Focusing on the significant few*

Next you need to prioritize risks for further study. You need to focus on the significant few rather than the insignificant many (see Figure 13.8). You should only focus on the numbers 4, 5 and 6 risks as calculated in Figure 13.9. The numbers 2 and 3 risks can be monitored in the background. In fact you should focus first on eliminating the number 6 risks, and reducing the number 5 risks to number 4 risks using the techniques described later. (The words in the cells of Figure 13.9 will be explained later when I talk about mitigating the risks.)

COMBINING RISKS

Now we can combine risk, determining their combined impact on the project. We can use a top-down (qualitative) approach or a bottom-up (quantitative) approach. The bottom-up approach is the quantitative risk analysis, using Monte Carlo analysis, which I will describe in the next section. However, we can make some further progress combining the risks using qualitative assessment. The top-down, qualitative, approach starts with a simple model for the project consisting of about 20 components. This can be the milestone plan (Figure 7.1), or the responsibility chart (Figure 8.8). You choose a model that illustrates the risks you want to investigate. Why about 20 components? It is a number that provides some value from the

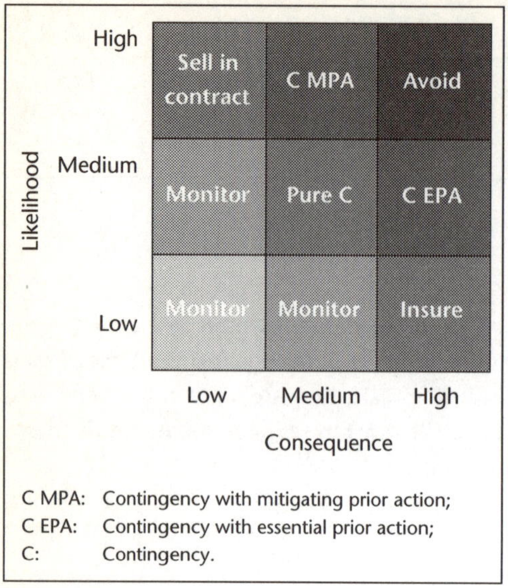

Figure 13.9 *Locating the significant few*

analysis, without being too many to overcomplicate the model. You then ask yourself two questions:

1 What is the risk of each component going wrong?
2 If it does, what impact will it have on all the other components?

You then ask yourself two more questions:

3 How do you eliminate or reduce the chance of each component failing?
4 And if you can't do that, how do you eliminate or reduce the impact on other components?

Now we see why 20 components. With 20 components, there are 400 impacts. If you have a sheet of paper describing each component and each impact, that is 400 sheets, roughly one ream. With 30 components, that is 900 sheets, roughly two and a half reams. But, you might say, if I am looking at the milestone plan, each milestone only has an impact on milestones dependent on it. Not so, unfortunately. The logic in the milestone plan represents what we expect to happen if everything goes well. But if something fails, it can cause something apparently unrelated to fail. For example, we make a design assumption in an early milestone. The logic represents what happens if those assumptions

The numbers at the centre top of Figure 13.11 are the duration of each package of work in months. Top left is early start, top right is early finish, bottom right is late finish, bottom left is late start, and bottom centre is float.

The plan shows a lead time of two months from *Design the web space, hardware and peripherals* to *Develop the web space and test*. What this means is that after the design starts, some development work can begin just one month into the design. Is there any risk in using this lead time? The answer is yes. The selection of the hardware may change the design of the web space. If we look at the plan, we see that both the web development and the procurement of the hardware take two months. So why bother? If we wait until the design is finished, we can do the development work while we are waiting for the hardware to arrive. Is there any risk in not using the two months lead time? The answer is yes. The development work is far more at risk than the delivery of the hardware. The latter might be exactly predictable at two months, or have very low spread of out-turns, whereas in the development work the tests might fail, requiring rework. If we can use the two months lead time we have a better chance of getting finished by the time the hardware arrives. Now, having identified the previous risk, we can try to cut the impact. In month 2 we will do the development work least likely to be affected by the design of the hardware, and month 3 work more likely to be affected, when the design of the hardware should be more stable.

Figure 13.10 *Top down risk assessment*

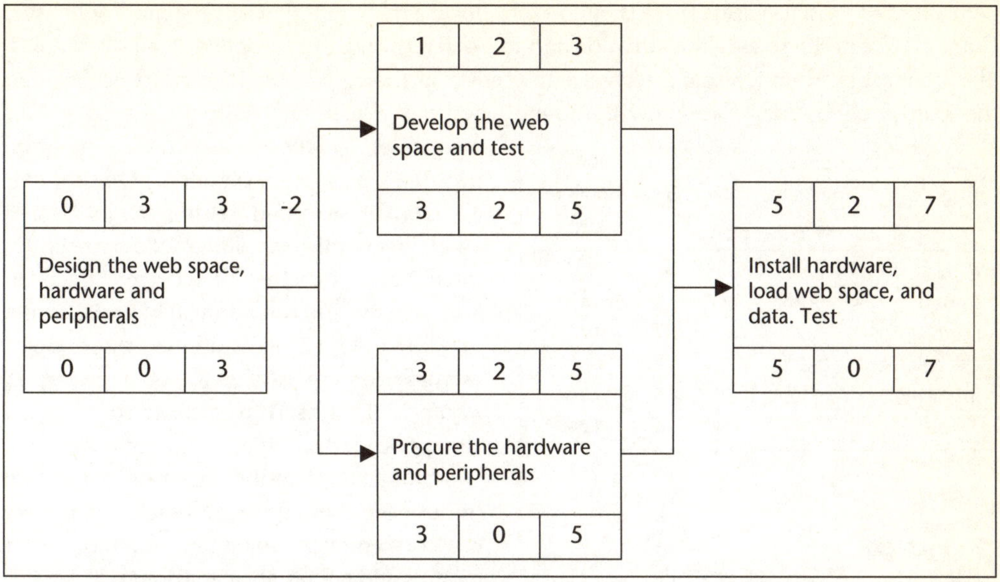

Figure 13.11 *Plan for a project to develop a simple web space*

are correct. However, we may find that we can't make them work. They then need changing in the whole project. Figure 13.11 shows a simple four step project to deliver a web space. The durations shown middle top are in months. The basic plan is seven months long. The top-down analysis might proceed as Figure 13.10.

QUANTITATIVE ANALYSIS OF RISK

You can make considerable progress with the qualitative assessment, and usually that is all you need. But occasionally your project is sufficiently large and complex to warrant quantitative analysis of the risk. A key point to make is that if your project is large enough and complex enough to warrant quantitative analysis of the risk, it is large enough and complex enough to use a computer programme to do it for you. The quantitative analysis is not something you do by hand. So it is worthwhile to understand how it works, but you don't need to know anything about the underlying mathematics. There are two steps in the quantitative analysis:

1 Three point estimating
2 Monte Carlo analysis.

THREE POINT ESTIMATING

You start with a project plan. If you want to analyse timescale, then a critical path network is needed. This could be in a proprietary package or an Excel spreadsheet. If you want to analyse cost, you need a cost model based on the cost control cube shown in Figure 11.9. Again this could be in a proprietary package or an Excel spreadsheet. For parameters or values in the model with significant risk, you develop a three point estimate, as illustrated in Figures 11.2 and 13.4. You estimate the most likely out-turn, the most optimistic and most pessimistic. It can be difficult getting people to make the spread between the most optimistic and most pessimistic wide enough to encompass all likely out-turns. It is suggested you make the spread include at least 90 per cent of all possible cases. There is often an irreducible minimum that sets the most optimistic. I cannot exceed the speed limit when driving to Henley, giving a most optimistic of 40 minutes. But the most pessimistic value is less easy to predict. In the case of my journey to Henley, I do the journey often enough to know that a most pessimistic value of 105 minutes accounts for most cases. It did once take me 135 minutes, but that was an exception. On another occasion I just missed getting caught behind an accident which would have held me up for three hours, but that would have been an insurable risk and not a spread of business risk.

Work pack	*Minimum values*	*Raw*	*Exp*	*Maximum values*
Path 1				
Design	2	3	3	4
Lead	-2	-2	-2	-2
Development	2	2	2.5	5
Installation	2	2	2.5	5
Totals	**4**	**5**	**6**	**12**
Path 2				
Design	2	3	3	4
Procurement	1	2	2	3
Installation	2	2	2.5	4
Totals	**5**	**7**	**7.5**	**12**
Project	5	7	7.5	12

Figure 13.12 *Three point estimating for Figure 13.11*

Figure 13.12 illustrates a three point estimate for the duration of the project in Figure 13.11. I need to calculate the duration along two paths. Some of the time Path 1 is critical, but most of the time Path 2 is critical (if I use the 2 months lead time). The project has a theoretical minimum duration of 5 months and a theoretical maximum of 12, but we shall see shortly there is no chance of achieving either 5 or 12, and that even 6 and 11 are unlikely. The expected out-turns for each activity are calculated using the 1:4:1 formula, giving an expected out-turn for the project of 7.5 months. In this case, because the two activities of work involving testing are heavily skewed to the worse, the 1:4:1 formula is inaccurate, and the expected duration is more like 8 months. Doing a cost estimate there is no need to add up along two paths, just sum over the four packages of work.

Three point estimating gives an indication of the range of possible outcomes for the project. But as we saw in Figures 11.2 and 13.12, the chance of achieving the extremes is slight. We need to do further quantitative analysis to calculate the likely spread of outcomes for the project, and the expected outcome. That is Monte Carlo analysis.

MONTE CARLO ANALYSIS

In all but the simplest cases, when it would be unnecessary, it would take an impossibly long time to work out theoretically the chance of achieving the spread of outcomes for the project. It is possible, but it would take forever. Thus a technique based on simulation and sampling has been developed to calculate a close approximation. This is called Monte Carlo analysis.

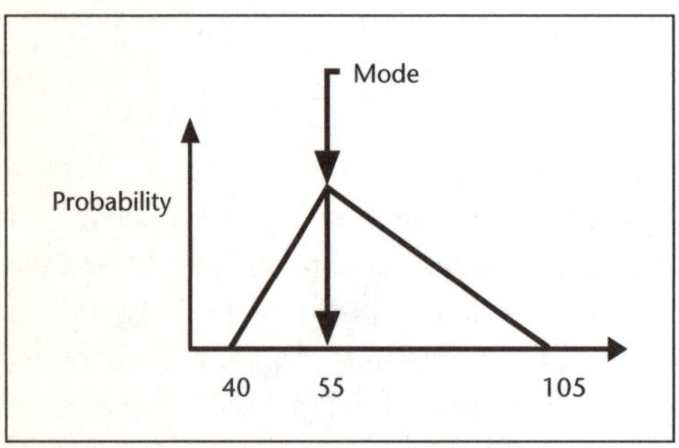

Figure 13.13 *Straight line (or triangular) probability distribution*

First, you also need to choose the probability distribution linking the three values for each estimate. It is common to choose a beta distribution (shown figuratively in Figure 13.3), or a straight line distribution, as in

Figure 13.13. Other possibilities include normal, skewed normal, stepped, and so on. Note, the 1:4:1 formula above is based on the assumption of a beta distribution, and this makes the most likely out-turn the P40 value. For my journey to Henley, a straight line distribution makes the most likely out-turn (55 minutes) the P25 value. The Monte Carlo analysis software you use will offer a choice of distributions, and give you guidance as to which are appropriate in your circumstance. You do not need to do the sums, just nominate the distributions.

Now you run the time or costs model a large number of times, typically several thousand. Every time the model runs, the software randomly chooses a value for each parameter with a three point estimate within the range specified, and using the specified probability distribution. Again, there is proprietary software to do this. There are a number of Excel add-ons to run Monte Carlo Analysis, notably @Risk® and Crystal Ball®. There are also add-ons to proprietary project management software systems.

The result is a spread of time or cost out-turns for the project. These can be presented as a point-wise probability distribution (Figure 13.14), or as a cumulative probability distribution (Figure 13.15). The former represents the probability that the out-turn will be a particular figure. The latter represents the probability that the out-turn will be less than a certain figure. The latter is more realistic.

This could not be done with the power of computers in the 1950s. Hence the need for the 1:4:1 formula, above. That is no longer necessary, with the ability to run the project plan thousands of times in a few seconds.

The value of Monte Carlo Analysis is it will indicate a number of things:

- a range of possible out-turns for the project, and the chance of achieving each
- a number of critical paths for the project, and what causes each one
- a number of cost drivers.

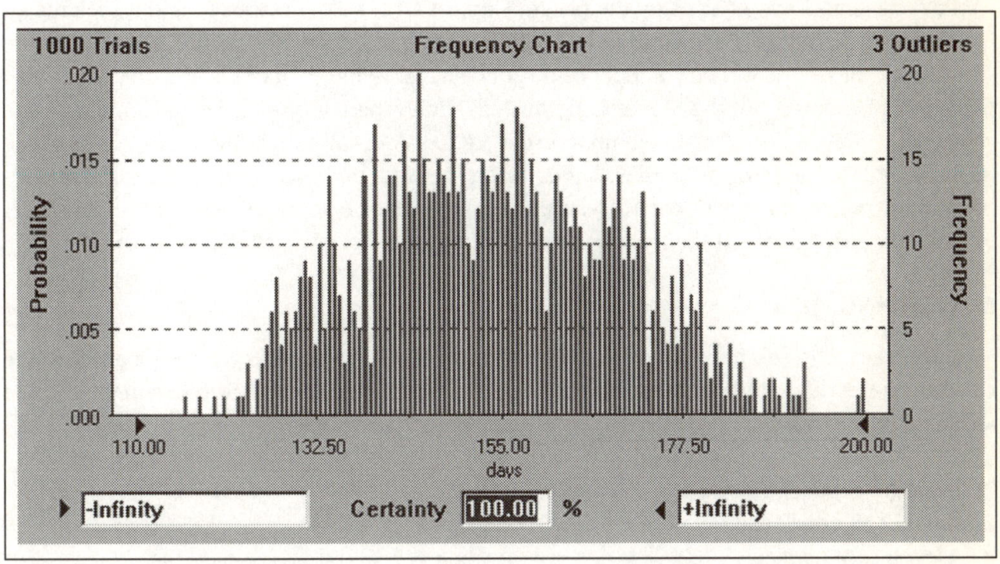

Figure 13.14 *Output (point-wise distribution) from a Monte Carlo Analysis using Crystal Ball®*

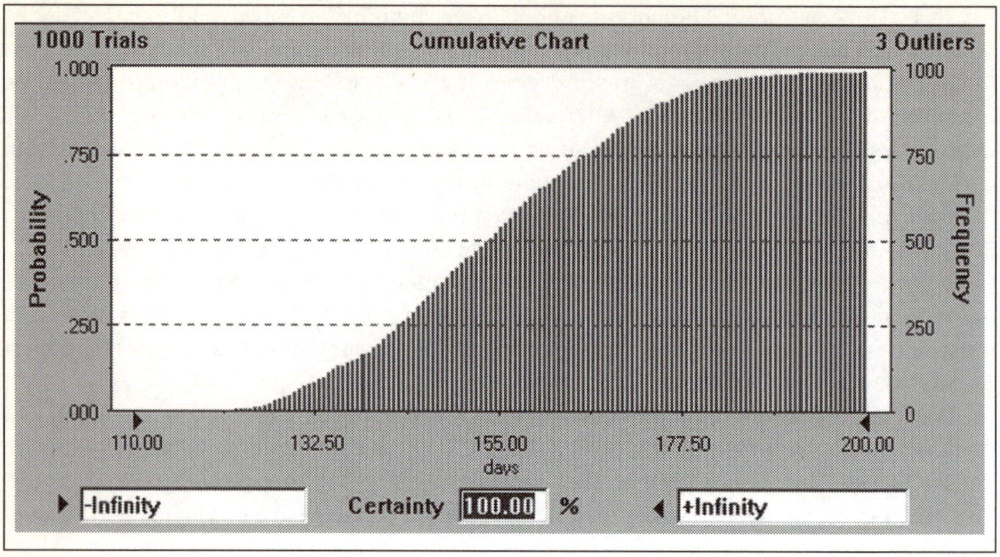

Figure 13.15 *Output (cumulative distribution) from a Monte Carlo Analysis using Crystal Ball®*

The team can then work on eliminating the various critical paths and cost drivers to try to achieve their desired outcomes. This is what the team on the Copenhagen to Malmö link did (Christensen and Rydberg, 2001). They identified likely risks, and conducted Monte Carlo Analysis on their plan. This indicated a 10 per cent chance of achieving their desired outcome. However, it also indicated the ten major risks, and that four of those were more severe than the other six (Figure 13.5). They then worked on eliminating or reducing the impact of those risks, and so were able to achieve the desired outcome for the project. That is using the quantitative analysis to improve project performance, not to frighten yourself out of the project.

I did a Monte Carlo Analysis on the plan in Figure 13.11. I did it manually, and it took me an hour working by hand. I assumed all four distributions to be stepped. The result is shown in Figure 13.16. You will see there is only a 5 per cent chance of achieving six months and only 2 per cent of exactly 11 months. But the Monte Carlo Analysis shows there is only an 18 per cent chance of achieving the raw estimate of seven months, it is a P20 value. Now when the project turns out to be eight months long instead of the planned seven, because the tests failed for technical reasons beyond the project manager's control, was that his or her fault? No, but it was their responsibility to make the client aware of the realistic duration of the project, given all the likely risks.

MITIGATING RISK

Now we need to develop a strategy for eliminating or reducing the risks we have identified. We can reduce the risks either by reducing their likelihood or by reducing their consequence. There are three basic strategies:

1 avoid (or reduce) the risk
2 pass the risk on
3 allow a contingency.

The 1987 edition of PMI's *Project Management Body of Knowledge* used the example of a cowboy being shot at. He can:

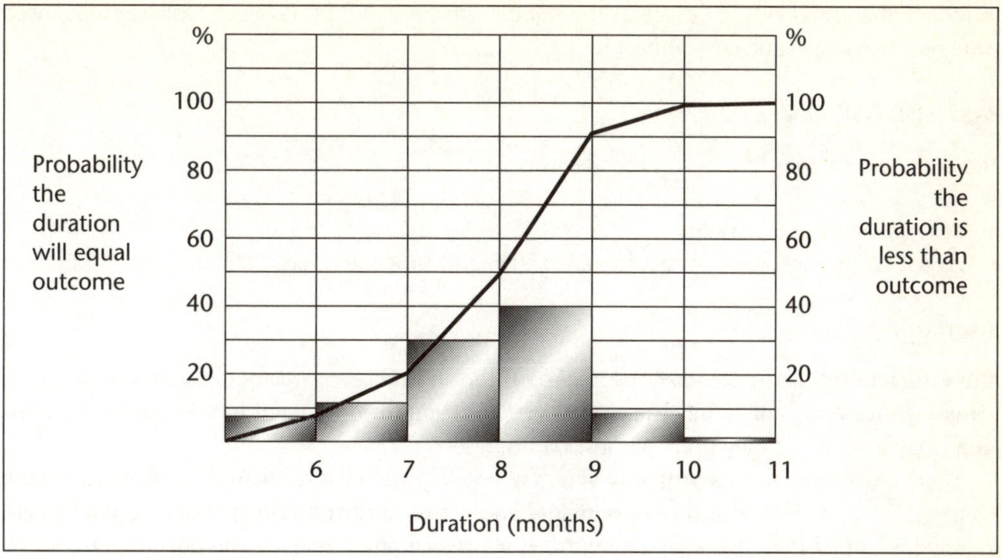

Figure 13.16 *Results of the Monte Carlo Analysis for Figure 13.11*

- take cover (avoid the risk of being hit)
- try to get someone else to stand in the way of the bullets (but there remains a risk that the bullets will travel on through the other person and still hurt the cowboy)
- allow himself to be shot and hope he gets to hospital in time to be repaired. (Viewing contingency that way, as a plan to fail and hope you can recover, the other approaches seem like a better idea.)

AVOIDANCE

This is the best strategy. Find another way of doing the project which:

- eliminates the risk altogether
- reduces the chance of its occurrence
- removes the impact of the risk on other parts of the project
- reduces such impacts.

How you do that will depend on the nature of your project and the nature of the risk. Sometimes you can find another way of doing the project which either costs you the same or less. At other times, there is a financial impact. If the change of the cost of the project is ΔC, and the change in the impact is $\Delta I = \Delta(I^*c)$, then it is worth implementing this strategy if $\Delta C < \Delta I$. For instance, if there is a risk with a 10 per cent chance of occurring, which will cost £1000 if it does, and there is a way of doing the project that reduces the chance to 1 per cent and the cost to £100, it is worth spending £99 to implement the strategy:

$$\Delta C \quad = \quad \Delta I \quad = \quad (0.1^*£1000 - 0.01^*£100) \quad = \quad £99$$

Risks in the top right hand box in Figure 13.9 (high likelihood, high consequence) have to be eliminated. For those in the centre top (high likelihood, medium consequence) you need to try to reduce the likelihood. For those in the middle right (medium likelihood, high consequence) you need to try to reduce the impact.

PASS THE RISK ON

There are two options for passing the risk on:

- take out an insurance policy
- pass it on through the contract to contractors and subcontractors.

Insuring the risk

Any insurable risk can potentially be passed to an insurance company, though an insurance company may not want to buy the risk off you, and you may not want to sell it to them. They won't buy it off you if they think it is just bad business.

There are at least two reasons why you may not want to sell it to them. The UK government insures none of its buildings for fire damage, and many companies don't insure company cars for anything other than the legal minimum. There is a common reason. The government has so many buildings, there are bound to be some fires each year. If they insure the buildings, at the start of the year they pay the insurance company a premium, and if the insurance company has done its sums right, during the year it pays back the premium minus their profit in claims. The net effect is the government hands over the insurance company's profit each year. It is better just to set aside in the budget an amount equal to the expected claims. It is the same with a large fleet of company cars. The other reason for not insuring company cars is that the company keeps control of the risk. If an employee is in an accident, and there is a 70 per cent probability that it was their fault, your insurance company might start quibbling with the other party. They then feel at a loss. In their view the accident was caused by your employee, and now your insurance company is quibbling and they are out of pocket. The third party will blame your company, not the insurance company. If you maintain control, you can just settle the other party's claim, and they may feel pleased and have positive feelings about your company.

Insurable risks in the bottom right hand box of Figure 13.9 (low likelihood, high consequence) are the best to insure. They are the insidious risks with a high spread of possible outcomes, as I said above.

Passing the risk through the contract

I have already discussed this. If the risk is one the contractor can control, it is sensible to pass it on, indeed the right thing to do. But where it is a risk that the owner can control it is best to retain it. That is the cheapest approach. The client may want to sell the risk to the contractor, and that is appropriate for risks in the top left hand box of Figure 13.9 (high likelihood, low consequence). These are highly predictable risks, so the contractor can allow a predictable contingency. But the contractor will charge a profit for buying it, just as the insurance company will, so it is a more expensive approach.

The modern approach, called partnering, used on complex projects where the client and contractor can together control the risk, is for the clients and contractors to pool their risk, and manage its reduction together. This is beyond the scope of this book, and you can read about it elsewhere (Scott, 2001).

CONTINGENCY

The final strategy is contingency – you plan to fail and hope to recover. There are two basic approaches. You can either develop a plan to recover should things go wrong, or you can set aside a sum of money to compensate for any losses should things go wrong. The latter is a form of internal insurance policy. I will concentrate on the former. There are three basic strategies of contingency:

Pure contingency

We develop a plan to recover should the risk occur. For example, the cowboy being shot at plans for his friends to take him to hospital should he be hit.

Essential prior action

Some work to implement the recovery plan is undertaken before the project starts, to make it quicker and easier to respond should the risk occur. This reduces the impact if the risk occurs, and is appropriate for risks in the middle right hand box of Figure 13.9 (medium likelihood, high consequence). Now it becomes a straight comparison between the cost of the essential prior action and the differential impact of the risk, as above under avoidance. For instance, the cowboy might pay to have an ambulance stand by, because he thinks there is a very high chance he will be hit, and so it is worth the additional expense.

Mitigating prior action

Something is done to reduce the likelihood of the risk, or change the nature of the impact to make the contingency plan work. This reduces the likelihood of the risk occuring, and is appropriate for risks in the middle top box of Figure 13.9 (high likelihood, medium consequence). The cowboy might wear a bulletproof vest. Again a straight comparison of the cost to the differential impact will say whether it is worthwhile or not.

CONTROLLING RISK

Once the project is underway, you need to monitor your risks and mitigation strategy at each project control cycle. The work up to now has just been laying the foundations for risk control. During the project you need to monitor:

- which risks are occurring
- the success of your risk mitigation strategy
- whether any changes need to be made to your mitigation strategy.

A risk register can be very useful for this purpose. Figure 13.17 is a suggestion for a possible register for the intranet at TriMagi, but this is something which is very particular to a project, and it is best that you develop your own. Possible additional columns might include columns for progress to date, future actions, responsibility, and ownership of risk. The status of risks on the register may rise and fall. One may rise, because you have entered the stage of the project where that risk is expected to occur, or because you have new information which increases the threat. One may fall, because you have developed a risk mitigation strategy to eliminate that risk, or because the time at which it would have occurred has passed, and it didn't happen.

TriMagi
Risk Register

Project:	Intranet Phase 1
Project Champion:	Martin Pacific
Project Manager:	Frances Seeker

Rank	*Milestone*	*Risk*	*Impact*	*L'hd H/M/L*	*Cons H/M/L*	*Strategy*
H	M1	Requirements compromised due to budgetary constraints	M2, M3, M4: Definition P2: Procedures designed	M	H	Ensure all data properly assessed in the inventory
H	P3	Fail to achieve user acceptance of new process definitions	D2: Design of procedures page P4: Optimization of processes	M	H	Communication plan Engage users Focus groups
H	P5	System does not work	P6: Go live H4: Install hardware H5: Migrate data	M	H	Monitor testing process Early testing Develop fall back plan
M	H5	Problems migrating data	H5: Site goes live	M	M	Ensure all data properly assessed in the inventory
M	P6	Training resources unavailable	P6: Go live	M	M	Identify back-up trainers

Author:	JRT	**Date:**	21 July 2003	**Issue:**	A

Figure 13.17 *Risk register for the intranet at TriMagi*

TriMagi **Risk Item Tracking Form**		
Project:	Intranet Phase 1	
Project Champion:	Martin Pacific	
Project Manager:	Frances Seeker	
Work area:	Procedures and systems	
Work area Manager:	Maria Street	
Milestone:	P3: New procedures piloted	
Milestone Manager:	Maria Street	
Risk item	Failure to achieve user agreement to process definitions	
Risk owner	Maria Street	
Likelihood	Medium	
Consequence	High	
Risk rating	High	
Milestones affected	D2: Document processing pages developed	P4: Procedures optimized
Impact	Page design invalid	Procedures need substantial modification
Mitigation Strategy	Communicate plans to users early Engage users in design of procedures Use focus groups	
Progress	Risk identified and mitigation strategy planned Communication strategy planned Focus groups established	

Author:	JRT	**Date:**	21 July 2003	**Issue:**	A

Figure 13.18 *Risk item tracking form for the intranet at TriMagi*

As well as the risk register, it can be useful to have a risk item tracking form, where details of individual risks are recorded. Again that will be very specific to the needs of your project, but a suggestion is given in Figure 13.18, for the intranet at TriMagi.

Remember, you may encounter risks you didn't think of. It is not possible to foresee everything. But if you are in control of the risks you did think of, you are better able to respond to those you didn't foresee. If you have no control over any risks, your project will go from crisis to crisis.

CHAPTER 14 *Controlling the Project*

Once the project is underway we need to control progress. There are those who think that once we reach this stage, the outcome is set. If the plan and risk analysis are well done, all we can do during project delivery is monitor achievement of the plan. It is now too late to make any improvement. There is some validity in this position. However, it is worthwhile to monitor and control progress. There are several reasons, including:

- As we saw in the last chapter, managing the risk can help to ensure we achieve the best possible outcome in terms of cost and time. I gave the example of the Øresund link between Copenhagen and Malmö. By predicting and then controlling risk they were able to achieve an outcome which at the start had only a 10 per cent chance of success.
- If you don't monitor progress, it is possible to lose control. It can be very difficult (though not impossible) to dramatically improve on the plan once the project is underway, but it is very easy to do much worse. Project control is a process whereby we ensure we deliver the plan we have set.

In this chapter I describe project control; first the requirements of effective control, and then the three steps in the process.

REQUIREMENTS FOR EFFECTIVE CONTROL

Figure 14.1 illustrates a four step control cycle. The steps are:

1 develop a plan
2 monitor achievement
3 calculate progress (and variances from the plan)
4 take action to recover progress as necessary.

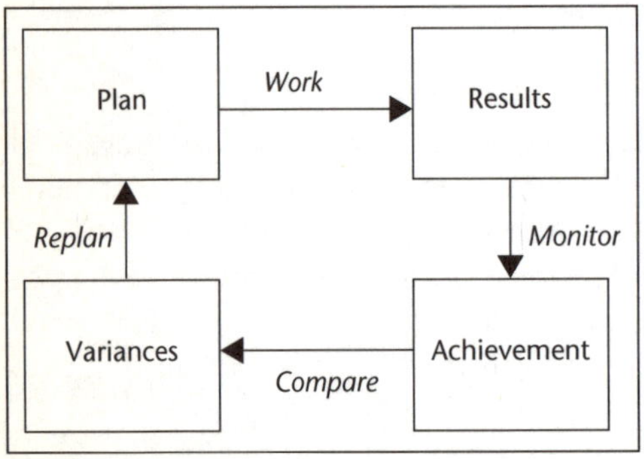

Figure 14.1 *Four step control cycle*

For the control process to be effective, each one of these steps needs to be effective:

- we must have an effective plan to do work to achieve results
- we must gather data which reflects actual progress
- we must be able to compare progress to the plan and calculate true variances
- we must be able to take action to recover the plan as appropriate.

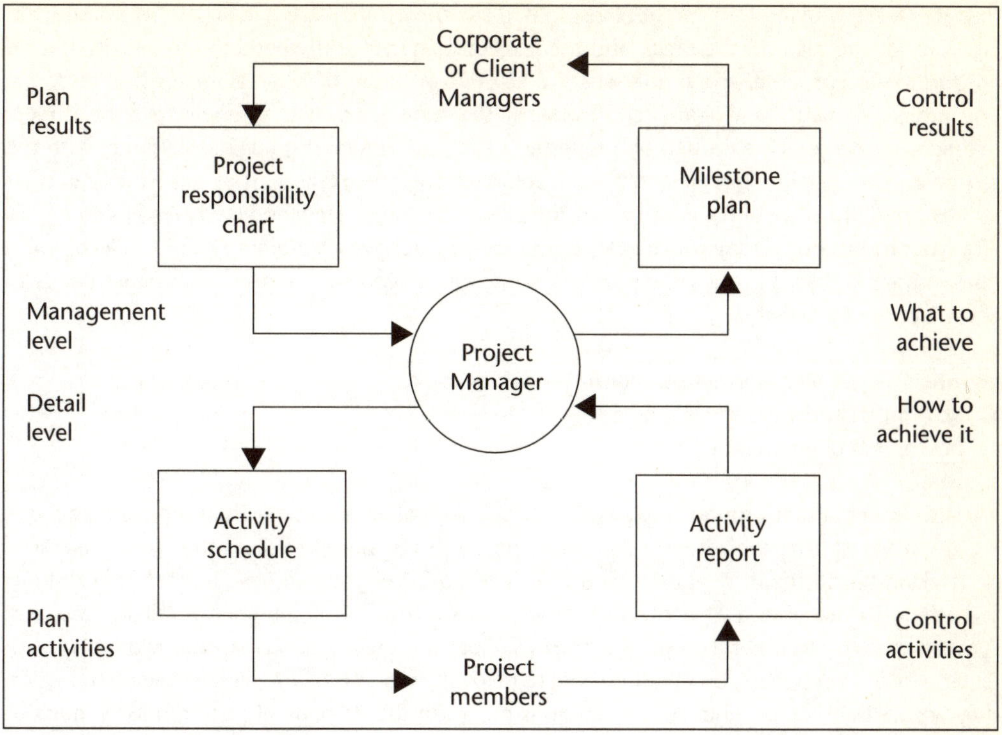

Figure 14.2 *Controlling progress at two levels*

The course up to this point has described the first step in this cycle. In this session I describe the other three steps. Figure 14.2 illustrates that control takes place at (at least) two levels:

1 one where the project team report progress to the project manager
2 one where the project manager reports progress to the owner (the client or senior managers).

These two reporting cycles should be at different frequencies. A ratio of about 1:3 is appropriate. On a project of several months duration, the lower reporting cycle will take place every one to two weeks, and the upper cycle once a month or once every six weeks.

GATHERING PROGRESS DATA

The gathering of progress data should satisfy several principles:

- reports should be made against the plan
- using defined criteria for reporting
- at specified intervals
- via simple reporting mechanisms.

Several of these are based on the idea that people don't like to volunteer their own failure, but also they will usually give a straight answer if asked a straight question. I have been involved in projects where the team said everything is going according to plan, but they and the project manager were working to different plans, so had a completely different idea of what that meant. So, you put the plan on the table, and the project manager asks whether each activity started and/or finished on time, and if not, when did it start or finish, or when is it expected to do so. The project manager and team report against the same plan. It is essential that the project manager should ask closed questions. Questions such as, 'How is it going?' will be met with the response, 'OK!' because people don't like to volunteer their own failure. They hope they can clear up any problems without having to worry the project manager. How often, when somebody asks after your health do you say you are OK, even though you have a streaming cold? It is a common human trait, and so it is the same with project progress reports. The project manager needs to know, activity by activity:

- when did it/will it start and/or finish?
- how much effort did it/will it take?
- how much did it/will it cost?

It is also essential that progress reports should be made at set intervals. Then the team knows it is time to report progress because it is time to report progress, not because the project manager is checking up on them. One thing you must not do is say you will have a meeting if there is something to talk about. That means you will have a meeting if someone is failing, and that someone has to volunteer their failure. They will not raise their hand just as their work begins to diverge from plan (when you might be able to recover progress). They will raise their hand when they are well off course, and all you can do is minimize the damage. If people make reports at predetermined intervals, then they can report progress honestly against the plan. Further I have said *predetermined* intervals, rather than *regular* intervals, because throughout the project you may need to change the frequency of reporting depending on the risk of the project at that point. Towards the beginning of the project you may report once every two weeks, but towards the end you may report weekly or even daily.

The last principle was that the reports should be simple. It is the team's job to do the work of the project, not spend their time filling in reports. The progress reports should therefore be kept simple. It is now quite common to give the project team a list of the activities they should be working on, with the start and finish dates, work effort and cost entered, and to either confirm the figures, or write in predicted values. These are sometimes called turnaround documents. In fact a very simple method is to give the project team members a trial time sheet for the week or fortnight, with the project activities they should be working on listed (together with the planned start and finish dates, and expected work effort). Then all the team member does is enters the number of hours worked on each activity day by day, and at the end of the reporting period (a week or fortnight), they say how much work they think is outstanding. The project control system can automatically pick up the first date at which they enter time against the activity as the start date. Then when they say the activity has no remaining work, the project control system can pick out the activity as finished, and take the last date with time entered as the end date. Finally the project manager or project controllers can also work out the predicted end date for work in progress, using the amount of work remaining. It is easy for the team members just to enter how much work they did day by day, and how much work is remaining at the end of the period. That is something they have to do for a number of other purposes anyway.

PROGRESS DATA REQUIRED

So, what progress data is actually required? It is necessary to gather:

- quantitative data to control cost and time;
- qualitative data to control quality, configuration and scope.

Quantitative data: I have mentioned the quantitative data required in the immediately preceding discussion. To control time we require:

- actual start and finish dates
- predicted start and finish dates
- percentage completion or predicted work remaining for work in progress.

In fact the percentage completion or predicted work remaining can help us calculate the predicted finish dates. If we know the percentage completion we can extrapolate the predicted finish date by assuming the duration is proportional to the work to be done. I believe it is better to ask the team members to predict the amount of work remaining and then calculate the remaining duration:

$$\text{\% completion} = \frac{\text{work done}}{\text{work done + work to do}}$$

$$\text{remaining duration} = \text{Original duration * \% completion}$$

$$\text{or} \quad \text{Elapsed time * (1 – \% completion)/\% completion}$$

Predicted start times of activities yet to start can be calculated from the predicted finish times of activities on which they are dependent.

To control cost, the information we need is:

- actual effort to date
- predicted effort of the work remaining for activities in progress
- other costs (other than labour as listed in Figure 11.1).

From the actual effort to date and other costs we can calculate the actual cost of work completed. For work that is finished we can add the total planned cost of that work to the planned cost of work complete. For work still in progress, we can calculate the percentage completion as described above, and add a proportion of the planned cost to the planned cost of work complete, as described in Chapter 11. Thus, the information above gives us enough information to perform the earned value analysis as described in Chapter 11.

Qualitative data: The qualitative data required is less specific, but includes:

- some measure of the result delivered at milestones or activity completion to compare to the measures set at the planning stage, as described in Chapter 10
- the causes of any delays
- whether responsibilities are being adhered to, and the project organization is working.

TriMagi ACTIVITY PLAN | **ACTIVITY SCHEDULE** | **REPORT**

Project:	Intranet Phase 1	**Author:**	Rodney Turner
Milestone:	D3: Personnel information pages designed	**Date:**	19 September 2003
Manager:	Ian Simons	**Checked**	Ian Simmons
Period:	Day	**Target end:**	25-Sep-03

X	eXecutes the work
D	takes **D**ecisions solely/ultimately
d	takes **d**ecisions jointly
P	manages **P**rogress
T	on the job **T**raining
I	must be **I**nformed
C	must be **C**onsulted
A	may **A**dvise

No	Activity name	Ian Simons	Jan Deptford	Procurement	Contractors	Personnel	Marketing	Selected users	Internal labour (d)	Subcontract (£k)
D31	Specify page based on agreed contents	P	X						5	
D32	Appoint contractors	Xd		Xd					3	
D33	Manage contractors	P								
D34	Design and develop pages	P			X				0	3.0
D35	Obtain approval – personnel	PX	X		X	C			5	2.0
D36	Obtain approval – marketing	PX	X		X		C		2	0.5
D37	Obtain approval – selected users	PX	X		X			C	2	0.5
D38	Make necessary changes	PD	X		X	d	d	d	3	1.0
	Total								20	7.0

No	1 (03-Sep)	2 (10-Sep)	3 (11-Sep)	4 (12-Sep)	5 (15-Sep)	6 (16-Sep)	7 (17-Sep)	8 (18-Sep)	9 (19-Sep)	10 (22-Sep)	11 (23-Sep)	12 (24-Sep)	13 (25-Sep)	14	15	Duration (d)	End date
D31																7	11-Sep-03
D32																2	11-Sep-03
D33																10	25-Sep-03
D34																7	22-Sep-03
D35																5	23-Sep-03
D36																2	24-Sep-03
D37																2	24-Sep-03
D38																3	25-Sep-03

Time now

No	Estimated Completion	Work done (d)	Work to do (d)	Quality acceptable	Responsibilities kept	Change required	External delay	Special problem
D31		7	0	Y				
D32		2	0	Y				
D33	26-Sep-03							
D34	23-Sep-03	6	2	Y				
D35	23-Sep-03	3	2	Y				
D36	25-Sep-03	2	2					
D37	25-Sep-03	2	2					
D38	26-Sep-03	3	3					

Figure 14.3 *Turnaround document against the activity schedule*

Turnaround documents: I described above how turnaround documents can be used to gather data simply and easily. In particular I described how data gathering could easily be built into the weekly or fortnightly completion of time sheets. Figure 14.3 is a turnaround document against the activity schedule shown in Figures 7.7, 8.10 and 12.5. I will describe in the next sections how this can be used to stimulate discussion about actual progress.

ANALYSING PROGRESS AND FORECASTING COMPLETION

The next step in the control process is to analyse progress. For the quantitative measures, cost and time, this means forecasting the cost and time to completion. For the qualitative measures, quality, configuration and scope, it means determining whether the correct standards are being achieved, and if not whether that will have any affect on the cost and time forecasts.

FORECASTING COST AND TIME TO COMPLETION

There is a principle of project management, called forward-looking control, which says that you can only control the future, you cannot control the past. The past is done, it is spent cost, and cannot be undone. If we are forecasting that our project will be overspent or late, we can only make savings in the future. The only value of the past is to learn from our mistakes.

Forecasting cost to completion

In Chapter 11 I introduced earned value analysis to forecast cost to completion. I won't repeat that here. I just want to reinforce that there are two ways of calculating planned cost of work complete:

1 as the sum of the estimates for the work completed (making an allowance for work in progress)
2 as the estimate for the work left to be done subtracted from the original estimate.

In Chapter 11, I said these would give the same answer if you made no allowance for possible changes in the cost of work left to do. The second method of calculating planned cost of work complete is consistent with forward-looking control because we adjust the estimate for the work left to do:

- if there has been an overspend in one area that is likely to be repeated, that can be included; for instance there may have been an increase in wage rates
- if there are changes, or shortfalls, or improvements, in the qualitative measures, that can be allowed for
- if our experience to date has shown a better, cheaper way of achieving our objectives.

The simplest way of working out the forecast cost at completion is:

Forecast cost at completion = Actual cost of work complete + Planned cost of work remaining

You can see how the data suggested above enables you to calculate these.

Forecast time to completion

The way to forecast time to completion is to schedule the rest of the project in the same way you scheduled it originally. If the project is on plan so far, you forecast it will be completed on the planned date. If non-critical work is delayed by an amount less than the float, you will probably forecast that you will complete on time, unless there are resource implications, that is the delay will cause a resource overload, causing something else to be delayed. If non-critical work is delayed by an amount greater than the float, or critical work is delayed, then that will have an impact on the completion date. You will need to declare a delay, unless you can find a way of shortening the time required for the work remaining. This you may be able to do by running more work in parallel (if resources will allow it), or by shortening the duration of future work. Durations of future work can be reduced by adding additional resources, or by using experience to date to find a better way of doing it.

QUALITATIVE MEASURES

These tell us whether we need to adjust the forecast of time and cost, increasing the estimates if there is a shortfall in quality and configuration, or decreasing them if we find an easier way to achieve our objective than planned. Also monitoring the quality and configuration ensures we achieve the standards as planned.

STIMULATING DISCUSSIONS

To forecast completion well, you need to stimulate good discussion in the control meeting. This can be achieved by having the team report progress verbally against the plan. The plan can be projected on to a white board, by photocopying it on to a transparency and using an overhead projector, or by using a beamer (data projector). Figure 14.4 shows how the discussion might go against Figure 14.3. Although I strongly recommend control meetings, because they are an essential part of control, I also recommend that they should be kept short. One hour a week, or two hours once a fortnight, are appropriate amounts of time for control. Ways of doing this are by focusing the discussion around the plan (as suggested in Figure 14.4) and by identifying problems and assigning responsibility for solving them, rather than trying to solve them in the meeting.

The team, including the contractor, meet at 4.00 pm on Friday 19 September. The previous meeting was a week ago, on Friday 12 September. At that point D31 and D32 had finished on time; D33 and D34 had started. It was already clear, as a result of the discovery work done in Milestone M4, that the design and development work might take a day longer than expected.

Ian Simons asks the contractor to report on progress. She says she has now spent six days, and as expected the work will take eight days, not seven. So there are two days remaining and she will finish on Tuesday next week, 23 September.

D35 has now also started. Ian asks Jan to report progress on obtaining approval of personnel. Jan says she has spent three days and expects it to take two more as planned. Only minor modifications have been identified.

D36, D37 and D38 are due to start on Tuesday next week. Ian asks Jan to comment. She says that because D34 is taking a day longer than expected, they will all start a day late, on Wednesday, but experience on D35 indicates they will take the planned time. In particular the changes identified so far indicate that the time allowed for D38 is realistic. Thus the milestone will be achieved a day late, a week today.

Figure 14.4 *Active control meeting*

Figure 14.5 is another simple tool that can stimulate discussion. It shows that the project timescale can be on time or late, and the cost can be as planned or overspent. That helps identify the cause of problems:

1 If both time and cost are as planned, that is good.
2 If the timescale is slipping, but the cost is as planned, that means the team are not working; you are therefore looking for external delays, such as information or materials or tools not arriving, or people delayed by working elsewhere.
3 If the cost is slipping, but the timescale is as planned, that means the team are having to do small amounts of additional work but they are able to cope within the timescale.
4 If both are slipping, then the team are suffering larger overspends or delays.

		Time	
		As planned	Late
Cost	As planned	All is well	External delays
	Overspent	Small extra work	Large extra work

Figure 14.5 *The interplay between cost and time*

I did an audit in one company on a project which had gone disastrously wrong, and while talking to the people in the contracts department, one person said, 'Those idiots in estimating forget to include the printers in the estimate in every project!' I asked him if he had ever been back to tell them after a project. 'No! D'oh!'

Figure 14.6 *Estimates are wrong*

If the work is taking longer than planned or costing more, does the fault lie with the estimates, or with the performance of the project team? It can be either, though usually there is some indication of which. If project after project the work takes longer than expected, it tends to suggest a mistake in estimating. However, if the estimates represent industry norms, it suggests something is seriously wrong with productivity on projects in the company. Figures 14.6, 14.7 and 14.8 illustrate this issue.

I worked with a small software consultancy that was trying to overcome a severe problem of job overruns. Jobs were estimated by principals or directors and project managers were told they were not to come back halfway through a job and say that the estimate was never achievable. They were told that once they had accepted the job, they had accepted the estimate, and if they wanted to challenge the estimate, they were to do so *before* starting the job. The project managers said that challenging estimates made by their seniors could be career limiting. The reply was that if they had a successful track record of managing projects, they could challenge about one estimate in five. Principals and directors were former project managers and so they knew how much time jobs took – almost all estimates were tight, but achievable. But nobody is perfect so the odd mistake was made. If a successful project manager challenged the odd estimate, it would be assumed that a mistake had been made; if somebody was challenging every estimate, then it would be rightfully career limiting. But if it was found that every estimate that had been challenged (by different project managers) had been made by the same principal, then that would be career limiting for that principal.

Figure 14.7 *Is challenging the estimates career limiting?*

> I worked in a software house. They said that every project was three times overspent. I asked why they didn't just estimate the cost of each project and then multiply by three. The answers I received ranged from 'the estimates would be wrong' (even though they would be more accurate) to 'we would never win a contract' (but at least they would make a profit on those they did win).

Figure 14.8 *Estimating software development*

TriMagi					MILESTONE PLAN	MILESTONE REPORT	
Project:					Intranet Phase 1		
Project Champion:					Martin Pacific		
Project Manager:					Frances Seeker		
Date	**P**	**M**	**D**	**H**	**Milestone name**	**Report date**	**Milestone report**
18 Aug		M0			When the managing director and personnel manager approve that the project is ready to start	29 Aug	Project started 18 August
26 Aug		M1			When the overall content and style of the web space has been agreed	29 Aug	Completed 26 August, 1 day late. system slightly larger than expected, but not critical
28 Aug				H1	When the current inventory of hardware and data has been identified and logged	29 Aug	Completed 26 August, 1 day early. Fewer exceptions identified than expected.
02 Sep		M2			When the content of the home and news pages has been agreed	12 Sep	Started and finished 1 day late, see M1. Since hardware is critical will not cause overall delay
02 Sep		M3			When the content of the document processing pages has been agreed	12 Sep	Ditto
02 Sep		M4			When the content of the personnel information pages has been agreed	12 Sep	Ditto
03 Sep	P1				When existing procedures have been reviewed and revised procedures written	12 Sep	Started and finished 2 days late due to extra work identified at M1. Nor critical
09 Sep		M5			When the overall content has been agreed ready for design	12 Sep	Proceeded to design 5 September
15 Sep				H2	When the hardware requirements have been defined	12 Sep	Finished 12 September. As predicted, lower requirements than originally expected
15 Sep	P2				When new jobs required by the revised procedures have been designed	12 Sep	Expected to finish 16 September. Taking longer due to increased reuirements, see M1
22 Sep				H3	When the hardware has been designed	12 Sep	Expected to start 15 September. Order should be placed on time
25 Sep			D1		When the home and news pages have been designed and developed	12 Sep	Work started. Expected to finish one day late, see M1
25 Sep			D2		When the document processing pages have been desinged and developed	12 Sep	Ditto
25 Sep			D3		When the personnel information pages have been designed and developed	12 Sep	Ditto
29 Sep	P3				When the new procedures have been piloted and adjustments approved	12 Sep	Piloting will begin next week, one day late
07 Oct			D4		When the site has been assembled		
14 Oct	P4				When the procedures have been optimized and adjustments made to the web site		
17 Oct			D5		When the site has been signed off and is ready to be deployed		
17 Oct	P5				When the user trial is complete and the operation of the procedures and sites tested and approved		
11 Nov				H4	When the new hardware has been installed		
11 Nov				H5	When the data for personnel information has been entered or migrated		
12 Nov	P6				When the site goes live		
14 Nov		M6			When the success of Phase 1 has been reviewed, a report produced and Phase 2 can begin		

Figure 14.9 *Control report at the milestone level*

REPORTING TO SENIOR MANAGERS AT THE MILESTONE LEVEL

Once progress data has been gathered and analysed at the activity level (the lower cycle in Figure 14.2), the project manager must summarize that information and pass it on to the client

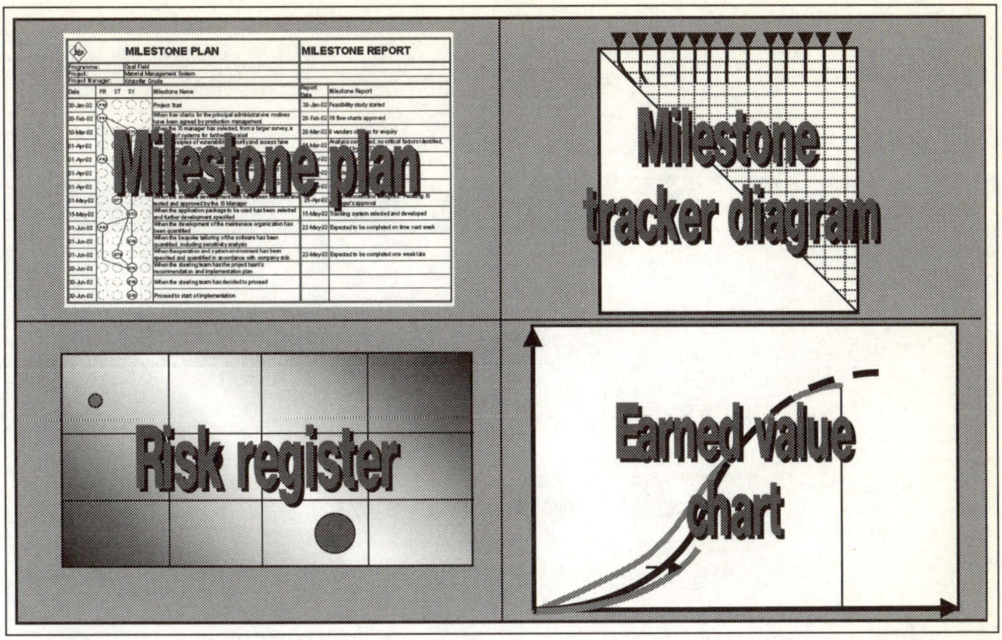

Figure 14.10 *Project performance tracking sheet*

or senior managers (the upper cycle in Figure 14.2). The report to senior managers can be made against the milestone plan, Figure 14.9, as suggested in Figure 14.4. This is usefully supported by the milestone tracker chart, Figure 12.7, and the earned value S-curves, Figure 11.14. These three diagrams provide a highly visual picture of progress on the project which is all the senior managers need. They can be combined into a single one page report, together with the risk register, Figure 14.10, or into a project dashboard, Figure 14.11. With this information, you should be able to keep them off the backs of the project team members, feeding them only more detailed information where there is a problem that requires their involvement (see Figure 14.12).

TAKING ACTION AND RECOVERING PROGRESS

The final step in the control process is to take any necessary action to recover progress. If the project is not going according to plan, there are four basic actions available:

1 rearrange the plan
2 slip the dates
3 add resource
4 reduce the ambition.

I used to say the last three meant you sacrificed time, cost or quality. Once I was doing a course where one of the delegates said that with the current focus on quality, they were not allowed to sacrifice quality. I then realized that 4 doesn't say reduce quality, it says do less work. The delegate was right. Once you have set the quality standard, that is sacrosanct. The work you do

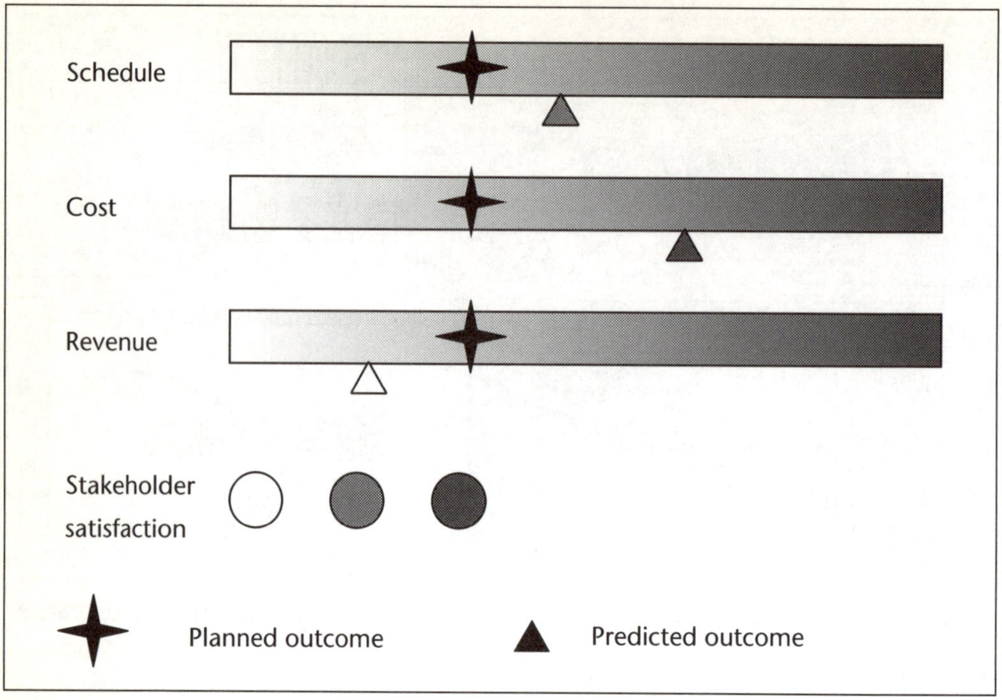

Figure 14.11 *Project dashboard*

> I did a course in a medium-sized electronics company. During the course, one of the in-company tutors claimed that the managing director reviewed progress on the 30 largest projects once a month. The course delegates would not believe this. I explained that with the project performance tracker sheet, Figure 14.10, or with the project dashboard, Figure 14.11, he would be able to satisfy himself that progress was satisfactory on, say, three-quarters of the projects after spending about 10 minutes on each one. Then he could spend up to an hour interrogating the one quarter worst performing ones, the whole process just taking one day.

Figure 14.12 *Reporting to senior managers*

must be to that quality. But sometimes you can reduce the work, and achieve something within your original timescales. I discuss this further below.

REARRANGE THE PLAN

The first option is to find another way of doing the project that enables us to achieve our original objectives within the time and cost targets. Sometimes, for instance, you had planned to do two activities in a certain order, just because both required the same scarce resource, and so had to be done in series and not in parallel. The one you scheduled first then gets delayed by some external circumstance. So you just do the other one first. It is for this sort of reason that I do not believe in overcomplicating the logic. It is best to keep as many degrees of freedom as possible, and you should certainly not use the logic to reflect resource constraint. This option is equivalent to avoiding the risk (see Chapter 13). It is a way of doing the project that enables you to achieve the original scope within the original time and cost targets.

SLIP THE DATES

Next you can just accept that the project will be delayed. Perhaps you rearrange the plan, and manage to recover some of the lost time, but perhaps not all.

ADD RESOURCE

The next option is to sacrifice the cost by throwing resources at the problem. However, sometimes this has the opposite effect to what is intended. Brooks in his famous book, *The Mythical Man-Month* (1995), proposes Brooks's Law:

> Adding resource to a software project that is going late, delays it further.

The reasoning is simple – people currently working on the project have to take time out to brief new people joining. You might think that you can overcome this by just asking the current people to work overtime. However, there is ample evidence that people's productivity falls as they work longer hours. Somewhere around 48 hours a week, their productivity falls to such an extent that the total amount of work done is less than someone working a 40 hour week. So by and large, adding people to the project doesn't work, unless you can get the extra people to work on bulk work that requires little briefing by the current team members. If you are falling behind, what you can try to do is carve out some of the work that is sufficiently independent of what has been done, so that the people it is given to don't need briefing on what has gone before.

REDUCING AMBITION

If all else fails, you can consider doing less work. Sometimes this is a viable option (Figure 14.13). You find you cannot produce all the desired outputs from the project in the time or cost available. But you can produce something of value, finishing the rest at a later date. It is usually not viable to do less work for the original budget; that is not cost effective. But perhaps for resource constraints you do less work in the original planned time, and then achieve the rest later.

WHICH IS PREFERABLE?

Which of these, sacrificing time, cost or functionality, is best? What should a team do if faced with two apparently equivalent options? The answer is it depends on the project, AND the project team should decide what is right for them as the project starts. It is so easy to convince yourself to follow the easy course in the middle of the project, not the course that is necessarily right. So you need to go right back to your decisions about success criteria, key performance indicators and success factors (see Chapter 6), and base your decisions on what you decided there.

I did a start-up workshop on a project in British Telecom where they faced the issue of reducing ambition. The project was to merge several computer databases and several customer helplines. Prior to this there was one database associated with each helpline, and vice versa. It would annoy customers with two queries to have to ring two helplines, and sometimes the data held was not consistent. So the idea was to have one database, and one helpline where the customers could raise all of their queries. (This is not as bizarre as it might sound. The increasing power of computers in the late 1980s made the single database possible.)

The plan was to implement both the one database and one help-line in nine months. However, they realized they could not achieve that. So they implemented the single database in nine months, and then customers could ask several queries at each line. They merged the helplines six months later. The single database enabling multiple question from each call was a customer quality issue; the single helpline was a question of internal efficiency. So they dealt with customer quality first and internal efficiency second.

Figure 14.13 *Reducing ambition*

RECOVERING FROM A CRISIS

Every now and again a project goes so badly it slips into a crisis. There is a human syndrome of spiralling into a worse and worse mess. Things start to go badly, so you work hard to put them right. That makes you tired, so you make more mistakes. So you work harder, which makes you more tired, resulting in yet more mistakes. If you find yourself in this situation, you need to break the cycle by taking a day's rest. Go and sleep on your problem. It is amazing how much clearer it is after you have had a good night's sleep. There is now ample psychological evidence that our brains clarify our problems subconsciously while we are asleep, making us able to address them much more clearly once we have woken up. Denis Healey, the previous Labour Chancellor of the Exchequer (Minister of Finance) in the UK, proposed his first law of holes:

> If you find yourself in a hole, stop digging!

What good advice. Leave your problem, sleep on it and then come back with a fresh mind. Then apply the ten step problem-solving cycle shown in Figure 1.4 to try to solve the problem in a structured way. Sometimes even another start-up workshop can help solve the problem. Of course from the hyperactive you get the same reaction to the idea of leaving their problems as you do to the idea of holding a start-up workshop. 'I don't have time to go and sleep on my problems, I have a fire to fight, holes to dig, dragons to slay!' They are the very people who need to leave their problems, to stop digging themselves into deeper and deeper holes, but they are the ones who will carry on and make a bigger and bigger mess.

Every now and again you may be faced with the decision of abandoning the project. I take a very simple view of this – predicted future cost *must* be justified by predicted future benefit. That is forward-looking control. You cannot undo what has been spent. Don't use what you have spent to justify carrying on. If either the predicted costs are rising or the predicted benefits are falling, such that you will no longer make a profit, stop!

CONCLUDING REMARKS

Ogård and Gallstad (1999) say

> You get what you measure

I spoke in Chapter 6 of deciding key performance indicators (KPIs) for the project, and measuring those as suggested in Figures 14.10 and 14.11. Whatever you focus on will be what the project achieves and delivers, so you do need to know and understand your KPIs and measure those. Similarly, if you measure the right KPIs, you should be in a position to make the right decisions to recover the project, as I have just suggested.

CHAPTER

15 *Project Close-out*

The last stage of the project life cycle is project close-out, called deployment in Chapter 2. This is when the project metamorphoses into a routine operation, where the new web space is commissioned and handed over to the users for them to run long term. With a diverse project team, it is particularly important to ensure that their work is integrated at the end. Also with a wide range of users and stakeholders, you need to ensure that they all accept the web space as it is delivered. As the project comes to an end, the project team need to ensure that:

- the work is finished and loose ends tied up, without losing control of cost and time
- the web space is commissioned and handed over to the users, and the users and their managers sign off any acceptance certificates
- the web space is operating to solve the problem for which it was developed, and delivering the benefit that was used to justify its cost
- the team is disbanded in a way that looks after their personal needs
- any learning from the project is recorded to improve the performance on future projects.

I will discuss each of these topics in turn.

FINISHING THE WORK

There is a version of Sod's Law that says:

> The first 90 per cent of the work costs 90 per cent of the budget; and the last 10 per cent of the work also costs 90 per cent of the budget.

There are two reasons why this happens:

1. The first is that the team have been lying about progress, saying everything is going according to plan when it is not. Milestone tracker charts, earned value analysis (Chapters 11 and 12) and reporting against the plan (Chapter 14) should stop that happening.
2. The other reason is the project manager holds on to resources that have finished their input, just in case they are needed. This practice is both wasteful for the project and wasteful for the organization. Further, the devil makes work for idle hands, so people whose input is finished must be released, or they will start to make changes which will be costly and delay the project.

The following can help bring the project to an end in a timely and efficient manner:

- producing checklists of outstanding work to ensure all loose ends are tied up
- planning and controlling at lower levels of work breakdown

- holding more frequent control meetings to ensure problems are identified and solved early
- planning the rundown of the project team as the work tapers off to ensure that people are released for other work
- creating a task force with responsibility for completing outstanding work
- closing contracts to ensure no unnecessary costs are booked
- supporting the project manager by using a deputy with finishing skills.

As you approach the end of the project, you look at what tasks need to be done to complete outstanding work. Instead of waiting for a fortnight to find out what work has been achieved, you need to create daily lists of outstanding work, to complete the web space and associated PSO changes, hand it over to the client and commission it. This leads to planning at a lower level of work breakdown, and holding more frequent control meetings. At the end, the risk of delay becomes greater, and so it becomes appropriate to review progress more frequently, weekly, daily, or even twice daily.

As the project nears its end, you require fewer resources. That is what gives the S-curve its classic shape. However, to ensure the most efficient completion, you must plan the release of resources in advance. You do not want them turning up one day, and sitting around until you realize they are not needed, because that is inefficient for both the project and the organization as a whole. You tell people one or two weeks in advance that they will not be required on a certain date. You also tell the resource providers, so that they can make full use of their people when they are released.

As the teams run down, it is essential to combine people into cross-functional task forces, to retain natural *hunting packs*. In Chapter 8, after Frame (1995), I described these task forces as *surgical teams*. There are several reasons for using them. People work best in small teams, and as the number of people reduces, the number of managers must be reduced, with teams merged. It is also natural to give the task forces checklists to complete, rather than spreading the work over disparate groups. As the project comes to an end, the work of different professionals needs to be integrated, and putting them together in a task force achieves that. Closing contracts with suppliers and subcontractors is another way running down the team (see Figure 15.1).

The skills needed to close a project can be different to those to start it up and run it. Therefore it may also be appropriate to change managers in the final stage. However, if this change is to be seamless, the new manager must be a former deputy (or team leader), who has been involved for some time.

> A delegate on a course told me he had been telephoned by the Accounts Department two years after a project had finished to be told it was overspent. He was asked what was he doing about it. He asked how this could be because the project had finished two years previously, it was underspent then, he had closed all the account numbers and no further work had been done. The Accounts Department said it was not company policy to close account numbers, and people were still charging their time, so what was HE doing about it. It wouldn't happen to Dilbert.

Figure 15.1 *Closing account numbers and contracts*

TRANSFERRING THE WEB SPACE

Key issues in transferring the web space to the users include:

- planning for the transition;
- ensuring the users accept the web space;
- training the users in the operation of the web space;
- ensuring a definite cut-over;
- recording the as-built design;
- ensuring continuing service or maintenance of the web space;
- appointing super-users.

I should say that although these are done at the end of the project, they must be planned early; in particular, the acceptance criteria must be agreed during design. You must not have post-completion justification of what is delivered, trying to force the users to take what is delivered, rather than what was agreed in design. Likewise, you must not let users try to impose new requirements at the end.

Planning for the transition: There must be a clear understanding of how responsibility for the web space is to transfer from the project manager to the operations manager. This will happen during the commissioning process, which, as we saw above, should be planned at a lower level of work breakdown than its construction.

Ensuring the users accept the new web space: At the end of the project the users must be given the opportunity to agree that the new web space meets the specification. There must be clearly agreed acceptance criteria against which it is accepted. On a strict contractual relationship the operations manager should sign completion certificates to accept the product.

Training the users in the operation of the new web space: The users will usually not be experts in the operation of the new web space. They will therefore require training in its use. This should be planned as part of the project, indeed, it is probably too late if it is not addressed until close-out. However, it is in this transition stage that much of the training takes place. Training will be in the use of the web space, but may also include simple maintenance procedures.

Ensuring a definite cut-over: There are two types of definite cut-over required:

- from project team to users
- from old system to new system.

The first of these is non-controversial, the second is. At the planned transition (and as acceptance certificates are signed), there should be a definite cut-over, at which responsibility is transferred, and the new web space accepted by the users. It is also important from a reliability point of view that there is clear ownership at the web space. Either the project manager should be in control or the operations manager should be in control.

The other definite cut-over is from old system to new system, if the new web space is replacing an existing system. At midnight one night the old system is turned off, and the new one used from then on. Some people say there needs to be parallel running as the new system proves itself. But with parallel running the new system will never prove itself, as the users will continue to use the old one they know and love. There must be cold turkey as they are forced to use the new system. By all means operate the new system in a pilot with trial data; have a small group of users run it in parallel with real data in the engineering or research department as a final test. But when it is commissioned it must be solely in charge. In Chapter 2 I described how replicating the functionality of the old system can aid this cut-over, but how that can be expensive and delay the adoption of new functionality.

Recording the as-built design: It is important that the as-built design is recorded. This requires the incorporation of all design changes into the final configuration. This is part of configuration management (see Chapter 10).

Ensuring continuing service or maintenance of the new web space: The users may be trained to undertake simple service or maintenance, and operating manuals may help them. But it is usually impossible for them to become experts in the technology of the new web space, and so it is necessary to ensure appropriate systems are in place to provide back up and support throughout its life. During handover these systems need to be implemented, but they should be designed during the design stage.

Appoint super-users: It is common to appoint two or three super-users, who are assigned to the project team early on and given higher level access rights, somewhere between ordinary user and administrator. These super-users build up a higher level of knowledge of the system, and can be the first line of technical support for other users, giving local support and reducing the need for users to contact the help desk or designers.

OBTAINING THE BENEFIT

Many project managers view their job as finished when the new web space is handed over. However, making sure it is being used to deliver benefit is the final step in the control process, undertaken at the top of the project hierarchy, the integrative level. Whether this final step is the responsibility of the project manager or project champion depends on the project, but should be agreed as part of the project strategy at the start. It will probably be the champion who is held accountable if the owner does not receive adequate return on investment, and so the onus rests on the champion to ensure it happens. There are four steps in the control process (see Chapter 14):

1. **Create a measure:** There must be a clear definition of purpose of the new web space and expected benefits. This is a clear statement of the criteria by which the project will be judged to be successful, stated as part of the project strategy, and defined as part of the project definition (see Chapters 5 and 6).
2. **Monitor achievement:** Following commissioning, you check to see whether the new web space is delivering the expected benefit. It should be delivering the expected functionality and the expected revenue stream.
3. **Calculate variances:** Determine the cause of any difference between the expected benefits and those obtained. This requires measuring the revenue stream. The cause may be that the users are not using the product to its full capacity, either deliberately or inadvertently. Or it may be that the expected market take-up of the new product is not what was expected.

4 **Take action:** Hopefully a small amount of fine tuning of the web space, or a small amount of additional training of users is all that is required to achieve the actual benefit. Projects are risky, because they are novel and unique, and so it is likely that the design carried some small imperfections which can be easily corrected. This is often the case with web design. Rarely, improvement will require another project.

DISBANDING THE TEAM

Over the last three sections, I considered work-related and strategic issues of close-out. However, the team members may face the end with mixed feelings. The cycle of team formation and maintenance discussed in Chapter 4 can see them going into mourning at the end of the project, and performance dropping. Performance can rise as they look forward to new opportunities, or drop if they face unemployment. This can impact badly on them and the project. It is the task of both line and project managers to manage this emotional response, so that staff are retained and reintroduced into the normal work environment. When considering the motivation of project staff, remember they belong permanently to the organization and only temporarily to the project. This means that while the project may not need them once their contribution has finished, the organization for which they work may value the team members even more because of new skills they learned and may want them for future projects. Retaining project team members is vital and so the process of disbanding the project team must be managed in a caring way. Key elements in this process include:

- planning the rundown of resources;
- returning resources promptly to their line managers;
- holding an end of project party;
- holding a debriefing meeting;
- rewarding achievement;
- disciplining underachievement, and
- counselling staff.

1 **Planning the rundown of resources in advance:** This, as explained above, is important to achieve an efficient end to the project. It is also important for the motivation of the project team. People feel more motivated to complete their work if they know they are to be transferred immediately to new work. That is only possible if their release has been planned, so that their line managers have been able to plan their future work.

2 **Returning resources promptly to their line managers:** The organization gets optimum use of its resources if they are returned promptly to normal duties after completion of the project. Line managers of people seconded to the project are more likely to treat future requests for resources favourably if those people are used efficiently, which means releasing them at the earliest possible opportunity.

3 **Debriefing meeting:** A project close-out meeting can be as important as a launch meeting, as part of the life cycle of the project team. It fulfils two purposes:

The most obvious is that it can be used to review the performance of the project, to see if there are any lessons that can be used for future projects. This is something that project-based organizations are very bad at. Learning in project-based organizations requires four steps:

- lessons must be captured in the post completion review
- they must be recorded
- they must be distributed to the rest of the organization
- they must be used on future projects.

There is an attenuation at each of these steps, with 80 per cent of projects conducting post completion reviews, 60 per cent recording the lessons learnt, 40 per cent distributing them to the rest of the organization, and 20 per cent reusing them on future projects. Some organizations, in particular, are very poor at inducting apprentice project managers in the lessons learnt in the organization, with the result that organizations find themselves repeating the same old mistakes, with a very strong sense of déjà vu.

The close-out meeting marks the end of the period of working together, and allows people to show their grief, or frustration, or pleasure at having been a member of the project.

I conducted a close-out meeting for a project for which I had done the start-up meeting. The close-out meeting lasted three days, the project manager debriefing the entire team on the first day, and her two lieutenants on the second day. They conducted a mini start-up meeting on the third day. The meeting was held in an expensive hotel to the West of London. It was January so at 'only' £150 per night the rooms were half price. The night before the meeting we had a dinner to celebrate the success of the project, and the project manager's boss was opening champagne at £100 a bottle. I asked how he could afford it, and he said the project had been budgeted to cost £10 million, but in the event it had cost £9 million. He was making use of a bit of the underspend to say thank you to the team.

Figure 15.2 *End of project party*

4 **End of project party:** The use of 'festivals' is an important motivator on projects. They should be used to mark important project milestones, especially the end of the project. The difficulty is choosing the timing of a party, so the maximum number of people can come, before being dispersed to new jobs, but when they actually have something to celebrate. The end of project party can be combined with the close-out meeting (Figure 15.2).
5 **Rewarding achievement:** The team members are likely to react favourably to future requests to work for the project manager if their contribution is rewarded. The end of project party is part of that (Figure 15.2). However, it is equally important that a person's achievement is recognized by those who matter, especially the manager who writes their annual appraisal, so that their contribution to the business can be recognized. An important part of this process is winning the appraising manager's commitment to the project, so that they view a success as an important achievement during the year.
6 **Disciplining underachievement:** It is also important to discipline poor performance so good performers do not feel their effort was in vain and poor performers know how to improve. For this reason the disciplining process should be positive, guiding people as to how to perform better. Of course, it might be possible to take corrective action during the project, so the earlier this is done the better. There is a line in Shakespeare's play *Hamlet*, 'You have got to be cruel to be kind.' Giving people feedback can help them improve in the future.

7 **Counselling of staff:** The fifth stage of team development is mourning, as the project fades into history and the team with it. This is not very good for the ego or self-esteem of the team members, who find that overnight they may be reduced to 'has-beens' unless they go immediately to another project or line job. For those who are not so lucky, a counselling session can be of tremendous value. Whilst this may incorporate some of the activities mentioned above, it often encompasses much more. For example:

- it offers a chance for the individual to review career objectives;
- it offers scope for skills consolidation in the form of theoretical training to supplement the practical experience;
- it shows caring by the organization, the key factor in the whole exercise.

REVIEWING ACHIEVEMENT

The post-completion review fulfils two essential steps for the project, both of which I have previously described:

- it can be used to ensure that the as-built design is properly recorded
- it can be used to capture learning from the project.

Lessons learnt can be obtained from:

- a comparison of final costs and benefits for feeding back to the estimating process, and to the selection of future projects
- a review of the technical achievement on the project for feeding back to the design and selection of future projects
- a review of the successes and failures of the project and the lessons learned, for feeding back to the management of future projects.

CHAPTER 16 *Managing Programmes and Portfolios of Projects*

Since Chapter 4 I have focused on the single project, describing how to define, plan and manage it. However, many web-delivery projects often take place as part of a larger programme or portfolio of projects. In Chapter 3, I emphasized how the implementation of a new web presence might lead to other changes in the business, changes to the people, systems and organization structure. However, rather than undertaking all of those changes as a single large project, it is sometimes more convenient to break them into several sub-projects, each sub-project delivering a component of the larger system. Also, the flexibility of web technology makes it easy to break a large web space into a number of sub-projects delivering elements of the space. So an organization might undertake a very large web implementation as a programme consisting of sub-projects to deliver elements of the web space, or corresponding PSO changes. The organization undertakes a programme of work to deliver the overall, strategic objectives, and breaks the programme into sub-projects, each delivering an element of the higher order system. At other times, an organization, especially a contract organization, or a back office doing development work for the front office, may undertake several projects using the same limited resource pool. The projects are not related in any way, other than that they share common resources. The projects are managed together as part of a portfolio for management convenience.

In this chapter I describe additional tools required for the management of a programme or portfolio of projects. In the next section, I define programmes and portfolios of projects, and consider some of the issues associated with their management. I then consider the management of a programme of projects, explaining how to ensure the projects deliver a coherent end of objective for the programme, and describing some of the roles associated with programme management. Finally, I describe how to manage the interfaces between projects in a programme, and how to prioritize resources between the projects in a portfolio.

DEFINITIONS AND ISSUES

Many books on project management are written about projects as stand-alone entities. They inherently assume that a project is a large unitary endeavour, with independent objectives, isolated from other projects and operations, and with a dedicated team. That is often the case with large engineering, building, or construction projects, and in my view represents about 10 per cent of project activity. Chapters 4 to 15 of this book tended to take that focus. However, many web-delivery projects take place as part of a larger programme or portfolio of projects, with shared objectives, integrated with each other, and other projects and operations and sharing resources from a common resource pool. That represents about 90 per cent of project activity, and since the projects in a programme or portfolio tend to be smaller, it represents about 99.9 per cent of projects by number. It is now common to differentiate between programmes and portfolios of projects (APM, 2000):

A programme is a group of projects which deliver a higher level strategic objective, not delivered by any of the projects on their own.

A portfolio is a group of unrelated projects brought together for management convenience, usually to prioritize resources or manage interfaces between them.

Some people say a programme is a special case of a portfolio, where the projects share a higher order objective. To an extent I disagree with this. With a programme the higher order strategic objective comes first, and the projects defined to deliver it. A programme is also usually a temporary organization, terminated when the objective is achieved. With a portfolio, you have a collection of projects which need prioritizing. And a portfolio may be permanent as new projects come and go. A group of projects is managed together as part of a programme or portfolio to reduce uncertainty and deliver additional benefit. The types of additional benefits you can gain are:

1 *Projects get finished:* A common syndrome when you don't prioritize resources is that projects keep on being interrupted. A project was meant to follow the dotted path in Figure 16.1, but keeps on losing its resources. Because it takes a time to work up momentum again, and some work has to be repeated, the delay is longer than the time it was without resources. When it loses resources for the second time it ought to be stopped. Prioritizing resources enables the project to follow the grey line. An aeroplane won't take off from the airport it is leaving from until the flight path is cleared through to the destination. Projects should be the same. The reality of life is that you may occasionally need to change priorities, but if you are prioritizing you are in control.

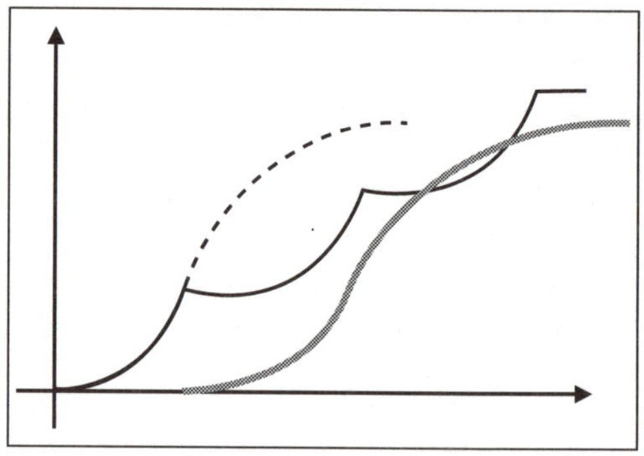

Figure 16.1 *Planning the flight path from take-off to landing*

2 *The higher order strategic objective is achieved:* The whole is greater than the sum of the parts.
3 *Interfaces are coordinated and risks managed:* The interrelationships between projects may be risks, or projects may share risks. By managing projects together you can reduce risks and achieve your objectives more effectively and more efficiently.
4 *Resource utilization is economized:* By taking a portfolio-wide view, resource utilization can be optimized across the portfolio ensuring resources are used to maximize profit overall. Like projects, programmes and portfolios are non-linear coupled systems which need to be optimized as a whole, and not project by project.

INTEGRATING PROJECTS IN A PROGRAMME

When the delivery of business strategy and development objectives requires the organization to undertake several related projects, it is best that the projects are managed as part of a programme of projects. Figure 1.8 shows the programme as the link between the organization's development objectives and individual projects. This concept may seem obvious, but it is surprisingly new in the project management community. The Office of Government Commerce

(OGC), produced the first edition of its project management procedure, Prince (OGC, 2002), about ten years ago, but has only recently issued the equivalent guideline for programme management (OGC, 1999). There are many advantages of grouping projects into programmes (or portfolios) which I now consider. I will then describe some of the roles associated with programme management.

ADVANTAGES OF PROGRAMME (AND PORTFOLIO) MANAGEMENT

Aligning projects with business strategy

In both Chapters 1 and 3, I stressed the need to ensure that the web-delivery projects we undertake are aligned with business strategy. If projects are undertaken individually, it is easy to get carried away with enthusiasm, and do projects which aren't strictly necessary, or in the worst case damaging. By maintaining the level of breakdown between development objectives and project objectives, the organization can define programme objectives to deliver its business objectives, and then ensure all the projects undertaken are aligned to those programme objectives. If any projects arise that are not, it is easy to decide whether those project objectives are important, in which case new development objectives need to be created, or whether the project should be cancelled. Similar decisions can be made with portfolios of projects. I discuss below the role of the project portfolio committee, which proritizes resources between projects depending on their strategic significance.

Refining understanding

An essential difference between programmes and large projects is that the objectives of a programme are less clear and specific. Often an organization has a strategic aim without clearly understanding how it will ultimately be achieved. Only as it works towards that aim can it refine its understanding of how that aim will be achieved. Early projects in the programme will refine the understanding of the final objectives. Grouping the projects into a programme enables them to be given clear precise objectives, while leaving the ultimate objective less clear. As the programme progresses, the final objective can be redefined as new projects start without great upheaval to projects in progress.

Achieving intermediate returns

Grouping the projects into the programme also makes it easier for the organization to achieve intermediate returns. I said above that the whole is greater than the sum of the parts. If the projects are managed separately, there is a risk that the higher order strategic objective won't be achieved until all the projects are integrated at the end. Managing them as part of a programme allows early projects to be integrated to achieve some of the higher order benefit early on.

> I worked with a systems integration contractor, developing military systems. They prioritized projects by date of receipt of order. They received an order from the Indian army for a system costing £5 million, needed in two years time. The next day they received an order from the British army for a spare part costing £50 000, needed yesterday, which would take two weeks to deliver. The spare part waited two years until the order for the Indian army was complete before it gained priority.

Figure 16.2 *Not focusing on smaller projects*

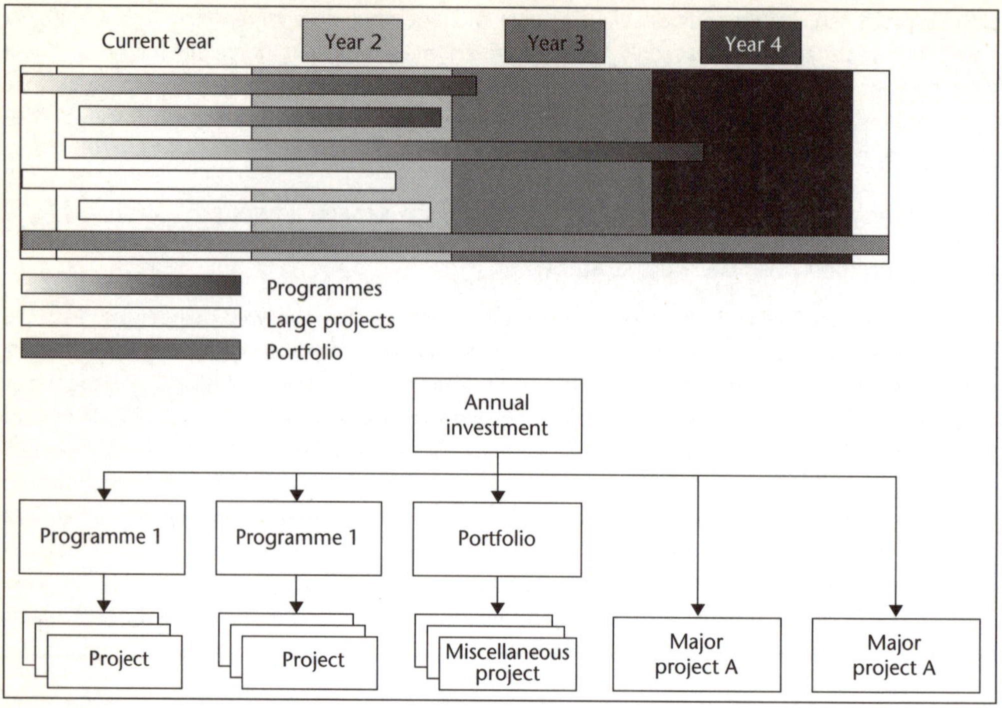

Figure 16.3 *Focusing on smaller projects*

Not forgetting smaller projects

There is a common syndrome in projects that the large projects gain the priority, simply because they are large. Small projects get forgotten about (see Figure 16.2). By grouping projects into programmes or portfolios, the programmes and portfolios can be given priority, and resources, alongside the large projects being undertaken by the organization (Figure 16.3). Each programme and portfolio can be given its own resource pool to manage.

Coordinating projects in a programme

Grouping projects in programmes facilitates the managing of interfaces between projects and the reduction of risk. A simple tool for coordinating the interfaces between projects in a programme is the impact matrix shown in Figure 16.4. A responsibility chart can be used for this purpose. The projects in the programme are listed across the columns and down rows, and interfaces between them identified. Grouping the projects into sub-programmes can minimize the number of interfaces between the sub-programmes. In that way you mitigate the risk of the interfaces. (The impact matrix is drawn as a half matrix, because it is assumed that we do not distinguish the direction of the interface.)

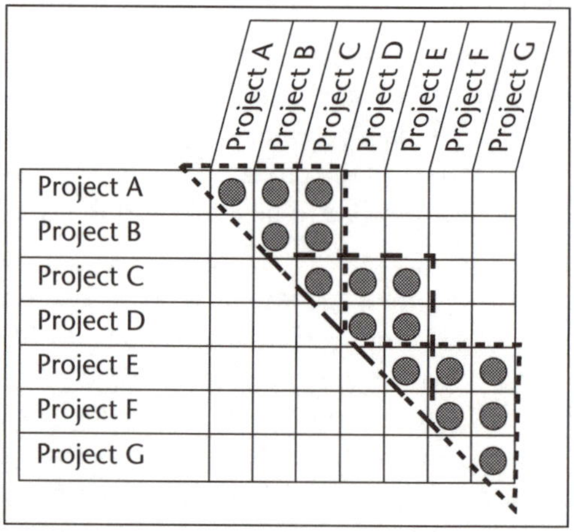

Figure 16.4 *Impact matrix*

MANAGING THE PROGRAMME

Structure

As with a project, a programme will have a manager and a champion. Figure 16.5 represents the relationship between them and the project manager and champion as suggested by the OGC (1999). The programme champion, often called the programme director, is responsible for delivering the benefits for the programme. The programme manager is responsible for ensuring the individual projects take place and deliver their benefits, and for integrating those into the programme's deliverables. As before, the project manager is responsible for ensuring their project is completed to time and cost, delivering its performance objectives. The project champion is responsible for ensuring the project delivers its business benefit as part of the overall programme. The lines in Figure 16.5 are intended to indicate reporting relationships, not hierarchical relationships. The project champion may in fact be the programme manager, or one of the business managers.

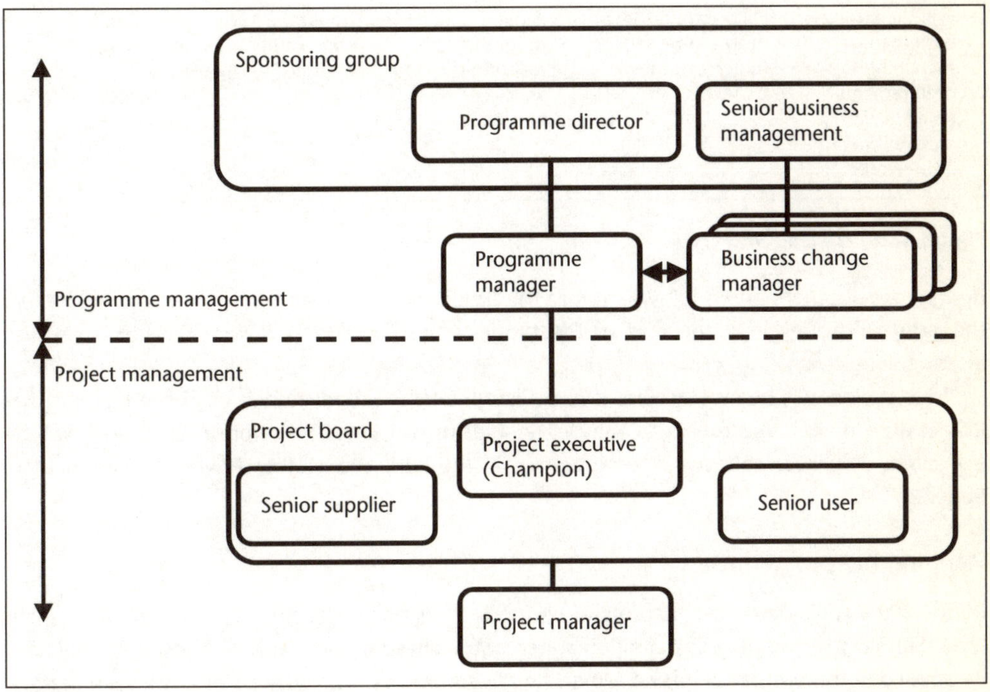

Figure 16.5 *Managing programmes*

Life cycle

As with a project, a programme will follow a life cycle. In fact with a programme of projects, the life cycle tends to be at the programme level. The individual projects tend to be much more homogeneous. Following the Prince 2 life cycle in Figure 1.7, start-up and initiation are done at the programme level. The individual projects are like stages of the programme, following implementation, delivery and transition to the next project. This is shown figuratively in Figure 16.6.

Following the life cycle for web projects in Chapter 2, discovery is done at the programme level, as initial design. That will define a number of projects, each of which will go through

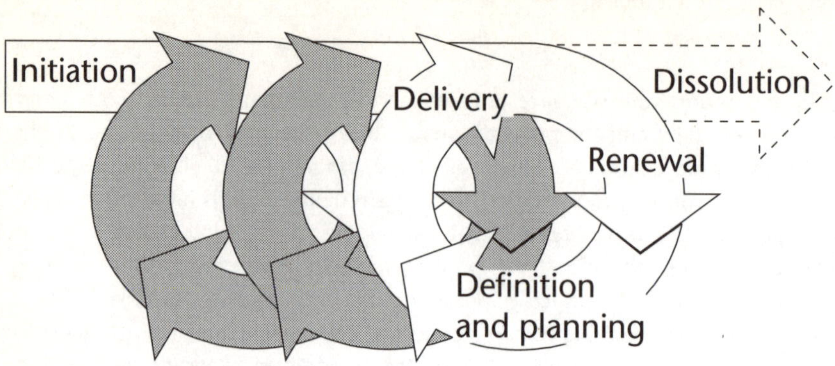

Initiation	Definition and planning	Delivery	Renewal	Dissolution
Will the business benefit from managing the requirements delivery with a programme framework?	How should the programme seek to achieve the benefits?	Is the programme realizing the anticipated benefits?	Should the programme continue?	How should remaining work or projects be reallocated?

Figure 16.6 *The programme cycle*

design, development and deployment into the programme. Further deployment will be done at the programme level, at the end of the programme, but also part way through to realize intermediate benefits.

Each project will be evaluated as it is delivered. One great advantage of web projects is that it is easy to make adjustments to the deliverables in real time. Therefore each project will be evaluated, as will be the overall programme, at the end, and at the delivery of intermediate benefits.

Planning the programme

Many of the tools described before can be used for planning the programme, but at a higher level. Particularly, the project definition statements, milestone plan and responsibility chart can be applied at the programme level. What is quite common is to have a summary level milestone plan for the programme (with an accompanying responsibility chart), and operational milestone plans for each project. A given project will be represented in the summary level plan by either a single milestone, or a few milestones, or even a whole area of work depending on its size. The milestones that appear in the summary level plan in the programme will be key milestones in the operational level plan at the project level.

PRORITIZING RESOURCES IN A PORTFOLIO OF PROJECTS

In this section I describe how to prioritize the resources between projects in a portfolio (or programme). Many organizations maintain a project portfolio committee to select projects for a programme. The third stage gate in Figure 3.11 is where projects are considered by the project portfolio committee. Having selected projects, it is then important to maintain a portfolio resource plan, both to help with the selection of future projects and to manage the assignment of resources to those projects selected. I will also describe selection of projects and the portfolio resource plan.

In an organization undertaking many web projects, the construction projects may be managed as individual projects, or managed as part of a programme of projects consisting of the development of the new web space, as well as supporting changes to people, systems and organizations. The remodelling and maintenance projects, on the other hand, would ideally be made part of a portfolio. A dedicated team would be created to manage the projects in the portfolio, and projects would be assigned to the portfolio, and resources assigned to the selected projects as described below. However, these are not strictly projects as described in Chapter 1. They are temporary activities assigned to the permanent organization, the portfolio. But regardless of whether you view them as projects or temporary activities assigned to the permanent organization, the techniques below can be used to select 'projects' and assign resources to them.

SELECTING PROJECTS FOR THE PORTFOLIO

In order to be able to properly select projects for the portfolio you need three things:

1 You need to know how many resources you have available to assign to new projects.
2 You need to know the resource requirements of the projects you plan to do.
3 You need to have a way of prioritizing projects.

The techniques described below for assigning resources to projects should forecast resource availability, so I won't discuss that any further now. I assume you know how many resources you have to assign to new projects. The techniques described in the earlier chapters, particularly Chapters 11 and 12, will enable you to work out the resource requirements for each project. The technique below for assigning resources assumes you know it, so it is taken as a given.

Next you need to be able to rank order projects according to priority. One method of ranking projects will derive from the investment appraisal process. Investment appraisal techniques are not discussed in this book, but you can read about them in Turner (1995) or Lock (2000b). From the investment appraisal process you will be able to rank projects according to internal rate of return (IRR) or payback. For IS and innovation projects, and therefore web projects, option pricing works better than IRR (Akalu, 2003). You may favour projects with fast payback, those that generate cash in the short term, rather than those that make profits in the long term. This will particularly be the case with remodelling projects, and may even be the case with some construction projects. Another method of ranking projects might be according to strategic importance. I suggested in Chapter 1 you could classify projects according to whether they are:

- stay-in-business projects
- repositioning projects, or
- performance improvement projects.

Many maintenance projects may be stay-in-business projects, while not generating much in the way of cash or profit per se. So they won't score highly against IRR or payback but will score highly against strategic importance.

Having prioritized the projects you are now ready to select those that you can do. This will be the role of the project portfolio committee. This is a committee of senior managers above the dotted line in Figure 16.5. The project portfolio committee can now be quite brutal. They list the projects in rank order, and keep adding them to the portfolio in that order until all available resources are consumed. There are no resources available to do the others. But it is not quite as blunt as that last statement. It might be that one of the projects that didn't quite make it is higher priority than one currently underway. In that case, the project underway needs to be cancelled, and the new project adopted. Also, one that didn't quite make it could be retained in the list of proposed projects, and reconsidered the next time the committee meets. The portfolio committee may meet once every three to six months. I worked with a company from the financial services industry making data products to supply over their own network. Their stage gate model is shown in Figure 3.11, and the meeting of the portfolio committee is stage gate 3. Their committee met once every three months. You might recall that I said in Chapter 3 that only two in eight projects adopted by the portfolio committee made it past the next two stage gates and were actually worked on, and only one was eventually released to market. I also worked with a company making electronic components for computers, where the committee met only once every six months.

ASSIGNING RESOURCES TO PROJECTS IN THE PORTFOLIO

Figure 16.7 illustrates the process of assigning resources to projects in the portfolio. But before describing this process, I will describe what doesn't work.

What doesn't work

The technique used in the past to assign resources to projects in a portfolio was as follows:

Individual projects were planned to determine their resource requirements. Then they were included in a gigantic plan, a plan of plans of all the projects. The resource availability was added to the system. Then the computer was told to schedule all the projects within the resource availability. The problem was you had to give the computer some rule for prioritizing one activity over another when there was a resource clash. And computers being dumb things, they would then apply that rule without question. Some of the rules proposed in the past were:

1 Projects are rank ordered in priority. What happens? The highest priority project gets all the resources it needs. The next struggles by. The next follows the start-stop-start-stop profile in Figure 16.1.
2 Priority is given according to float of the activity. What happens? Every activity is scheduled by late start. It can only get priority when it has no float.

Nothing works. This technique abdicates management responsibility to the computer, which doesn't have the intelligence to make fuzzy decisions. I still get papers submitted to the *International Journal of Project Management* suggesting new prioritizing rules. I send them straight back saying that their approch is 1980s project and portfolio management.

Master project scheduling

So what I propose is a technique I dubbed 'master project scheduling' (see Figure 16.7).

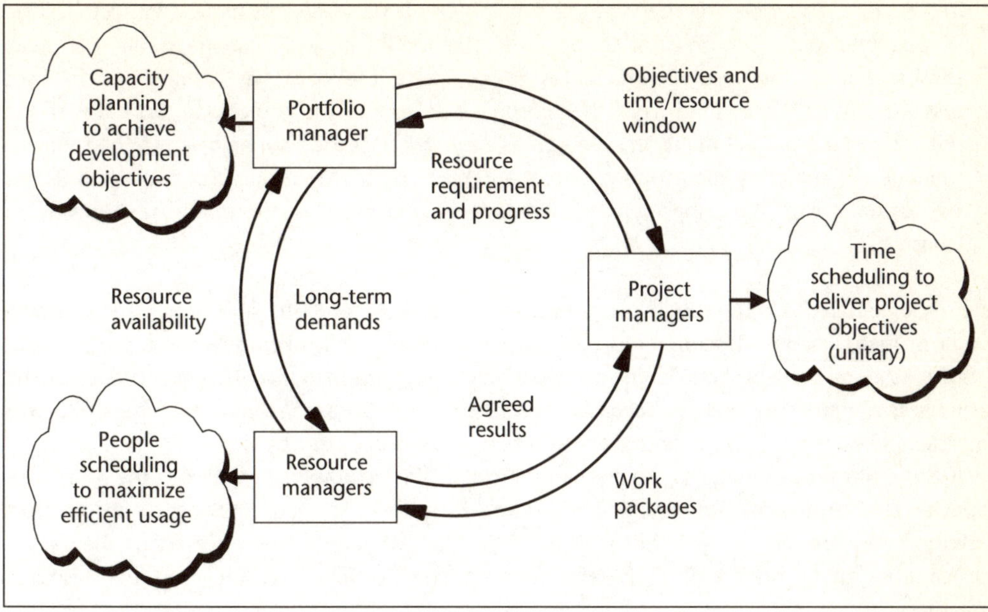

Figure 16.7 *Master project scheduling*

1 Individual projects are proposed to or by the portfolio directors. If the projects in the portfolio are internal development work, then the projects may be proposed by people in the front office or back office. If the firm is a contractor doing work for external clients, then the projects will be proposed by external clients, via the sales department.
2 Yes, individual projects are planned, and the resource requirements determined. This is done by project managers.
3 But instead of adding the complete project plans to the giant plan of plans, each project is added to the portfolio resource plan as a single activity, with idealized resource requirements. I call this portfolio resource plan the master project schedule, or rough-cut capacity plan.
4 The total resource requirement is compared to the resource availability, as determined by the resource managers. Projects are eliminated as described above, so that the resource requirement and resource availability roughly balance. Then steps have to be taken to smooth out the requirement to more closely match the availability. The requirement will probably have peaks and troughs, with the requirement sometimes exceeding the availability, sometimes being less. For an organization doing internal development work, projects need to either be delayed, or extended, to smooth out the peaks and troughs. For an organization doing work for external clients, delaying the start or taking longer over projects is not an option. The client wants the project by the due date. Then the peaks and troughs need to be smoothed out using temporary workers. It is typical for a contract organization's staff to have between 20 per cent and 40 per cent temporary workers at any one time.
5 A start date, finish date and resource profile is determined for the projects in the portfolio. Projects are then given to project managers to manage within the time and resource window.

6 The project managers will manage the projects using standard techniques. Projects will be broken into packages of work to be undertaken. The project managers will then seek resources from the resource managers to complete the packages of work. Sometimes resources will be seconded from the resource pool on to the project, to work under the direction of the project manager. Sometimes the work packages will be given to the resource managers so that they can assign resources and take up the responsibility of managing. These two options were described as the secondment and coordinated matrix respectively in Chapter 8.

The resource balance in the rough-cut capacity plan will be accurate to say ± 5 per cent. But with the error magnification described in Chapter 13, as the work is broken down into projects and the projects are then broken down into work packages, the resource demands made on the resource managers may only be accurate to ± 50 per cent. So the resource managers still have considerable work to do balancing the assignment of resources day by day.

It is the resource managers who are caught in the pincer movement between the rough-cut capacity plan and the resource demands made by project managers. But it is the project managers who are seen to fail if it doesn't work. So it usually falls to them to manage the rough-cut capacity plan, even though it falls between the portfolio directors and the resource managers.

If you are dealing with homogeneous projects with artisan labour, this usually works very well. Even though several resources need to be smoothed, if the projects are homogeneous, then if one resource is smoothed, so are the others. Web projects involve professional knowledge workers, and the projects tend to be heterogeneous. Smoothing one resource makes another even more unbalanced. It is not easy. But if you are not doing it, you are not in control.

Also if you do find the unexpected happens, and you need to reassign resources, you are able to do it and avoid Figure 16.1. The unexpected is the reality of projects. You may need to reduce the resources for a project a bit, but you know what is happening and reduce the impact.

Any of the standard software packages can be used to maintain the portfolio plan, but dedicated packages have also been developed.

THE PORTFOLIO OF PORTFOLIOS

Large project-based organizations, undertaking a large number of projects, may break them into many programmes, portfolios and major projects as illustrated in Figure 16.3. The assignment of resources to individual projects will be done at the portfolio level. But resources need to be prioritized between the portfolios, programmes and major projects. To do that the organization needs to maintain a board level committee, a board investment committee, which will prioritize resources within the portfolio of portfolios. But that is taking us out of project, programme and portfolio management and into strategic management and so it is a useful place to stop.

So, may I wish you happy projects, happy programmes, happy portfolios.

APPENDIX **1**

Pro-forma Project Definition Report

Euro Projex

Project Definition Report

Project: **Project Champion:** **Project Manager:**	

Contents

1 Project context	Background
2 Project definition	Purpose/scope/objectives Work areas
3 Project strategy	Key performance indicators (KPIs) Mission statement
4 Work definition	Milestone plan Work-package definition Work-package scope statements
5 Organization	Departments involved Project roles Responsibility chart Stakeholder register
6 Project plans	Resource estimates Network and bar chart Quality plan Risk register
7 Project control	Planning and control system
8 Project appraisal	Cost estimate Revenue estimate Project appraisal

Author:	JRT	**Date:**	21 Jan 2004	**Issue:**	A

Reproduced from J. Rodney Turner, *Managing Web Projects*, Gower, Aldershot, 2004.

Euro Projex

Project Definition Report

Project: **Project Champion:** **Project Manager:**	

Background

Author:	JRT	**Date:**	21 Jan 2004	**Issue:**	A

Euro Projex

Project Definition Report

Project: **Project Champion:** **Project Manager:**	
Purpose **Why?**	
Outputs **What?**	
Scope **How?**	
Areas of work	

Author:	JRT	**Date:**	21 Jan 2004	**Issue:**	A

MILESTONE PLAN

Project:

Project Champion:

Project Manager:

Date		Milestone name

MILESTONE REPORT

Report date	Milestone report

Short name	End date

Euro Projex

Project Definition Report

Project: **Project Champion:** **Project Manager:**	

Work Areas	**Milestones**
A:	A1: A2: A3: A4: A5: A6:
B:	B1: B2: B3: B4: B5: B6:
C:	C1: C2: C3: C4: C5: C6:
D:	D1: D2: D3: D4: D5: D6:

Author:	JRT	**Date:**	21 Jan 2004	**Issue:**	A

Euro Projex

Milestone Scope Statement

Project: **Project Champion:** **Project Manager:** **Work area:** **Work area Manager:** **Work-package:** **Work-package Manager:**	
Milestone number and name	
Measure of achievement	
Draft activity list	

Author:	JRT	**Date:**	21 Jan 2004	**Issue:**	A

PROJECT RESPONSIBILITY CHART

PROJECT SCHEDULE

Project:	0
Project Champion:	0
Project Manager:	0

Period: **Target end:**

X	e**X**ecutes the work
D	takes **D**ecisions solely/ultimately
d	takes **d**ecisions jointly
P	manages **P**rogress
T	on the job **T**raining
I	must be **I**nformed
C	must be **C**onsulted
A	may **A**dvise

No	**Milestone name**																	1	2	3	4	5	6	7	8	9	10	11	12	13	14	15	d (Duration)	**End date**
	0																																	
	0																																	
	0																																	
	0																																	
	0																																	
	0																																	
	0																																	
	0																																	
	0																																	
	0																																	
	0																																	
	0																																	
	0																																	
	0																																	
	0																																	
	0																																	
	0																																	
	0																																	
	0																																	

Reproduced from J. Rodney Turner, *Managing Web Projects*, Gower, Aldershot, 2004.

ACTIVITY PLAN

ACTIVITY SCHEDULE

Project:	0
Milestone:	
Manager:	

Period: | **Target end:**

X	e**X**ecutes the work
D	takes **D**ecisions solely/ultimately
d	takes **d**ecisions jointly
P	manages **P**rogress
T	on the job **T**raining
I	must be **I**nformed
C	must be **C**onsulted
A	may **A**dvise

No	**Activity name**														1	2	3	4	5	6	7	8	9	10	11	12	13	14	15	d (Duration)	**End date**

Euro Projex

Stakeholder Register

Project:
Project Champion:
Project Manager:

Stakeholder name/group	*Objectives*	*Aware Y/N*	*Influence Y/N*	*Support Y/N*	*Influence strategy*
Stakeholder 1					
Stakeholder 2					

Author:	JRT	**Date:**	21 Jan 2004	**Issue:**	A

Reproduced from J. Rodney Turner, *Managing Web Projects*, Gower, Aldershot, 2004.

ACTIVITY PLAN

Project:	0
Milestone:	
Manager:	

X	e**X**ecutes the work
D	takes **D**ecisions solely/ultimately
d	takes **d**ecisions jointly
P	manages **P**rogress
T	on the job **T**raining
I	must be **I**nformed
C	must be **C**onsulted
A	may **A**dvise

No	**Activity name**									Labour	Material	Sub-contract	Plant and equipment	Overhead and admin

ACTIVITY SCHEDULE

Period:		**Target end:**	

1	2	3	4	5	6	7	8	9	10	11	12	13	14	15	d (Duration)	**End date**

Reproduced from J. Rodney Turner, *Managing Web Projects*, Gower, Aldershot, 2004.

PROJECT ESTIMATES

Project:	0
Project Champion:	0
Project Manager:	0

		0	0	0	0	0	0	0	0	0	0	0	0	0	0	Sub-contract	Materials	Plant and equipment	Overhead and admin	Duration
No	**Milestone name**	d	d	d	d	d	d	d	d	d	d	d	d	d	d	£k	£k	£k	£k	d
	0																			0
	0																			0
	0																			0
	0																			0
	0																			0
	0																			0
	0																			0
	0																			0
	0																			0
	0																			0
	0																			0
	0																			0
	0																			0
	0																			0
	0																			0
	0																			0
	0																			0
	0																			0
	0																			2
Sum	0	0	0	0	0	0	0	0	0	0	0	0	0	0	0	0.0	0.0	0.0	0.0	2

PROGRESS REPORT

	Labour						Labour					
	Labour estimate	Actual	Estimated remaining	% complete	Earned value	Calculated remaining	Cost total	Actual	Estimated remaining	% complete	Earned value	Calculated remaining
No	hrs	hrs	hrs	%	hrs	hrs	£	£	£	%	£	£
	0	0	0	0.0	0	0	0.0	0.0	0.0	0.0	0.0	0.0
	0	0	0	0.0	0	0	0.0	0.0	0.0	0.0	0.0	0.0
	0	0	0	0.0	0	0	0.0	0.0	0.0	0.0	0.0	0.0
	0	0	0	0.0	0	0	0.0	0.0	0.0	0.0	0.0	0.0
	0	0	0	0.0	0	0	0.0	0.0	0.0	0.0	0.0	0.0
	0	0	0	0.0	0	0	0.0	0.0	0.0	0.0	0.0	0.0
	0	0	0	0.0	0	0	0.0	0.0	0.0	0.0	0.0	0.0
	0	0	0	0.0	0	0	0.0	0.0	0.0	0.0	0.0	0.0
	0	0	0	0.0	0	0	0.0	0.0	0.0	0.0	0.0	0.0
	0	0	0	0.0	0	0	0.0	0.0	0.0	0.0	0.0	0.0
	0	0	0	0.0	0	0	0.0	0.0	0.0	0.0	0.0	0.0
	0	0	0	0.0	0	0	0.0	0.0	0.0	0.0	0.0	0.0
	0	0	0	0.0	0	0	0.0	0.0	0.0	0.0	0.0	0.0
	0	0	0	0.0	0	0	0.0	0.0	0.0	0.0	0.0	0.0
	0	0	0	0.0	0	0	0.0	0.0	0.0	0.0	0.0	0.0
	0	0	0	0.0	0	0	0.0	0.0	0.0	0.0	0.0	0.0
	0	0	0	0.0	0	0	0.0	0.0	0.0	0.0	0.0	0.0
	0	0	0	0.0	0	0	0.0	0.0	0.0	0.0	0.0	0.0
	0		0	0.0	0	0	0.0	0.0	0.0	0.0	0.0	0.0
Sum	0	0	0		0	0	0.0	0.0	0.0		0.0	0.0
Forecast cost at completion	0				0		0.0				0.0	

Euro Projex

Risk Item Tracking Form

Project: **Project Champion:** **Project Manager:** **Work area:** **Work area Manager:** **Work-package:** **Work-package Manager:**	
Risk item	
Risk owner **Likelihood** **Consequence** **Risk rating**	
Milestones affected **Impact**	
Mitigation Strategy	
Progress	

Author:	JRT	**Date:**	21 Jan 2004	**Issue:**	A

Euro Projex

Risk Register

Project:
Project Champion:
Project Manager:

Rank H/M/L	*Milestone*	*Risk*	*Impact*	*Likelihood H/M/L*	*Consequence H/M/L*	*Strategy*

Author:	JRT	**Date:**	21 July 2004	**Issue:**	A

Reproduced from J. Rodney Turner, *Managing Web Projects*, Gower, Aldershot, 2004.

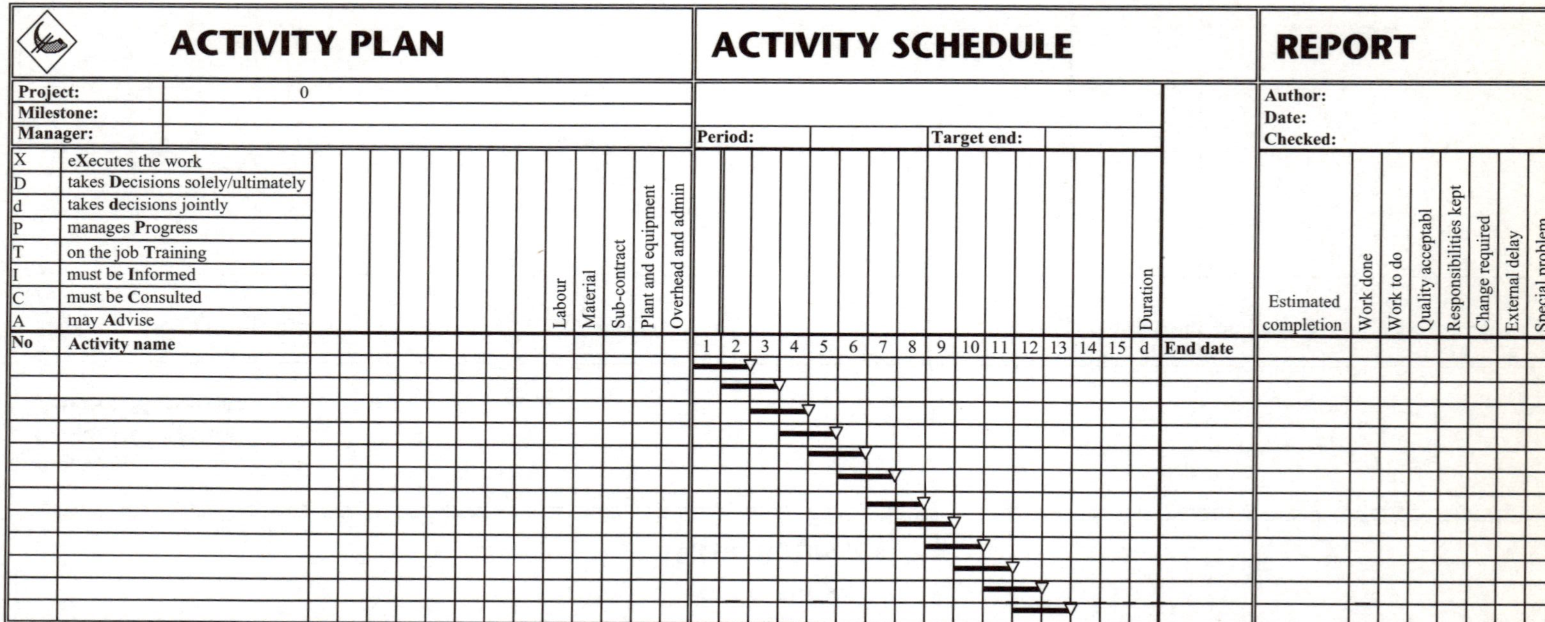

ACTIVITY PLAN | **ACTIVITY SCHEDULE** | **REPORT**

Project: 0
Milestone:
Manager:

Period: **Target end:**

Author:
Date:
Checked:

X	e**X**ecutes the work
D	takes **D**ecisions solely/ultimately
d	takes **d**ecisions jointly
P	manages **P**rogress
T	on the job **T**raining
I	must be **I**nformed
C	must be **C**onsulted
A	may **A**dvise

Labour, Material, Sub-contract, Plant and equipment, Overhead and admin

Duration

Estimated completion, Work done, Work to do, Quality acceptabl, Responsibilities kept, Change required, External delay, Special problem

No	**Activity name**	1	2	3	4	5	6	7	8	9	10	11	12	13	14	15	d	**End date**

Reproduced from J. Rodney Turner, *Managing Web Projects*, Gower, Aldershot, 2004.

Bibliography

Adams, J. L. (2001), *Conceptual Blockbusting: A guide to better ideas*, 4th edn, Boulder, CO: Perseus Publishing. ISBN: 0 7382 0537 0.

Akalu, M. M. (2003), *Projects for Shareholder Value: a capital budgeting perspective*, Ph.D. Dissertation, no 299, Tinbergen Institute Research Series, Erasmus University, Rotterdam.

Andersen, E. S., Grude, K. V. and Haug, T. (1995), *Goal Directed Project Management*, 2nd edn, London: Kogan Page. ISBN: 0 7494 1389 1.

APM (1997), P. Simon, D. Hillson and K. Newland (eds) *Project Risk Analysis and Management Guide*, High Wycombe: Association for Project Management. ISBN: 0 9531 5900 0.

APM (2000), M. Dixon (ed.) *Project Management Body of Knowledge*, High Wycombe: Association for Project Management. ISBN: 0 9034 9401 X.

APM (2002), M. Stevens (ed.) *Project Management Pathways*, High Wycombe: Association for Project Management. ISBN: 0 9034 9400 1.

Bicknell, D. (2002), 'Tightening the net', *Director*, **56**(3) October, 97–104.

Bower, D. and Skountzos, F. (2003), 'Partnering, benchmarking and alliances', in J. R. Turner (ed.) *Contracting for Project Management*, Aldershot: Gower.

Brooks, F. P. (1995), *The Mythical Man-Month*: 20th anniversary edn, Reading, MA: Addison Wesley. ISBN: 0 2018 3595 9.

BS ISO 10 006 (1997), *Quality Management – Guidelines to Quality in Project Management*, Geneva: International Standards Organization. ISBN: 0 5802 8801 3.

BS6079-1 (2000), *Project Management: Guide to Project Management*, London: British Standards Institute. ISBN: 0 5802 5594 8

Christensen, P. J. and Rydberg, P. (2001), 'Overcoming obstacles, strategic risk management in the Øresund Bridge project', *PMNet*, **15**(11).

Cleland, D. I. and King, W. R. (eds) (1988), *Project Management Handbook*, 2nd edn, New York: Van Nostrand Reinhold. ISBN: 0 4422 2114 2.

Coase, R. H. (1964), 'The regulated industries: discussion', *American Economic Review*, **54**(May) 194–197.

Cooke-Davies, T. (2002), 'The success factors on projects', *International Journal of Project Management*, **20**(3) 185–90.

Fangel, M. (1991), 'To start or to start-up? – that is the key question of project initiation', *International Journal of Project Management*, **9**(1) February.

Fangel, M. (ed.) (1987), *The Handbook of Project Start-up: how to launch projects effectively*, Zurich: The International Project Management Association.

Fayol, H. (1949), *General and Industrial Management*, London: Pitman (out of print).

Fleming, Q. W. and Koppleman, J. M. (2000), *Earned Value Project Management*, 2nd edn, Sylva, NC: Project Management Institute. ISBN: 1 8804 1027 3.

Fong, P. S. W. (2003), 'Knowledge creation in multidisciplinary project teams: an empirical study of the processes and their dynamic interrelationships', *International Journal of Project Management*, **21**(7), 479–86.

Frame, J. D. (1995), *Managing Projects in Organizations: how to make the best use of time, techniques and people*, San Francisco, CA: Jossey-Bass. ISBN: 0 7879 0160 1.

Gareis, R. and Huemann, M. (1998), 'International research project PM-benchmarking: benchmarking the PM-process', *Project Management: The Professional Magazine of the Project Management Association Finland*, **4**(1) Summer, 34–9.

Gates III, W. H. (2000), *Business @ the Speed of Thought: Using a Digital Nervous System*, New York: Warner Business Books. ISBN: 0 4466 7596 2.

Graham, R. G. (2003), 'Managing conflict, persuasion and negotiation', in J. R. Turner (ed.) *People in Project Management*, Aldershot: Gower.

Handy, C. B. (1995), *The Age of Unreason*, Business Books. ISBN: 0 8758 4301 8.

Hartman, F. T. (2001), *Don't Park your Brain Outside: a practical guide to improving shareholder value with SMART Management*, Newtown Square, PA: Project Management Institute. ISBN: 1 8804 1048 6.

Jiang, J. L., Klein, G. and Ellis, T. S. (2002), 'A measure of software development risk', *Project Management Journal*, **33**(3) September.

Johansson, H. J., McHugh, P., Pendlebury, A. J. and Wheeler, W. A. (1994), *Business Process Reengineering*, Chichester: Wiley. ISBN: 0 4719 3883 1.

Kerzner, H. (1999), *Project Management: a systems approach to planning, scheduling and control*, 6th edn, New York: Wiley. ISBN: 0 4712 8835 7.

Kulik, P. and Samuelsen, R. (2001), 'E-project management for the new reality', *PM Network: the Professional Magazine of the Project Management Institute*, **15**(3) March.

Lock, D. (2000a), 'Managing time', in J. R. Turner and S. J. Simister (eds) *The Gower Handbook of Project Management*, 3rd edn, Aldershot: Gower.

Lock, D. (2000b), 'Project appraisal', in J. R. Turner and S. J. Simister (eds) *The Gower Handbook of Project Management*, 3rd edn, Aldershot: Gower.

Müller, R. (2002), 'Managing information technology projects: a training and communication challenge', in A. Jain (ed.) *IT Business in a New Light: the projectized way, Proceedings of the First Software Project Management Congress*, Bangalore, India, May CEPM/PMA, Delhi: Centre of Excellence in Project Management.

Murray-Webster, R. and Thiry, M. (2000), 'Managing programmes of projects', in J. R. Turner and S. J. Simister (eds) *The Gower Handbook of Project Management*, 3rd edn, Aldershot: Gower.

Ogård, L. and Gallstad, I. (1999), *Total Inre Effektivitet*, Konsult Förlaget.

OGC (1999), *Managing Successful Programmes*, London: The Stationery Office. ISBN: 0 1133 0016 6.

OGC (2002), *Managing Successful Projects with PRINCE 2*, 3rd edn, London: The Stationery Office. ISBN: 0 1133 0981 4.

Onanbanjo, A. (2001), *Key Features of E-business projects (E-projects), which Differentiate them from IT Projects*, MBA Dissertation, Henley Management College.

Partington, D. (2000), 'Implementing strategy through programmes of projects', in J. R. Turner and S. J. Simister (eds) *The Gower Handbook of Project Management*, 3rd edn, Aldershot: Gower.

Pharro, R. (2000), 'Processes and procedures', in J. R. Turner and S. J. Simister (eds) *The Gower Handbook of Project Management*, 3rd edn, (CD-ROM and hardback) Aldershot: Gower.

Pinto, J. K. and Slevin, D. P. (1988), 'Critical success factors in effective project implementation', in D. I. Cleland and W. R. King (eds) *Project Management Handbook*, 2nd edn, New York: Van Nostrand Reinhold. ISBN: 0 4422 2114 2.

PMI (2000), *A Guide to the Project Management Body of Knowledge*, (CD-ROM) Newtown Square, PA: Project Management Institute. ISBN: 1 8804 1025 7.

Rahschulte, T. (2001), 'E-opportunities', *PM Network: the Professional Magazine of the Project Management Institute*, **15**(3) March.

Rees, D. (2003), 'Managing culture', in J. R. Turner (ed.) *People in Project Management*, Aldershot: Gower. ISBN: 0 5660 8530 5.

Reid, A. (2003), 'Managing teams: the reality of life', in J. R. Turner and S. J. Simister (eds) *The Gower Handbook of Project Management*, 3rd edn, Aldershot: Gower.

Scott, B. (ed.) (2001), *Partnering in Europe: incentive based alliancing for projects*, London: Thomas Telford. ISBN: 0 7277 2965 9.

Turner, J. R., Grude, K. V. and Thurloway, L. (1996), *The Project Manager as Change Agent*, London: McGraw Hill. ISBN: 0 0770 7741 5.

Turner, J. R. (1999), *The Handbook of Project-based Management*, 2nd edn, London: McGraw Hill. ISBN: 0 0770 9161 2.

Turner, J. R. (ed.) (1995), *The Commercial Project Manager*, Maidenhead: McGraw Hill. ISBN: 0 0770 7656 7.

Turner, J. R. (ed.) (2003a), *People in Project Management*, Aldershot: Gower. ISBN: 0 5660 8530 5.

Turner, J. R. (ed.) (2003b), *Contracting for Project Management*, Aldershot: Gower. ISBN: 0 5660 8529 1.

Turner, J. R. and Simister, S. J. (eds) (2000), *The Gower Handbook of Project Management*, 3rd edn, Aldershot: Gower. ISBN: 0 5660 8397 3.

van Fenema, P. C. (2002), *Coordination and Control of Globally Distributed Software Projects*, Ph.D. Dissertation, Erasmus Research Institute in Management, Erasmus University, Rotterdam.

Wateridge, J. F. (1995), 'IT projects: a basis for success', *International Journal of Project Management*, **13**(3), 169–72.

Wateridge, J. F. (2000), 'Project health checks', in J. R. Turner and S. J. Simister (eds) *The Gower Handbook of Project Management*, 3rd edn, Aldershot: Gower.

Index

About the Author

Rodney Turner is Professor of Project Management in the Department of Marketing and Organization of the Faculty of Economics, Erasmus University, Rotterdam, and a director of EuroProjex, the European Network for Project Excellence, and Goal Directed Project Management Systems Ltd. He is also a visiting professor at Henley Management College and adjunct professor at The University of Technology, Sydney. After leaving Oxford University, where he completed his doctorate and was a post-doctoral research fellow at Brasenose College, he spent several years with ICI working on engineering design, construction and maintenance projects in the petrochemical industry. Next, he worked as a consultant in project management with Coopers and Lybrand, where he was exposed to all types of projects in all types of industries, before joining Henley Management College. He has been with Erasmus University since 1997. Rodney works as a project management consultant. He lectures worldwide, and has published several books and papers on project management, including the best-selling *Handbook of Project-based Management*, and *The Gower Handbook of Project Management*. Rodney Turner edits the *International Journal of Project Management*, is Vice-President and past Chairman of the Association for Project Management, and immediate past Chairman of the International Project Management Association.

rodneyturner@europrojex.co.uk

Other books by Rodney Turner published by GOWER

The Gower Handbook of Project Management, 2000, edited with Steven Simister, ISBN: 0 566 08138 5, (Hardback), ISBN: 0 566 08397 3, (CD-ROM).

People in Project Management, 2003, editor, ISBN: 0 566 08530 5 (paperback).

Contracting for Project Management, 2003, editor, ISBN: 0 566 08529 1 (paperback).

John Clare's Guide to Media Handling
John Clare
0 566 08298 5

Making the Connections
Using Internal Communication to Turn Strategy into Action
Bill Quirke
0 566 08175 X

How to Measure Customer Satisfaction 2ed
Nigel Hill, John Brierley and Rob MacDougall
0 566 08595 X

The Goal
A Process of Ongoing Improvement 2ed
Eliyahu M. Goldratt and Jeff Cox
0 566 07418 4

Benchmarking
Sylvia Codling
0 566 07926 7

The New Guide to Identity
How to Create and Sustain Change Through Managing Identity
Wolff Olins
0 566 07737 X

It's Not Luck
Eliyahu M. Goldratt
0 566 07627 6

GOWER

Join our email newsletter

Gower is widely recognized as one of the world's leading publishers on management and business practice. Its programmes range from 1000-page handbooks through practical manuals to popular paperbacks. These cover all the main functions of management: human resource development, sales and marketing, project management, finance, etc. Gower also produces training videos and activities manuals on a wide range of management skills.

As our list is constantly developing you may find it difficult to keep abreast of new titles. With this in mind we offer a free email news service, approximately once every two months, which provides a brief overview of the most recent titles and links into our catalogue, should you wish to read more or see sample pages.

To sign up to this service, send your request via email to **info@gowerpub.com**. Please put your email address in the body of the email as confirmation of your agreement to receive information in this way.

GOWER